UNBURIED LIVES

LAURIE A. WILKIE

✦⇒◉⇐✦

UNBURIED LIVES

✦⇒◉⇐✦

The Historical Archaeology

of Buffalo Soldiers

at Fort Davis, Texas,

1869–1875

University of New Mexico Press Albuquerque

First paperback printing 2023

ISBN 978-0-8263-6299-5 (cloth)
ISBN 978-0-8263-6567-5 (paper)
ISBN 978-0-8263-6300-8 (electronic)

Library of Congress Control Number: 2021941184

Founded in 1889, the University of New Mexico sits on the traditional homelands
of the Pueblo of Sandia. The original peoples of New Mexico—Pueblo, Navajo,
and Apache—since time immemorial have deep connections to the land and have
made significant contributions to the broader community statewide. We honor the
land itself and those who remain stewards of this land throughout the generations
and also acknowledge our committed relationship to Indigenous peoples.
We gratefully recognize our history.

Cover illustration: JWJ MSS 54 / Randolph Linsly Simpson
African-American collection / Yale University Library
Designed by Mindy Basinger Hill
Composed in Garamond Premier Pro and Trajan Pro

TO MARK COOPER EMERSON,

who has traversed this project with me

from beginning to end, bottom to top.

⊷⊜⊶

AND TO TAJMA HASSAN,

a talented archaeologist and an incredible person,

who profoundly shaped this work.

CONTENTS

—➤══◉═══◄—

ILLUSTRATIONS

⟶⇒◉⇐⟵

TABLES

ACKNOWLEDGMENTS

There are no existing photographs of Corporal Daniel Tallifero, Company I, Ninth Cavalry, the man whose death both haunts and anchors this work, and details of his life are vague. At a time when speaking the names of those lost to racialized violence is so important, we cannot even be sure how to pronounce his name. Tallifero, and several other spelling variants, are common in Virginia, linked to old planter families; the "T" in Booker T. Washington's name stood for Tallifero. Despite its spelling, the name is commonly pronounced something closer to "Tolliver," a name more commonly seen as a Black family surname. While documents show his name spelled in multiple ways, it is always a form of Tallifero, and both Daniel and his mother are identified with that particular spelling, even though there is no clear evidence that either of them could write. The only document found with Daniel's mark were his enlistment papers, marked with an X. Though there are no photographs of Daniel, it has not been difficult to see his face, just one of too many faces—Trayvon Martin, Oscar Grant, Eric Garner, Byron Williams, George Floyd—who come to mind when considering the corporal's death.

I did not start this project with the intention of writing around Daniel Tallifero and his death. I was aware of his case from the secondary literature, and it seemed unfortunate that a soldier fell so neatly into the worst white supremacist stereotypes of Black manhood. On seeing the documentary record first-hand, however, I was astounded that the story has persisted as it has, indeed, being elaborated upon in many ways. It was of the greatest luck (fate?) that as the archaeological part of the study commenced, the deposits encountered around the unfinished barracks dated to the years immediately before and following Tallifero's death. What I thought might be a footnote became instead a framing point for the work, leading me to interrogate the racialized landscapes of military life in a fine-grained way. In short, the archaeological record encouraged my admitted obsession with the Tallifero case rather than dampening it.

In the manner of obsessed people, I talked incessantly about the case, involved others in the archival search for records that no longer exist, talked through the different possibilities, and shared little tidbits of archival and material evidence that accumulated like archaeological deposits not just about the early morning of November 20, 1872, but also about the complex entanglements between the people, places, and things of the post between 1869 and 1875. I have accumulated many debts during the course of this project, not a small part of which are owed to those who have been subjected to my rantings, encouraged me, and helped me along the way. There are many more whom I can mention in this space, and I apologize to anyone who hasn't been specifically called out, but please know you have been appreciated greatly during this long process.

First, the staff (past and present) of the Fort Davis Historic Site, particularly John Heiner, Regina Heiner, John Morelock, and Donna Smith; the Texas State Archaeology Office; state parks archaeologist Tim Roberts; the Texas SHPO; NPS archaeologists Jacquelin St. Clair and Jim Bradford; WAAC staff member Kim Beckwith; Center for Big Bend Studies, Sul Ross State University archaeologist Andy Cloud; and former director of the Sul Ross State University Museum of the Big Bend, Larry Francell were just a few of the Texas-based experts who helped make the project happen and proceed successfully. Likewise, the staff at the County Assessors Offices of Brewster, Jeff Davis, and Presidio Counties were extremely helpful. A thanks as well to the Buffalo Soldier Museum of Houston, whose representatives fortuitously visited remote west Texas with high school students during our excavations.

Fieldwork would not have been possible without an exceptional crew of graduate student staff and undergraduate student apprentices. I could not have hoped for better codirectors than Katrina Eichner and Erin Rodriguez, who both completed dissertations out of the broader Fort Davis research; interested readers should seek out those works. Katrina in particular was and is a close collaborator, always pushing me, and whether we were butting heads or commiserating, missing or meeting deadlines, exchanging archival references, sharing photos or ideas, it has been and continues to be a productive relationship—even, despite it all, a good friendship. Alyssa Scott, David Hyde, and Mario Castillo supported the project as graduate field directors. David, in addition to directing the barracks excavations when I had to absent the field for a bit, was an excellent karaoke partner (it's amazing how little of the "House of the Rising Sun" lyrics we actually knew). Alyssa's support has been essential as a sounding board and reader, and generally less shocking to the ears of the listener. Elizabeth Flores, Jenifer Davis, Jackson Huang, Chandler Fitzsimon, Nick Perez, Shauna Smith, Jesse Pagels, Victoria Sandsor, Carlisha McCord, and Thomas Banghart were incredible team members in the field and field lab, and many of them continued with the project in Berkeley's Historical Archaeology lab. Jenifer, Chandler, Jackson, Nick, Shauna, and Elizabeth also completed outstanding senior honors theses on the project, covering aspects of the project not covered here.

Archival work was facilitated by the staffs at Sul Ross State University's Archive of the Big Bend, the National Archive and Records Administration, and the Denver Public Library and made possible by research support from the Stahl Fund of the Archaeological Research Facility, the Richard and Rhoda Goldman Distinguished Chair of Social Sciences Fund, and funds from Berkeley's Committee on Research.

Amanda Guzman, Nick Eskow, Leah Grant, Alexandra Farnsworth, and Christopher Lowman were part of my obsessive search for NARA records related to Fort Davis, but particularly for Daniel Tallifero specifically at different times. Amanda and Nick in particular have fielded text inquiries at odd times as I sought outside perspectives on whether materials were as significant as I thought (or hoped). Nick, Leah, and I did a lot of side-by-side scanning of documents at NARA, and we still occasionally discover things on our respective phones that we forgot about.

While visiting in Columbia, South Carolina, I was able to drop in at the South Carolina Institute of Archaeology and Anthropology, where director Steven D. Smith was more than generous with his time and resources. He and his colleagues were essential in ensuring that I got right things about Civil War–era military gear (all errors are my own!)

Colleagues and audiences at Notre Dame, Boston University, Bard Graduate Center, UCLA, South Carolina University, and, closer to home, at the Townsend Center and the Archaeological Research Facility at Berkeley listened to presentations based on different aspects of this research and provided very welcome feedback. To them I remain indebted. Likewise, Mark Tveskov at the University of Southern Oregon has been generous in including early aspects of this research in an edited volume and including me in conference sessions, leading to valuable and thought-provoking interactions with a number of colleagues. Also at conferences (and sometimes over text or during visits), Maria Franklin, Nedra Lee, Audrey Horning, Ayana Flewellen, Mary Beaudry,

Whitney Battle-Baptiste, Alex Jones, Jerry Howard, Eleanor King, Kat Hayes, Teresa Bolger, Bonnie Clark, Kathleen Corbett, Edward González-Tennant, Terry Weik, Justin Dunnavant, Mark Hauser, Douglas Armstrong, Carolyn White, Leland Ferguson, Eleanor King, Steve Silliman, Kelly Fong, Meredith Chesson, Robb Mann, Kelly Goldburg, and so many others have listened to me try out versions of the alternate interpretations of the Tallifero documents; some of the nights, particularly in Boston, got pretty late and blurry, so I apologize profusely to those I've missed—looking at you Texas contingent. Meredith Chesson has been a supporter of this research from the very beginning, providing emotional and reading support, and I owe her greatly.

Here at Berkeley, anthropology faculty and other colleagues, including Cori Hayden, Charles Hirschkind, Sabrina Agarwal, Bill White, Rosemary Joyce, Kent Lightfoot, Kira Blaisdell Sloan, Ayana Flewellen, Justin Dunnavant, John Chenoweth, Pascale Boucicaut, Natasha Fernandez, Nico Tripcevich, Jun Sunseri, Rus Sheptek, Gekka Chapman, and Saba Mahmood have at different times hashed out different ideas with me, displaying remarkable patience.

The "UCB Writing Group," as we are known on Google Drive, has suffered through multiple versions of some of these chapters and have seen at least one iteration of the entire manuscript. Thanks also go to Martha Diaz-Longo, Tajma Hassan, Jarre Hamilton, Katie Kinkopf, Christopher Lowman, Alyssa Scott, Elena Sesma, and Evan Taylor; the work is so much improved by their thoughtful and considered feedback.

Jiyoon Lee was crucial in helping format and proofread the manuscript in preparation for submission, and her thoroughness, attention to detail, and endless good humor were so greatly appreciated.

I would like to thank the different people I have worked with at UNM press. This project was contracted with the help of Clark Whitehorn, and Elise McHugh delivered the project into the hands of Michael Millman, who has been extremely supportive and has shepherded the manuscript through review through the strange days of Covid lockdowns. I want to thank Katherine White, James Ayers and others from the marketing department. Richard Feit, as copyeditor extraordinaire, has succeeded in wrestling my unwieldy prose into something lovely.

No one has endured more than my family. Alex has been called upon to help with Photoshop, zip files, lost documents, and many other indignities that come with being an only child of an academic who has questionable technical skills. Thank you to my sister, Merebeth Wilkie Antino, who was willing to try her hand at imagining Fort Davis moments we have no visual record for. Mark, my beloved husband, has been endlessly patient and supportive, providing a listening ear, car service in west Texas, archival support in Denver, and even an emotional support puppy (thank you, Wynfred), and since 2010, when the idea to study Fort Davis first struck me, has listened to more about Fort Davis than any living soul not researching the place should endure.

Finally, my deepest gratitude to the buffalo soldiers who lived and served, among other places, at Fort Davis. You have inspired me and humbled me as I learned about your experiences and lives. I hope I have done your collective memories justice.

IMPORTANT PERSONS
IN THIS WORK

TABLE 0.1. *Soldiers in the Narrative,*
with Military Unit Membership and Rank

COMPANY K, NINTH CAVALRY
(*June 1868–April 1871*)

Rank	*Name*
Lieutenant	James T. Birney
Sergeant Major	William Henderson
Sergeant	Henry Browler
Corporal	John Shanks (married to Nancy Burch)
Private	George McIsaac
Private	Buck Taylor

COMPANY B, TWENTY-FOURTH INFANTRY
(*November 1869–May 1871*)

Rank	*Name*
Private	William Donaldson

COMPANY F, TWENTY-FOURTH INFANTRY
(*June 1870–April 1872*)

Rank	*Name*
Corporal	Samuel McKinney
Private	Calvin Dudley
Private	Lemuel Johnson
Private	William Jones

COMPANY I, NINTH CAVALRY *(June 1871–April 1875)*

Rank	Name
Captain	Frank Bennett
Lieutenant	W. W. Tyler
Sergeant	John Hewey
Corporal	Daniel Gigsby
Corporal	Daniel Tallifero
Private	Squire Bartley
Private	Albert Dennis
Private	Moses Digous
Private	Richard Roper
Private	Richard Thompson

COMPANY G, TWENTY-FIFTH INFANTRY
(July 1870–September 1875)

Rank	Name
Captain	J. W. Patterson
Lieutenant	Wallace Tear
Sergeant Major	William F. King
Sergeant	Henry Washington (wife Mary)
Sergeant	Joseph Chapman
Sergeant	Jonas Cox
Corporal	Squire Jackson
Private	Henry Cuff (married to laundress, wife's name unknown)
Private	George Dallas
Private	Elijah Fillmore
Private	Courtney Sullivan

TWENTY-FIFTH INFANTRY BAND

Musician	Eli Smallgood
Musician	George Brown
Musician	Peter Hicks

COMPANY E, TWENTY-FIFTH INFANTRY
(May 1872–May 1880)

Rank	Name
Captain	David Schooley
First Lieutenant	Frederick Augustus Kendall
First Sergeant	John Sample
Sergeant	Anthony Jackson (married to Lucinda)
Sergeant	John A. Martin
Sergeant	Edward McKenzie (married to Minerva)
Corporal	Griffin Collins
Corporal	John Williams (married to Annie Williams)
Private	William Johnson
Private	Martin Pegee/Pedee (Sample's Bunkie)
Private	Henry Sappho
Private	William Smith
Private	Joseph William Stevenson
Private	James Wilson
Private	Gatewood, Scott (Wilson's Bunkie)

COMPANY D, TWENTY-FIFTH INFANTRY
(November 1872–July 1876)

Rank	Name
First Lieutenant	Edwin J. Stivers
Sergeant	John Moore
Private	Henry Butcher
Private	Jordan Hudson
Private	James Lusk
Private	Solomon Powell
Private	Alfred Taylor
Private	Charles Southerner

PROLOGUE

On November 20, 1872, a Black soldier was shot to death at Fort Davis, Texas. The commanding officer reported the death the following day to the assistant adjutant general for the Department of Texas, claiming that an officer's wife killed the man as he was attempting to enter her quarters while her husband was away. The commanding officer strongly implied that rape was the motive.[1] Many historians writing the history of buffalo soldiers, a name commonly used to describe Black regulars serving on the frontier, have recounted this incident uncritically.[2] A small number have questioned whether burglary rather than rape was the motive.[3]

Not a single historian has considered the possibility that the commanding officer lied.

UNBURIED LIVES

1

BLACK SOLDIERING
MATTERS AT FORT DAVIS
Taking an Archaeological Approach to Frontier Life

First. You are a man, although a colored man. If you were only
a horse, or an ox, incapable of deciding whether the rebels are right
or wrong, you would have no responsibility, and might like the horse or
ox go on eating your corn or grass, in total indifference, as to which side
is victorious or vanquished in this conflict: You are however,
no horse, no ox, but a man, and whatever concerns man should
interest you. . . . Manhood requires you to take sides, and you are mean
or noble according to how you choose between action and inaction.

FREDERICK DOUGLASS, 1863, "Why a Colored Man Should Enlist."[1]

Marquis De Lafayette Cotton started drinking in the early morning on July
14, 1872, or perhaps he simply continued his efforts from the previous night.[2]
When Cotton arrived at the house of Calvin Robinson near the post of Fort
Davis, Texas, at 9 a.m., he was already "drunk and accompanied by another
two bottles of liquor." As Cotton, in the emphatic manner of the inebriated,
assured Robinson that he would soon leave, William Donaldson, a former
soldier, approached the house on horseback. Both Cotton and Robinson were
white. Donaldson was Black.

William Donaldson was one of a number of Black veterans who had settled
in the small settlements of "the Creek" and Chihuahua, reaching no farther
than one mile from the safety of the post.[3] Along with Mexican American
residents of the town, the veterans worked as laborers or ran businesses like
restaurants and saloons that catered to the military population. Donaldson

left the military in December 1869, having served his term in Company B, Twenty-Fourth Infantry. When he enlisted in Nashville, Tennessee, he would have expected to serve in the South to support Reconstruction efforts.[4] He probably hadn't planned on living in the West, but in 1869, convinced that it was too provocative to have Black soldiers overseeing white southern populations, Congress voted to move all Black military units west of the Mississippi River. When discharged, Donaldson stayed in the area, near friends and a life that had become familiar and that was so very different from life under enslavement. As of 1870, Donaldson was working as a laborer and living with two other men, a white cook and a mixed-race shoemaker. The multiethnic settlement of Chihuahua contrasted with the primarily white households that settled closest to the post.[5]

Donaldson's horse immediately drew the drunk man's attention.

"I'll give you ten dollars for that horse," Cotton offered. Donaldson declined. Cotton, not to be deterred, made a second offer of fifteen dollars, adding under his breath, "That is as much as the son of a bitch is worth or any of his breed." He then wandered off, oblivious to the impact of his words.

Donaldson was incensed. "That is something that I won't take from anybody," he fumed at Robinson. Robinson was confused; he had heard nothing offensive, and he asked what Donaldson meant. "That old man called me a son of a bitch!" Donald said. Robinson tried to convince the angry man that Cotton was referring to the horse, not his owner, but failed to sway him. Donaldson rode off, returning shortly to Robinson's house with another mounted Black man, an unidentified soldier. Donaldson wanted Robinson to help find the old man, but Robinson refused and watched the men ride off.

Cotton had not gone very far. He was found by another town resident lying in the road nearby, "raving like a crazy man."[6] The old man was being helped to his feet as Donaldson approached, still on horseback. Donaldson was again told by a bystander that the old man was "crazy drunk" and couldn't be held accountable for his words. Donaldson was momentarily appeased and rode off.

Cotton's momentary savior this time was a white man named George Fitzsimon, who walked to a nearby home-based saloon. Cotton followed him. When Fitzsimon sat down to have a drink, Cotton also entered the house, walked to a bedroom, and promptly passed out on a bed. Donaldson, as fate in a small town would have it, also wanted a drink and came to the same establishment. An afternoon of fuming convinced Donaldson beyond doubt that Cotton had called him, not his horse, a son of a bitch.

FIGURE 1.1. A confrontation over a horse. Illustration by Merebeth Wilkie Antino.

Seeing Donaldson entering and knowing the inevitable confrontation that would ensue, the saloon/homeowner, a Mexican man named Mendosa, and Fitzsimon tried to prevent the former soldier from seeing Cotton. They failed and pushed an angry Donaldson out of the house. Guns were drawn and shots fired (whether intentionally or not was a subject of debate at the inquest). Cotton heard the fight, pulled a gun of his own, and fired at Donaldson, who returned fire through the closed door. Cotton forced his way out of the house, and another unidentified man came to take Donaldson away. Bystanders climbed to the rooftops of houses for safety and watched. Donaldson was seen to take another shot at Cotton, who, unhurt, continued walking. One witness, describing Donaldson as "shooting a cap" (firing an unloaded gun) at Cotton, wasn't sure that Cotton had been hit.

Around three o'clock in the afternoon, Henry Greenleaf, a white man, was sitting on the porch of merchant Daniel Murphy, also white, at the edge of the post when he saw Donaldson again catch up with Cotton. The old man was sitting in the road as the younger man approached and drew a pistol.

"Why did you shoot me?" Donaldson demanded.

Cotton retorted that Fitzsimon had shot him.

"Liar!" exclaimed Donaldson. "You both shot me!" He fired the pistol at Cotton, who now ran.

Cotton, now visibly shot, was dragged into Murphy's house and brought into the parlor, where he lay on the floor. Murphy's family members examined Cotton's wound and sent for the post surgeon. Donaldson came to the house still looking for Cotton and was met by Murphy, who blocked his entrance. Donaldson complained to Murphy about the shot he had taken to the shoulder. Murphy told him to go see the doctor and expressed his disapproved of the goings-on. Donaldson lingered in the area, trying to find out what was happening and brandishing his weapon. Cotton died in Murphy's house the following morning, but not before identifying "a Black man, very stout and riding on a horse and wearing a badge on his shoulder," as the person who shot him. Donaldson was taken into custody, and after a military inquest, he was sent to civilian authorities in San Elizaro, Texas.

Soldiers, not Horses

What possessed William Donaldson on that July day to escalate a slanderous remark to deadly violence? The happenings of July 14, 1872, near the post of Fort Davis may seem a strange starting point from which to begin an examination of Black masculinity and citizenship at a Texas fort. In this incident, we can see how the quest for recognition of one's manhood and humanity shaped frontier life. The deadly argument between a former soldier and a drunk white man over a horse could simply be attributed to the influence of cheap whiskey. Some readers may be unsettled by the notion that verbal slurs could so quickly escalate to gun violence. And that is why this is an excellent place to begin the story of Fort Davis. For to truly enter this time and place, we must orient our gaze to how words and actions were experienced in the past, a past whose objects and technologies were entangled in relationships that are distinctly different from those of today.

Foremost, the insult to Donaldson was to his manhood. Men in nineteenth-century US lived in a world where two genders were highly segregated, and women who held particular social and kinship roles (mother, wife, sister) were elevated to the pinnacles of moral righteousness. In what is sometimes called the "cult of true womanhood," the purest of women were seen to embody all that was morally righteous and to require the protection of men to maintain their virtue and reputations. In a patriarchal society, the reputation of a kinswoman or spouse was a direct extension of a man's good name, and no woman was more important in this symbolic hierarchy than mother.[7] Court-martial transcripts of Fort Davis are filled with examples of soldiers—Black and white, enlisted men and officer alike—violently fighting a man who had slighted his mother. Indeed, "son of a bitch" seems to have been the most vile insult one man could hurl at another.[8]

For Black men serving at Fort Davis, many of whom had been born into enslavement, slander against one's mother had an additional subtext. The conditions of enslavement often separated children from mothers, and as demonstrated by interviews with formerly enslaved people undertaken in the 1930s and '40s by the Federal Writer's Project, many who experienced childhood in bondage had few memories of their parents or curated vivid memories of loved ones separated by sale or death. Boys who grew to manhood under enslavement understood all too well the particular sexual, physical, and emotional acts of violence endured by Black women protecting their families.[9] William Donaldson had been born in Tennessee in 1846, served in the Sixty-Fourth Regiment, United States Colored Infantry, mustered out in March 1866, and immediately enlisted in the peacetime army that same year.[10] We do not know his history before entering the service, but his reaction to this insult suggests a man nursing deep wounds, a man whose wounds would not allow him to ignore that "one word."

Cotton insulted not only Donaldson's mother. His words, in referring to the worthlessness "of his breed," denied Donaldson's humanity, equating him to an animal. While others insisted that the words were referring to the horse, Donaldson would have known in his gut that the slight had been intentionally ambiguous. Enslaved people had been treated for centuries as animals, as either subhuman or not-quite-human.[11] Military life, too, often mimicked the more dehumanizing aspects of enslavement. Punishments for military transgressions went beyond confinement and could include corporal punishments in the form of flogging, hanging by thumbs, branding, and carrying logs around the parade ground.[12]

At a post with a large cavalry presence, horses were a particular site of struggle between Black enlisted men and white soldiers; Black soldiers recognized that horses were often valued more by white officers than they were. This point was dramatically made in 1869 when William L. Henderson, a sergeant major for the Ninth Cavalry, who despite a distinguished record of service in both the Civil War and the frontier was reduced to the rank of private in a court-martial. His crime? Henderson was accused by a white officer of "running his horse too quickly" and using an improper "tone" to said officer.

In his defense, Henderson sought not to counter the charges against him but to appeal to his record of distinguished service:

> I entered the service on the 25th day of December 1863, during the Rebellion. I was sent to Rikers Island as a soldier in the 20th US Colored Infantry after reporting to General Jackson. I was detailed as Acting Post Hospital Steward of the Camp of Recruits, which place I remained until the 20th of January when I was relieved by Hospital Steward Pennington and ordered to report to Regimental Headquarters of the 20th US Colored Infantry as Acting Sergeant Major, and at the organization of the Regiment on the 3rd day of February 1864, I was appointed Sergeant Major of the Regiment, which position I held until the 17th day of October 1865, the muster out of the Regiment in New Orleans. I remained out of the service until the 22nd Day of October 1866, when I again entered the US Service in the 9th US cavalry and was appointed Sergeant Major from my enlistment which position I have held up to the present date. I never was placed under arrest before for any disobedience of orders or any disrespectful language to my superiors or officers placed over me.[13]

Henderson's decision to dedicate his defense narrative to his Civil War service is not surprising. In late 1868, Black military veterans were still recognized as essential contributors to the Union's victory.[14] While Henderson was restored to the rank of sergeant major on July 1, 1869, no doubt the memory of the humiliation lingered.[15] In both the court-martial of William Henderson and the unfortunate encounter between veteran Donaldson and Cotton, we see examples of Black men's continued struggle for manly respect and an acknowledgment of their humanity.

Racial and gender oppression is enforced through the systemic denial of a group's humanity. Bodies are sorted into the categories of human, not-quite-human, and subhuman. Metaphors equating people to animals are commonly used in racialized discourses to denote the less-than-human qualities of the targeted subject.[16] Members of marginalized groups are not unaware of this labelling process, and it is not surprising that Sergeant Major Henderson and veteran Donaldson would be sensitive to language or practices that equated them to, or rendered them as less than, a beast of burden.

Several times in their inquest testimony, white men expressed concern over Donaldson's anger. His irritation at being offered a low-ball price for a horse that wasn't for sale and his offense at the foul language were dismissed

FIGURE 1.2. Sergeant Major William L. Henderson and Hospital Steward Thomas H. S. Pennington of the Twentieth U.S. Colored Troops Infantry Regiment. Photographed in Boston, circa 1864. Photograph by W. H. Leeson. Liljenquist Family Collection of Civil War Photographs, Library of Congress, LC-DIG-ppmsca-40621 (digital file from original item, front) LC-DIG-ppmsca-40622 (digital file from original item, back). Digital Id ppmsca 40621//hdl.loc.gov/loc.pnp/40621. Accessed June 1, 2020.

or minimized by others in the conversation. Donaldson was quick to draw his gun, but despite several shots being fired by both sides, hitting the target didn't seem to be the intent so much as emphatically punctuating one's argument with gunfire. Sergeant Major Henderson's words demonstrate his anger through indignance. He drew a weapon familiar to nineteenth-century men of a particular social standing and education—the righteous sword of rhetoric. Each of these men engaged in a form of self-defense of manly honor recognizable across racialized and class boundaries. But because both men were Black, their anger was seen as threatening.

This leads to my final reason for beginning this consideration of military life at Fort Davis with these two men: much corrective history of the buffalo soldiers has been hagiographic in nature. The early works of authors such as Steward, Nankivell, Fowler, and Leikie focused on military exploits with special attention to examples of battle valor and medal recipients.[17] This is important work. But hagiography raises its own challenges. Real, embodied humans rarely conform to the arbitrary measures of character that are imposed on them. Elizabeth Leonard's book on Black service begins with the account of a conversation she had with her son, who was upset that Black soldiers had been involved in the Indian wars. Shouldn't they have known better? Shouldn't they have been naturally aligned with the cause of indigenous peoples?[18]

During this research, I have been confronted by people asserting that this history is not important, explaining to me that Black soldiers were dupes to the imperialistic policies of the US government and no better than the white soldiers who participated in genocide of native peoples. I would suggest that this notion that Black soldiers should be held to higher standards is just a new version of the pressure that Black soldiers themselves struggled under to be the best soldiers possible. Further, this kind of simplistic attitude misses the complex histories of Native American and African/African American entanglements, which include many instances of alliances and conflict alike, a subject that deserves distinct consideration. The nature of the archaeological and archival evidence from Fort Davis makes it an inappropriate place for such a study. Suffice it to say, Black soldiers were part of the settler colonialist system that waged genocidal policies against native peoples—but they were also facing their own history of victimization within that same political structure. As Le'Trice Donaldson suggests, arguments like this distract from the real work of social uplift, or "race work" accomplished by Black men in the military.[19] Further, a focus on the limited military campaigns shifts our gaze from the necropolitical webs in which Black soldiers were enmeshed. Necropolitics, an idea that arises from the postcolonial theorizing of Achille Mbembe, describes the process by which states create communities of "fellows" and "non-fellows" and instill structural and institutional practices that naturalize the abuse, neglect, or even death of non-fellows.[20] Black men saw soldiering as a means to assert their role as fellows, or full citizens, in American society; white military men and the institution often saw and treated them differently.

This work is not interested in putting black or white hats on Black or white men. In the past as in the present, people made decisions based on their experiences, hopes, and understandings of the possibilities available to them. In that messiness, we see the hallmarks of being human. My intent is to account for the diversity of embodied experiences that were represented within the segregated Black units at Fort Davis. I am interested in their humanity, in all its lovely and complicated reality. Some readers may prefer the way William Henderson directed his anger; others may respect the choices made by William Donaldson. But whether their actions might be deemed, after Douglass, "mean or noble," the anger and the humanity of each of these men (and the others with whom they served) deserves to be recognized.

Not all extant scholarly literature on the Black regulars is limited to works that praise them. Two other important genres of research exist. First, there are social and political histories incorporating the experiences of buffalo soldiers into broader tapestries of western history, attempting to look at the complex intersectionalities among race, class, and military rank in frontier situations.[21] There is also the work of military historians attempting to present a more holistic sense of the Black military experience.[22] A thread to this research, however, has been the narrative that while there were undoubtedly racist people in the military, the institution itself was progressive compared to other aspects of US society. While this is in several respects true, there is also overwhelming evidence of the ways that Black men faced inequitable circumstances in their day-to-day lives and in the course of their career trajectories in and beyond the military.

To uncover those inequities as experienced in the day-to-day, however, requires an anthropological rather than an historical approach. Anthropologists focus on the mundane practices and performances that compose the routines of the everyday, the doings of life that create the communities, institutions, and structures in which we find our gendered, raced, social, political, and economic selves entangled.[23] Anthropologists are inherently interested in questions of scale. What are the articulations between a person and a community, a city, or a nation, or between different institutions? Soldiers confronted a heavily hierarchical system in joining the military, and they needed to navigate a variety of interconnected administrative organizations within the institution, all while moving through their day-to-day lives as men, citizens, and soldiers in a highly racialized society.

This study is specifically an anthropological archaeological intervention in Black soldiers' lives. It is an anthropological perspective to the everyday that deploys archaeological techniques and the study of material traces. Archaeology is well suited for understanding intimate relations, for the traces left behind by men, whether those traces are to be found in the ground, in architectural remains, in oral histories, or in archival collections, largely relate to the challenges of surviving day-to-day life. The archaeological approach taken here extends to the archive, a place usually seen as the domain of historians. Archaeologists are attentive to context—where things are found, how they have come to be preserved (or not), the things with which they are associated, the ways things have come to be together—and this kind of perspective to the archive is essential when dealing with the traces left by people who for one reason or another have been defined as non-fellows by the powers that control the archive. The archive itself requires excavation. Nowhere was this more apparent than when working through the records of the National Archive, whose curation and cataloging systems are themselves artifacts of past inequities and exclusions based on racialized assumptions and practices.[24]

Through the study of the practices and day-to-day routines of frontier military life, it is possible to see the entangled interplays of race, class, gender, sex, and rank at play in face-to-face interactions. We see the ways that inequities became naturalized at the level of the post and enforced or challenged at other levels of the military hierarchy. Institutions do not somehow create themselves unbidden and unconnected to the actions of those persons who comprise them. I understand the social world as emerging through routinized practices and procedures and self-conscious performances of self that serve to create (and contest) those things in society that seem unyielding and normative.[25] I am interested in how persons and communities recognize the malleability of what is deemed normative and reshape and reconfigure the world to make spaces for themselves.[26] Objects, words, thoughts, and practices are all the stuff of humanity that situate social relationships in the built and natural worlds.[27]

Archaeological materials and an archaeological approach to archival remains draws our attention from the white officers and allows our gaze to focus on the men who saw opportunities in post-slavery America to create new selves on the western frontier. The archaeological materials date to the years immediately following the Civil War, when Texas was still being reconstructed and Black regulars served in that Reconstruction. It was a time of violence but also a time of hope, a time before the contested election of 1876 marked the abandonment of Black people into the hands of a vengeful white South and a North intent on healing the white supremacist order. Citizenship and equality still seemed achievable dreams, and the men of the Black regulars sought those rights in differing ways, traces of which they left in the soil of the west.

Martial Citizenship and the Necropolitics of Military Life

The military is an institutional space that engages in the enforcement of US social, economic, and political policies, both beneficial and detrimental. The military was a crucial space for remaking what it meant to be a Black man after the end of enslavement. Military service has long been tied to ideas of citizenship rights in the US. Rooted deeply in the American psyche is the notion of a martial citizenship. Full voting and other legal rights have historically been reserved for those who could fight for them on the battlefield, a narrative rooted in the American revolutionary past. Martial citizenship was enforced as both a masculine and a racialized space, with strict structures controlling who was able to participate in the military and in battle, practices that continue to be important sites of contest today. The participation of Black men in the military has a long history of regulation and debate surrounding it, from the American Revolution to the contemporary period.[28]

Military service, especially the right to bear arms in defense of one's country, was identified during the Civil War by Black activists like Frederick Douglass as a space for proving the worthiness of Black men for freedom and citizenship.[29] Military service, argued white abolitionists, would instill a sense of manly honor and discipline in formerly enslaved men. Thomas Higginson, who led a Black regiment from 1862 to 1864, argued that military service proved that formerly enslaved men possessed the fortitude, intellect, and patriotism to be US citizens.[30]

The military initially adopted policies to support the transition of enslaved men into citizens, such as the development of military schools to promote literacy. Sergeant Anthony Jackson, who served at Fort Davis, learned to read and write at a school run by the military chaplaincy at the military depot where he worked. Literacy allowed him to become a noncommissioned officer (NCO). Post schools were intended to be part of an active program of social uplift in the military, parallel to schools run by the Freedman's Bureau.[31] After the coordinated and long-running pay protests of the Fifty-Fourth Massachusetts Infantry during the Civil War, the military adopted the policy of equal pay for men of equal rank no matter their color. This practice continued in the frontier army and made the military one of the more progressive employers in the postwar period.[32] Training opportunities, the ability to earn a living wage, and the ability to participate in martial manhood made the postwar military an inviting opportunity for many Black men. Military service during the Civil War also allowed men to directly participate in their own emancipation, allowing them to wage war on the rebel forces fighting to keep them enslaved.

For men joining the peacetime military, their primary mission was to enforce US Reconstruction policy in the South. It was only after 1869 that enlistment necessarily led to posting in the West. Service in the West provided opportunities to continue to fight against enslavement. Human trafficking was part of the frontier world, with several indigenous groups actively involved in capturing and enslaving Mexican and US nationals.[33] The rhetoric surrounding the enslavement of white citizens, particularly women and children, was predictably hyperbolic, and for men who had not yet experienced first-hand the complicated realities of frontier politics and native-military-settler relations, the opportunity to "rescue" US citizens from Indian depredations was a way to prove one's manhood and citizenship worthiness. In short, there was much about military service that facilitated Black men in their quest to establish their credentials as men and humans.

The negative impacts of service cannot be ignored. In the Civil War, the blood payments demanded of Black soldiers to claim citizenship were quite distinct from those of white soldiers. Black soldiers were routinely murdered by Confederate troops if captured. A notorious example was after the battle at Fort Pillow, where captured Black soldiers were systematically massacred by Confederate troops.[34] In the "peacetime" military, Black soldiers continued to be the targets of violence at the hands of white citizens, who were often not brought to justice.[35]

Increasingly, US policy toward its Black citizens during and beyond Reconstruction was one of political disenfranchisement, economic oppression, and a withdrawal of legal protections that ensured life, liberty, and the pursuit of happiness. The US was invested in the killing of the Black body—socially, politically, economically, and physically. The military was part of this broader necropolitical agenda. It is no stretch to see in eugenics, the school-to-prison pipeline, and anti-Black police brutality the shadows of the Black military experience on the frontier.[36] Violent acts in the past do not remain in the past; they echo, they reverberate, they endure in memory and exhibit themselves in contemporary inequalities. Recent important works on historic sites of widespread violence against Black citizens, such as Edward González-Tennant's work at Rosewood, Florida, or ongoing work at Tulsa, Oklahoma, illustrate the ways that the past keeps a grip on the present.[37]

As an institution of the government, the military seems to have been an early space where practices of unequal education and health care, increased incarceration, and unequal access to public support programs (such as pensions) became normalized. The archaeology of Fort Davis shows that at the same time that Black soldiers at Fort Davis were facilitating the agendas of settler-colonialism as part of their own quest for citizenship rights, the military was engaged in institutionalizing unequal treatment of Black soldiers, treatment that led to crowded living conditions, under provisioning, neglectful medical care, unequal legal treatment, and a failure to adequately address violence committed by white civilians against soldiers. The military engaged in practices that contributed to greater rates of death among Black soldiers on the frontier than their white counterparts.[38] Military service was a site where Black men engaged in a struggle to assert their citizenship rights within an institution that normalized practices that contributed to their deaths.

In military posts, the rank-caste system separating commissioned and noncommissioned officers from enlisted men served to naturalize the order of racial difference.[39] Until Henry Flipper battled his way to become the first Black graduate of West Point in 1877, in the Black infantry and cavalry, commissioned officers were always white and NCOs and enlisted men always Black. Flipper's military career met its inglorious end at Fort Davis in 1882, when he was discharged for behavior unbecoming an officer following a court-martial for embezzlement (a charge not proven). With Flipper's removal, the proper order was restored to the frontier military.[40] As a result of the social isolation and crushing physical abuse, not all men who attempted to complete training at West Point were successful. Cadet Johnson C. Whittaker was court-martialed in 1881 and expelled from West Point after being found bound to his bunk and brutally beaten. He was essentially found guilty of beating himself unconscious.[41] An 1880 letter from the wife of Fort Davis commanding officer Colonel Benjamin Grierson illustrates an example of how officers commanding Black troops endorsed the military color line through their actions: "Fanny Monroe gave a Masquerade Party last week. Lt. Leavell said he wanted to personate Cadet Whittaker, and wanted to borrow your Cadet Uniform for the purpose. I loaned it to him, and he came in to show us how he looked, which was hideous. He had his face Blackened, and then painted red in the most savage style."[42] Officers could participate in dehumanizing Black soldiers in a variety of ways. Racial violence could be experienced in day-to-day interactions on post. Breaking through the glass ceiling of the military had its profound costs. Black graduates John Hanks Alexander and Charles Young, the second and third Black graduates, successfully navigated their postgraduate military careers at great personal cost. Johnson was dead at thirty from a stress-related illness; Young lived a lonely and solitary life in the service.[43]

Thus, the nineteenth-century military successfully fashioned itself as a white supremacist organization, one thought to be a reflection of the natural order found in global mankind, with white men holding the highest positions of power in civilization.[44] The frontier military, therefore, was a tool of civilization both within—with its efforts to uplift the lesser races of Africans who had joined its ranks—and without, first in its work to eradicate the native peoples of North America and later with it expansionist efforts in the Caribbean, Latin America, and the Philippines. Military service brought people of multiple ethnoracial ancestries together, enabling the development of multiracial societies while still promoting a power structure of white supremacy. These complications of settler colonialism and empire demand that the military draw our historical attention.[45]

Frontier military service did more than offer Black men secure pay and the opportunity to become a lesser kind of white man. Service in the army exposed Black men to systems of racialization that were radically different from the one-drop rule that characterized the American South whereby a single Black relative in an extended family tree was enough to deem a person Black. In contrast, the *casta* system of the Spanish world, still very much a part of the Tejano communities of the Rio Grande borderlands, allowed for social mobility. Instead of the Black/white bifurcation that classified all bodies in the South, in the *casta* system, native, Black, and white bodies and all the possible outcomes of their mixing were read through the lens of economic class. While *negro* remained toward the bottom of the system, mixed ancestry, strategic marriage, and economic success were factors that could allow a person or a person's children to advance socially.[46]

Many Black regulars stayed on the frontier after their enlistment and married local Hispanic women, with their descendants among the prominent pioneers of west Texas towns. James Watts, who left military service with the Tenth Cavalry after a gunshot-caused amputation of his arm, is one such example. Discharged at Fort Concho, Watts followed his company to Fort Davis, where he became a saloon and brothel owner. He married a local Latina, and after the closure of the fort in 1891 moved just over twenty miles away to Alpine, where he opened the Mexican Grocery Store and became a respected business owner who self-identified as of "Filipino and Irish ancestry."[47] The Wattses are listed as one of the pioneer families of Alpine on a local history wall. Veterans like Watts were able to remove themselves from Blackness.

For other men, military service provided an arena within which not only to question the social construction of race but also to begin to understand more fully the shared experience of racialization. Men from throughout the North American continent and several from the Caribbean and the East Indies served at Fort Davis. The post brought together men from diverse locales who shared the common experience of being Black in America. The men served alongside Black Seminole army scouts, men whose complicated ancestry had roots in both the horrors of African enslavement and the persecution of indigenous peoples. These were transformative interactions that led not only to an increased sense of diasporic solidarity (that could include indigenous peoples) but also to the configuration of a mode of political engagement that heralded a distinctive Black masculinity within the frontier military. Experiences that emerged out of military service gave men new ways to think about their personal relationships to race, class, masculinity, and, ultimately, other peoples of color. These opportunities emerged on posts in ways that the military powers had not anticipated.[48]

This book is shaped around the twin enabling and debilitating aspects of military service for Black men. Service provided Black men the opportunity to earn wages that were equal to those earned by white men and to demonstrate their commitment to the ideals of martial masculinity and citizenship. Military service was recognized by Black men and the broader Black community as a place of racial uplift and the rehabilitation of the white public perception of Black manhood. Through military service, the battle against prejudice could continue to be fought. Yet Black men strove for these goals within a military institution that was shaped by broader governmental policies that sought to deny racial progress. To clearly see these binary processes at work requires a microscalar examination of the lives of Black troops, their officers, and the broader civilian community.

The World of Nineteenth-Century Fort Davis

Nestled in the Davis Mountains in the vast expanse of Presidio County in west Texas, Fort Davis was first established in 1854 to guard travelers on the Overland Trail from bandits, Native American "raiders," and other threats to colonization and commerce. The post was named for the secretary of war, Jefferson Davis, a man who had not yet betrayed his country. The first fort was a scatter of unimpressive adobe buildings situated at the bottom of a steep canyon, a decision that more than one military expert questioned.[49]

A southern, enslavement-based economy, Texas was among those states that attempted to secede from the Union in 1861, and the federal fort at Davis was abandoned by the Union and held by Confederate forces. Eventually, both forces decided that the post was not a military priority and left the scattered adobe buildings to melt back into the high desert.[50] Following the cessation of hostilities, the military was distracted from the frontier by its role enforcing Reconstruction policies and providing peacekeeping in the conquered South. For the first time in US history, this peacetime military included in its ranks thousands of Black men. The presence of Black military men in the defeated southern states fueled white southern paranoia that they would be subjected to "Negro rule," and violence against and involving Black troops in the South was common. So as federal attention turned back to problems of securing

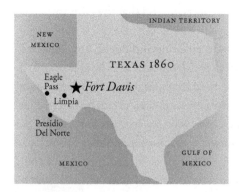

FIGURE 1.3. Location of Fort Davis in Texas. After County Map of Texas, 1860 . . . map, 19uu (https://texashistory.unt.edu/ark:/675 /metapth190739/:accessed July 5, 2020). University of North Texas Libraries, the Portal to Texas History, https://texashistory.unt.edu, University of Texas at Arlington Library.

CHAPTER ONE

FIGURE 1.4. Fort Davis as it appears today. Photograph by the author.

routes to the West and developing infrastructure for communications and travel in 1866 and 1867, Congress decided in 1869 that Black infantry and cavalry regiments should all be sent west of the Mississippi.[51]

The Black troops of the Ninth Cavalry under Colonel Wesley Merritt reoccupied Fort Davis in June 1867, beginning the slow process of rebuilding. The men of the post were again charged with protecting settler populations and commerce. They were also responsible for creating the infrastructure of the area, building and improving roads and installing telegraph lines. Two hundred miles east of El Paso and 402 miles west of San Antonio, the post was isolated. It is difficult to imagine the isolation of nineteenth-century Fort Davis from today's perspective. Today, Fort Davis is nestled with two other nearby towns, Alpine and Marfa, neither of which existed in 1867.[52]

Presidio County, which then included what is now Jeff Davis and Brewster Counties and extended to Mexican border, was a staggering twelve-thousand-plus square miles in size. The population in 1870 for this vast area was counted at 1,636 residents, not including the military men posted at Davis. Nearly half the counted population was described as "Mexican," a constituency most likely comprising people who had found themselves suddenly living on the other side of the border after the Mexican-American War and indigenous people descended from missionized Indians, who for obvious reasons found it safer to identify as Mexican. Previous to the reoccupation of Fort Davis, the 1860 census included a total of six Black denizens of the county—four enslaved men and two free Black men. Fort Davis's soldiers and their families at times brought the Black population of the county close to five hundred. Small Apache rancherias still dotted parts of the landscape, but the area was more commonly used for travel to Mexico by Comanche and Apache warring parties leaving the confines of reservations in Indian Country and New Mexico.[53]

By 1872, the officers' quarters of the post had been nearly completed, with ten of fourteen planned stone and adobe buildings built and two of four planned enlisted men's adobe barrack buildings occupied. Two additional barracks, left in an unfinished state, were being reclaimed by the earth as each rain of the monsoon season converted clay bricks to mud. The men of the Ninth Cavalry were housed in one of the barracks, but overcrowding in the other barrack building forced numerous men of the Twenty-Fourth and Twenty-Fifth Infantries to live in tents. Adjacent to the post was a cluster of small households comprising Mexicans, Anglos, former soldiers, and other immigrants. Colonel William Shafter, then commanding the post, estimated that no more than a few hundred people lived in these communities as of 1871:

> The one here [settlement] although containing about 150 Mexicans and perhaps 25 Americans can hardly be regarded as a settlement as the entire settlement depends of either the post and the stage line for their support . . . and were troops moved probably every person except those connected with the stage company would leave.[54]

Nor were large Native American populations visible. Shafter wrote:

> The Indians that occasionally appear in this vicinity are Apaches either from the Guadalupe mountains or from the vicinity of the Rio Grande south of here where they occupy is whatever is most convenient to them either side of the river. In the time that I have been here (8 months) the only large part of Indians that has been seen near the post was a party of about 20 Comanches who captured a train of work mules in June last about 25 miles west of here. These Indians came from and returned to the east side of the staked plains. Stealing parties of Apaches, usually on foot and numbering from 3 to 6 have been in the vicinity and stole a few cattle.[55]

Climatically, Fort Davis is situated in the Fort Davis Mountains of the Chihuahuan Desert in the Trans-Pecos region of west Texas. The climate within the Chihuahuan dessert is semiarid, with an average annual rainfall of 48 cm.[56] Fort Davis lies at 1,487 meters (4,878 feet) above sea level on a plain composed of quaternary alluvial fan deposits.[57] In the nineteenth century, the volcanic-formed Davis Mountains were recognized as having a pleasant climate, with even the summer months rarely achieving temperatures over the mid-70s Fahrenheit; today, climate change has taken its toll, and average temperatures from May to September are all in the mid-to high 80s. Oaks, junipers, cottonwoods, and pinyon pines dot the hills, and shrubs like cholla, yucca, acacia, sumac, and Apache plum are common, as are a number of grass species. Deer, pronghorn, javelina, bobcats, mountain lions, and the occasional bear were among the larger species living in the region, along with rabbits and a range of other small mammal species and birds.[58]

With its arid climate and cliffs of exposed volcanic rock and unobstructed horizons, the environment of west Texas must have seemed alien to men who, coming predominantly from the low-elevation, humid, claustrophobic South, may well have wondered if freedom could really look like this dry and alien place. In this sparsely populated, little-developed land, the Black regulars went about the work of making the area habitable for their officers, themselves, and the small number of local civilians, while protecting and developing infrastructure to enable the continued march of the US across the continent, all while presenting themselves as men worthy of citizenship.

Why Archaeology at Fort Davis?

In recovering archaeological materials, archaeologists are concerned with finding chronologically and spatially discrete deposits that can be associated with particular populations at particular times. Military posts are spaces of constant turnover in personnel. As a result, military occupations at most posts are characterized by archaeological deposits comprising the mixed trash of multiple companies of multiple regiments.[59] White troops always outnumbered Black troops, and at many places, it is impossible to separate the traces of distinct regiments and companies from one another. In remote and unloved west Texas, however, Black troops were banished to long periods in undesirable places. Their misfortune has made for a unique archaeological circumstance. From 1867 to 1880, Black troops and their white officers manned Fort Davis alone.

When Black troops reoccupied the post in 1867, the first fort was deemed too dilapidated to reoccupy, and the Black soldiers built new housing in a new section of the post on a new alignment. There is no archaeological overlap between the Black troops' occupation and previous occupants.

Through a combination of limited excavation in 2015 and the study of orphaned collections from the site, I have identified multiple discrete deposits associated with enlisted men stationed at the post between 1869 and 1880, with the most significant deposits dating mainly between 1869 and 1875 (table 1.1). Each of these deposits provides windows into the post's past. The materials from these deposits offer the possibility to address some of the silences of the historical record that characterize the daily lives of the Black regulars, counter misleading historical representations, and allow for a new contextualization of the extant archival and architectural records related to the Black regulars. These circumstances mean that the archaeology speaks to the practices and day-to-day experiences of a limited number of men over a short but important moment in American history—the years of Reconstruction. No previously studied fort has had such wonderful temporal clarity in its archaeological remains.

While the archaeology adds a unique dimension to the study of Black soldiers, I also bring a different perspective to the archival record. I see documents as particular kinds of artifacts, objects created for one purpose that have taken very different journeys in archival contexts. As an archaeologist, I work with objects and other traces of the past that have been preserved for study in the present. I consider any particular trace as a thing unto itself but also as part of a larger assemblage. Documents are not an assemblage separate from the archaeological materials; they are all part of the same assemblage, the full range of traces related, in this case, to the life worlds of Fort Davis.

Archaeological data is drawn from what we call the archaeological record. The archaeological record is a modern thing, a product of all the human and nonhuman interactions that have shaped things left behind in the past. Perishable items decay, scavengers drag away bones, ceramic and glass sherds get moved by tunneling gophers, kicked to the surface by aggressive lawn mowing, and kicked around—or picked up and carried away—by visitors. These kinds of actions that shape the remains that have been left to study are known as site formation processes.[60] Part of archaeological interpretation is understanding how and why the materials left for us to study are where they now are and how they got to be in the shape they are.

TABLE I.I. *Archaeological Deposits from Fort Davis*

TYPE OF DEPOSIT	DATE OF DEPOSITION	LIKELY ASSOCIATION
Barracks HB-20 and HB-21 dump	Used no earlier than 1869 and no later than the end of 1872	Ninth Cavalry, Twenty-Fourth Infantry (formerly Thirty-Eighth) and Twenty-Fifth Infantry (formerly Fortieth)
Hearth related to use of Sibley stove, in yard of HB-22. Interpreted as evidence of a tent or canvas house.	1872–1874	Married NCO and wife, Twenty-Fifth Infantry or Ninth Cavalry
Trash from small group using the interior of unfinished HB-22 barracks	No earlier than 1869, no later than 1876	Ninth cavalry, Twenty-Fourth or Twenty-Fifth Infantry, and friends
Yard midden associated with HB-22 barrack porch	1877–1880	Ninth Cavalry
Materials dropped in HB-22 barracks kitchen, under floor	1878–1880	Ninth Cavalry
Ashpit in yard of HB-22, possible slow-cooking feature and clean-out of stove associated with a second tent occupation.	1874–1876	Married NCO and wife, most likely associated with a tent occupation by married NCO and wife, Twenty-Fifth Infantry or Ninth Cavalry.

The archival record is also subject to site formation processes, but those processes are not always explicitly considered by scholars. Some documents get preserved; others do not. The National Archive includes categories of official records that were important to curate for all posts—letters and telegrams sent and received, Standard Orders, muster roles, post returns, court-martial transcripts, surgeon's records, and so forth. Not all the records of a post were preserved, and depending on the post, the quality of those surviving records will vary. Importantly, however, how these materials get cataloged and administered deserves consideration as its own kind of site-formation process. National Archive cataloguing processes, for instance, often render documents written by Black soldiers invisible in location aids and catalog systems.

There is a strange perception by some in the contemporary world that there exists some shining, knowable, single history that represents the truth of the past, and authors who present a new angle on a historical problem or population are too often viewed with suspicion. My own field of archaeology has sometimes been blindered by those who have sought to reconstruct the past as if that one historical narrative, fixed as though engraved, could be recovered if only we had better methodological tools.[61] This idealized past is often cited as being somehow superior to so-called revisionist histories, histories that attempt to demonstrate the rich diversity of lived experiences in the past.

This is not how historians think about their subject. Rather, they recognize that they are engaged in a pursuit of sources and in discussions about how best to understand them (historiography). History, in other words, is a process. Archaeological inquiry is similarly dynamic. We work with the available information, analytical tools, and those random ingredients of human insight and creativity to construct the best possible interpretation of evidence. The most elegant and carefully constructed piece of historical work can be undermined by the discovery of new documents; a simple set of radiocarbon dates on a new discovery can rewrite decades-old understandings of human prehistory. A carefully constructed argument is only as strong as its weakest evidence, and the weight of new information can cause the whole structure to topple.

Those archaeologists who work in time periods that have archival as well as archaeological sources have both the richness and the troubles that come with working with seemingly disparate kinds of evidence. After all, a broken plate dropped outside a barracks would seem to have little in common with a letter written by a commanding officer to army headquarters. Yet both are *things*, things that were created and used for a particular purpose at a particular moment, things that for whatever reason have survived the past to be contemplated in the present. And this last part—the ability to be observed in the present—is key. We are always working in an unknowable universe, always asking, What existed once that exists no longer?

Why some objects endure and others do not is not just a function of natural forces. Humans are the agents of this endurance, deciding what survives and what does not. Such decisions are neither neutral nor academic but are grounded in value judgements. Whose things are worth saving? Whose things can be destroyed? The answers to these two questions determine whose history can be studied.

Archives and museums are shaped by collecting policies that privilege the acquisition of certain things over others and curation policies that decide what should be saved or discarded. In the United States, architectural works, landscapes, and archaeological sites are in some ways more protected than archival materials.[62] We have a range of federal and state laws that attempt to ensure that in instances where federal or state monies are involved, resources that are threatened with destruction must be professionally evaluated and losses mitigated. The document trade, however, has no similar oversight. This means that we are especially dependent on the will of particular individuals or groups to preserve certain kinds of archives. When we are considering archives from which to understand the pasts of minority and subjugated groups, the implications should be obvious. In a world where "fake news" is a common argumentative trope and internet search engines shape knowledge through a focus on what information is most popularly accessed rather than most analytically supported, we need to vigilantly question what it is we think we know, from what sources we know it, and how those sources were created.

Together, these seemingly diverse lines of evidence represent an assemblage. To explain the notion of an assemblage brings us to a fundamental difference between archaeological and other approaches to history: archaeologists are less concerned with what people said than with what people did. Archaeological traces are produced by people *doing*. And by thinking about what they were doing, we inherently confront the contexts in which that doing was accomplished. A letter preserved in an archive is only one trace of the action of writing a letter, an activity that requires access to specific skill sets (reading, writing, etiquette standards), materials (pen, ink, paper, proper lighting, and a surface to writing on and a body to hold the pen, see the paper, and think the words), and other connected activities, like transporting the document from writer to reader. Writing a letter is an intentional act. The letter is part of an assemblage of connected things, people, and doings.[63]

In working through the material traces of the Black soldiers at Fort Davis, it has been important to interrogate the nature of the sources I am working with. Alexander Weheliye's masterful Black feminist work *Habeas Viscus*, particularly his concept of racializing assemblages, has influenced much of the thinking in this book.[64] Instead of thinking about issues of race or racism, Weheliye asks us to think about the process of racialization, or the way the idea of race comes about, as a set of sociopolitical strategies that are employed to sort people into categories of full humans, not-quite humans, and nonhumans (structural racism). Race is not a biological conception but the socially constructed product of a set of processes (racializing assemblages) that create and enforce inequality.

The idea that race is socially constructed is not new in academic circles, but it is often greeted with skepticism outside university campuses. After all, people think it is possible to look at a person and determine "what they are." For those readers who doubt the assertion (and without going into discussions of epidermalization and biological counters), I would point to Deborah Willis and Barbara Krauthamer's book, *Envisioning Emancipation*, in which they have gathered pictures of formerly enslaved people.[65] Among the photos they reproduce are a collection of images that were taken of children who had been enslaved in New Orleans. Copies of the photos were sold as part of a fundraising effort in 1864 to support education for formerly enslaved children. In these images, one sees children of every hue and physiognomy who were all classified as enslaved Negro persons. Clearly, physical biological attributes had very little to do with the state of Blackness and enslavement. Jim Crow laws emphasized that one drop of blood was enough to render a person Black, a powerful example of a set of legal and social practices that were part of an enduring racializing assemblage. Racializing assemblages serve to naturalize the kinds of necropolitical agendas I discussed earlier. But failures in archival collecting, curation, and accessibility that I alluded to above compose another kind of racializing assemblage—a set of processes that keep alternate stories of the past from easily being told. Those whose records are easily recovered and whose versions of the past are hidden is one form of racializing assemblage at play when studying Black soldiers.

Sergeant Anthony Jackson, a soldier we will encounter again, regularly wrote to his wife as his postings took him westward, far from their Alexandria home where she raised their children. When Mrs. Jackson first applied for a widow's pension, she submitted a packet of the most recent letters he had written her from about 1870 until his death in 1875. Unfortunately, as she noted in her second application, those letters were never returned to her when that application was denied. The archivists at the National Archive assured me that Mrs. Jackson's letters were probably tossed when the archive decided not to curate all failed applications (the index record for the failed pension exists, but the failed pension application does not). This kind of record destruction was a routine archival formation process that has done unspeakable violence to Black history. Still, one never knows when one might confront the carefully written letters of a Black regular when reviewing an existing pension file. These resources exist under the radar, so to speak, and are not cataloged as discrete objects. They are rendered invisible in finding aids, the stories they tell silenced until they are excavated from the archive.

Other kinds of practices shape the archival record in ways that provide more information than is typical for certain soldiers. It was not uncommon for people who had been enslaved to change their names several times during their lives, one of the ways that freedom was experienced. Pension applications by men who had changed their names provided detailed accountings of their lives and friendships as they attempted to prove they were who they claimed to be. Archival catalogs attempt to cross-reference names where possible when multiple names had been established for a person, but this is not foolproof. Martin Pedee, whom we will encounter in the next chapter, was remembered in an oral history published on a local church web page as having served in a US Colored troop during the Civil War.

When one visits the National Archive, the help desk associates point researchers to Fold3 and Ancestry to track down most service records. Pedee did not appear in those databases or on the National Park Service's wonderful digital website of Civil War soldiers. I decided on my last day at the archive in 2019 to skip the electronic resources and survey the old microfilm of index cards that were used to organize the pension files. My hope was to identify soldiers I hadn't found through other means. I came across a "Martin Pegee" who served in the same regiment and company as Martin Pedee. Pegee had a successful pension request. In pulling the file, I found that Martin had served as Pegee in the Civil War, Pedee in the frontier army, and at different points in his life went back and forth between the two similar names.[66] I would never have found this wonderful resource had I stuck to the digital archive alone. The National Archive recently had a volunteer day dedicated to digitizing records associated with buffalo soldiers, and hopefully, as a result of this and other efforts, such as the website of the Buffalo Soldier History Museum in Houston, more first-hand documents will emerge.

In these pages, I will draw on court-martial transcripts at length; these are another resource that remain underutilized. Court-martial charges and verdicts were published in a number of sources and are easily found. These publications, however, provide no account of testimony, names of witnesses, or details of defendant statements. To see that requires that one travel to the National Archive and Record Administration and pull individual court-martial transcripts—time consuming but rewarding work. In the details of trial transcripts, we hear the voices of Black soldiers but also clearly see the biases and blunders of the military judicial system. We can also see the many times when court-martial verdicts were overturned or mitigated higher up in the chain of command. This messiness and detail is smoothed out and erased in published summaries.

In pulling together this work, I have tried to draw on as many voices of Black soldiers as possible, allowing them and their friends, loved ones, and comrades to dictate as much of their stories as possible. Sometimes, this meant moving beyond the temporalities of the fort and following the men into other parts of their lives. For those whose voices remain muted, the eloquence of the other material traces they left behind will have to suffice.

The Organization of this Book

Each of the chapters that follow are like beads on a string; though they stand alone as vignettes about particular assemblages of people, things and events, when linked together they create something more complex, a woven story of a different kind about the death of one Corporal Daniel Tallifero at Fort Davis in the early morning of November 21, 1872. My interest is in bringing to light the kinds of interpersonal relationships and mundane routines, objects, and places that characterized the embodied social experience of living at Fort Davis during Reconstruction. Some of the individuals encountered in these pages will emerge again and again, linked to the multiple webs of people, places, and things that enfold the messiness of life, a messiness further complicated when people live and work together in isolated circumstances. I have included a chart providing a shorthand reminder of who particular people were for the reader to reference when it becomes difficult to keep actors distinct from one another (table 0.1). I hope by the time we reach the end, a number of these men will have made a deep impression on the reader.

Chapter 2, "Corporal Williams's Tent," continues our consideration of the geographic and social spaces of the fort and its environs. Corporal Williams served in the Twenty-Fifth Infantry, and his and his wife's tent became a locus for an event and resulting court-martial that stoked controversy and outrage among some members of the fort's community. The happenings at Corporal Williams's tent provide an important entrance for considering the myriad impacts of living conditions on the men's health and lives at the post and allows for the introduction of some of the strong characters who shaped post life during the time of this study.

Soldiers, as collective members of companies or as individuals, through their own efforts attempted to improve the living conditions of the camp. In chapter 3, "Private Stevenson's Pocketknife," the reader encounters the range of material culture that was accumulated and used by buffalo soldiers in their living and workspaces. Company funds were used to acquire goods that one may not associate with the rough-and-ready life of a frontier soldier—tableware, glassware, and bathware—that speak to the men's understanding of the role of genteel manners and presentation in the performance of nineteenth-century versions of martial manliness, which were very much situated in discourses on civilization and refinement. Likewise, unique personal items demonstrate how men presented themselves as individuals within an organization that encouraged communal identification.

While chapters 2 and 3 focus primarily on soldiers' experiences in and around the barracks, chapter 4, "Sergeant Hewey's Stick," provides a deeper consideration of the spatial and social structure of the broader post. Who were the actors who were potential allies or obstacles in military life? What was the nature of relationships with civilian populations, and how did soldiers move across the physical and social spaces of the post and the neighboring communities? The case of Sergeant Hewey and his stick, which may or may not have been a firearm, also provides the opportunity to further examine the complicated relationships of power between commissioned officers, NCOs, and enlisted men, while introducing more of the long-serving NCOs at Fort Davis during the period 1869–1875.

One of the promises of military life for Black men was an opportunity for an education. Chapter 5, "Private Johnson's Letters," reviews the contrast between the post's failure to consistently mount a post school before 1873 with the archaeological evidence of continued interest in education among the men. With the founding of a regularly offered school in January 1873, we see evidence of growing literacy not only in the archaeological remains from the barracks but also in the archival record of an increased presence of letters by soldiers. Soldiers clearly understood the revolutionary potential of an education in their quest for citizenship.

In chapter 6, "First Sergeant Sample's Eyesight," I consider more fully the range of intimate relationships between men and women and between men and other men and what was sanctioned and unsanctioned in military culture. Fort Davis was occupied at a time when notions of love and intimacy and the definition of gender and sex roles were being challenged. For formerly enslaved African American men, the naturalized conflation of citizenship and patriarchy that characterized white manhood was not a given, and men and women sought to define their relationships to one another on their own terms. The military was also structured in ways that depended on close relationships between men sharing the same rank. Close living quarters and life on patrol created circumstances that encouraged emotional and even physical intimacy at a time when "manly love" was a necessarily opaque construct.

Finally, in chapter 7, "Corporal Tallifero's Cap," we confront the event of November 21, 1872: the shooting death of Daniel Tallifero. This event was widely reported in the media of the time and has been regularly cited in the secondary literature. A look at primary sources related to the case and a consideration of fort life that emerged through the historical archaeology of Fort Davis suggest that the case deserves closer examination, an archaeological assessment that requires us to consider the complicated and interconnected interpersonal relationships that linked the lifeworld of the post. If the previous chapters are beads on a string, the Daniel Tallifero shooting is the clasp that holds them together.

I push for the strength of a historical archaeology that recognizes the agency of things and the thingness of documents as a powerful tool for recognizing racializing assemblages in the past. I document the active manipulation of the media by military officers to foil the efforts of Black men to claim citizenship rights and naturalize their deaths. While Daniel Tallifero died almost 140 years ago, the processes that facilitated his death and the slipshod investigation that followed are no strangers to us today. If we can render visible the racializing assemblages that made it easy to represent Tallifero as an embodiment of a stereotype and glorify his death, we may see ways to halt those same processes today. Daniel Tallifero's life mattered, and the relationships between people, places, and things that served to naturalize the inevitability of his death haunt us today.

CHAPTER ONE

2

CORPORAL WILLIAMS'S TENT
Frontier and Military Spaces

It was past ten o'clock on a rainy August night, 1872, punctuated with cracks of lightning. Sergeant Edward McKenzie made his way from the commissary to check on his relief for guard duty.[1] He made it as far as the flagpole on the parade ground when he heard someone scream "Murder!" Thinking at first that the sound had originated at the sentry at post 5, he soon realized the scream had come from Corporal Williams's tent.

Private Joseph William Stevenson, Company E, Twenty-Fifth Infantry, was lying in his bunk when he heard the scream. He recognized the voice of Mrs. Williams. Remembering that Williams was on guard duty, Stevenson jumped from bed without dressing, grabbed his small knife, and in his underwear, ran to the tent, located outside the barracks. Private Stevenson got to the tent first.

"Annie, what is the matter?" he asked. She told him that Martin Pedee had been in her tent—and not for the first time; he had been in it once before. She asked Stevenson to go around to Sergeant Sample's room to see if Pedee was in there. Stevenson headed toward Sample's quarters, located at the far north side of the barracks.

Sergeant McKenzie passed Stevenson and asked him what the noise had been. The private directed him to the tent.

"What is the matter with her?" the sergeant demanded.

"That damned Pedee was in my tent!" she responded. Looking at the rain and the dark, Sergeant McKenzie was skeptical.

"How in the devil do you know it was Pedee?" he asked.

"I know it well that it was him!" she said. "I could tell by feeling his head."

McKenzie asked if she had a light in her tent. She said that she didn't.

"How the devil could you tell by feeling of a man's head in so dark a night?" he asked, exasperated.

"Well, I don't know. I believe it was him. He was here before," Mrs. Williams said. "I wish you would go around to Sergeant Sample's room and wake up Sergeant Sample and see if Pedee is in there."

McKenzie told her he had been away from the guard house much too long but promised to tell her husband, Corporal Williams, to come back to the tent. As the sergeant left the tent, he could hear her say, "Goddamn it. I wish he was in hell or some other place."

Housing at Fort Davis, 1867–1875

Corporal Williams and his wife were not the only military personnel living in tents, though exact numbers are unclear. The earliest illustration of postbellum Fort Davis shows multiple lines of two-man shelter tents immediately east of where the barracks were eventually built.[2] In December 1868, the troops were still housed in tents when Private George McIsaac was deemed responsible for a carbine stolen from his tent. In his statement, McIsaac describes his tent as being occupied by himself and one other man, Private Hughes Davis. From this account, it appears that the men were living in a two-person tent typical of those used when on patrol.[3] Privates like McIsaac would have been moved to barracks as they became available. Black NCOs are recorded as living in barracks dormitories with enlisted men throughout the post's occupation, as revealed in court-martial testimony in multiple transcripts.[4] Only the highest-ranking NCO of a company would be eligible for private quarters, since each barracks was designed with a first sergeant's quarters. Yet given the overcrowding of barracks, these would have been in short supply.

Married men presented a particular challenge. The only enlisted men allowed to marry were NCOs, and to do so required permission of commanding officers. Commanding officers recognized the "civilizing" influence of marriage and women's domesticity within the post setting, but no distinct housing for married men was constructed at Post Davis until the 1880s. By the mid-1870s, married NCOs seem to have constructed two small neighborhoods of houses for their families, one near the quartermaster's corral and another in a remote area at the boundary of the fort reservation, now known as the "laundress quarters."[5] Many of the NCOs were married to women who were employed as

US military laundresses. Unmarried laundresses in the early postbellum post lived in tents close to the barracks.[6]

Pinpointing from testimony where the Williamses' tent was located in 1872 is a bit complicated. Corporal Edward McKenzie of Company E, Twenty-Fifth Infantry, described the tent "to the left of Company E's barracks." Private Henry Sappho was slightly more helpful, stating, "The tent was on this end of the barrack and I was at the other end of the barrack, the tent was across the road running past the opposite end of the barrack from where I was sitting." Since Sappho was sitting near Sample's quarters on the northern end of the barracks, the tent was at the southern end, on the same side of the barracks building as the guard house. An 1871 photograph shows a tent of the "canvas house" or "wall tent" style clearly nestled south of the mess hall and east of the dormitory.[7] That same photograph labels the northern half of the structure as "Co G."[8] A row of tents are seen well behind the barracks and may be the laundress tents. While we cannot know whether this was the Williamses' tent, that area was used as living space for people living outside the barracks.

Building the Post

Construction on the postbellum incarnation of Fort Davis commenced shortly after June 29, 1867, when Lieutenant Colonel Wesley Merritt of the Ninth Cavalry began the reoccupation of the post. Cavalry men were used to securing locally available materials, with a pinery developed twenty-five miles away, a stone quarry less than a mile away, and a limestone quarry (for mortar) thirty miles away.[9]

Little progress was made on construction before the department quartermaster called for a halt to all building due to budget shortfalls on March 30, 1869.[10] The 1869 fiscal yearend report for Fort Davis described the structures of the post as four completed officers' quarters (one major's, one captain's, and two lieutenant's quarters), a guard house and magazine, and the major quartermaster's building. Two sets of company quarters were partly built, and one structure, still floorless but roofed and windowed, was temporarily occupied by Companies C and K, Ninth Cavalry.[11]

A plan map from two years later, in 1871, represents the unrealized plans for the post. The imagined four company barracks and twenty officers' houses were planned. Barracks were situated on the east side of the parade ground, fourteen of the officers' quarters on the west side, and the remaining six split between the northern and southern edges. A pair of cavalry corrals and stables were constructed immediately to the east of the men's barracks. At the time that the 1871 map was drafted, two of the barracks were represented as completed, two still under construction, and nine of the officers' quarters complete, with others indicated as in process or planned. The commander's house stood in the center of the planned row and faced the flagstaff. The temporary hospital building was immediately behind (west of) the commander's house. Other standing structures included a stone guard house and a sutler's store, both immediately to the south of the parade ground, and a quartermaster's complex to the southeast of the southernmost barracks, consisting of the quartermaster's office and store, corral, commissary, and bakery. These were indicated to be "old adobe buildings," presumably from the first fort and reused when possible. The temporary hospital, for instance, was situated in a cluster of older buildings to the west of the parade ground. On the northern edge of the post was a post office and, by 1869, a building that could be used as a post church and school. Another adobe quartermaster store was located immediately to the north of the northernmost cavalry corral. The officer's quarters were being built from north to south along the parade grounds, while the barracks were being built from south to north. Only three of the nine officer's cabins faced occupied barracks.

Lieutenant Colonel James H. Carelton, acting assistant inspector general, provided a description of the post that accompanied this map and was tasked with the job of suggesting how to complete the construction of necessary buildings in the most economical way. He wrote on March 6, 1871:

> Ground plans of the post show which buildings are finished and occupied. The two buildings marked in red near the head of "mens [sic] quarters" are built up to the roof. If they are to be occupied, I do not think with proper management it would cost a large sum to put on the roofs and make them habitable. I recommend that the building nearest the walk from the flagstaff be roofed and occupied as office and store rooms and with grain and forage by the quartermasters and the other be made into a hospital . . . if the garrison of the post be one company of cavalry and two of infantry, which I shall recommend, two companies of infantry filled to 60, the present allowed strength, could occupy one of the sets of quarters already built and the company of cavalry, 84 strong, could occupy the other and have a saddle room and shop for the saddler in the same building.[12]

CHAPTER TWO

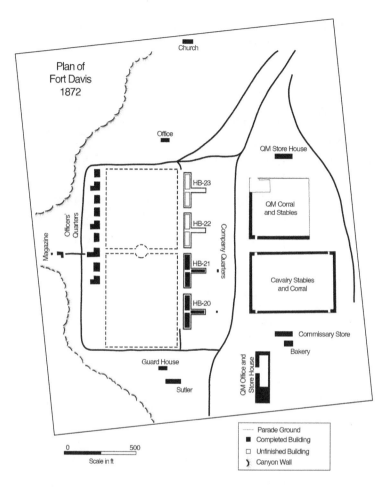

FIGURE 2.1. Map of the post, 1872, after "Plan of Fort Davis, Texas," 1871, in Greene, *Historic Resource Study*, 462. Illustration by the author.

Carleton's recommendations to reduce the planned housing for the enlisted men seems to have been partially followed. It would be in the fourth building where the quartermaster's storehouse would be situated, while the third building in the row would eventually become a completed barracks. Writing in 1881 to the adjutant general regarding post repairs, Shafter, again commanding the post drew on his historical recollections of building functions. "Building Number 4 [the fourth barracks building] was originally intended as a barrack for the companies but has been to this time used as a quartermaster's store house."[13]

TABLE 2.1. *Commanding Officers of Fort Davis from 1869 to 1876 (after Utley 1965)*

NAME	RANK	REGIMENT	PERIOD OF SERVICE
Wesley Merritt	lieutenant colonel and brevet major general	Ninth Cavalry	June 1, 1868–September 3, 1869
William Bayard	captain and brevet Major	Ninth Cavalry	September 3, 1869–October 10, 1869
James F. Wade	major and brevet colone	Ninth Cavalry	October 10, 1869–November 26, 1869
Edward Hatch	colonel and brevet major	Ninth Cavalry	November 26, 1869–December 15, 1870
John W. French	captain	Twenty-Fifth Infantry	December 15, 1870–February 12, 1871
Andrew Sheridan	captain and brevet major	Twenty-Fourth Infantry	February 12, 1871–May 18, 1871
William F. Shafter	lieutenant colonel	Twenty-Fourth Infantry	May 18, 1871–June 18, 1871
John W. French	captain	Twenty-Fifth Infantry	June 18, 1871–July 9, 1871
William Shafter	lieutenant colonel	Twenty-Fourth Infantry	July 9, 1871–October 5, 1871
Charles C. Hood	captain	Twenty-Fourth Infantry	October 5, 1871–November 1, 1871
William Shafter	lieutenant colonel	Twenty-Fourth Infantry	November 1, 1871–November 12, 1871
Charles C. Hood	captain	Twenty-Fourth Infantry	November 12, 1871–January 1, 1872
William Shafter	lieutenant colonel	Twenty-Fourth Infantry	January 1, 1871–May 26, 1872
George L. Andrews	colonel	Twenty-Fifth Infantry	May 23, 1872–July 31, 1872

NAME	RANK	REGIMENT	PERIOD OF SERVICE
Frank T. Bennett	captain	Ninth Cavalry	July 31, 1872–August 8, 1872
George L. Andrews	colonel	Twenty-Fifth Infantry	August 8, 1872–August 23, 1873
David D. Van Valzah	captain	Twenty-Fifth Infantry	August 23, 1873–September 1873
Zenas R. Bliss	major and brevet lieutenant colonel	Twenty-Fifth Infantry	September 1873–April 14, 1874
David D. Van Valzah	captain	Twenty-Fifth Infantry	April 14, 1874–September 8, 1874
George L. Andrews	colonel	Twenty-Fifth Infantry	September 8, 1874–April 25, 1876
Zenas R. Bliss	major and brevet lieutenant colonel	Twenty-Fifth Infantry	April 25, 1876–October 29, 1876

From the vantage point of 1871, it would be six more years before either structure was completed. In the years between, the adobe walls of these two buildings would slowly melt away.

Carleton's recommendation was in contradiction to the monthly inspection reports that continued to note that soldier housing was inadequate. Just two months earlier, the post adjutant requested that "sufficient double bunks be made for forty men of A Company 25th infantry."[14] The double bunks are worth a moment of consideration. The bunk, based on an example that was found at Fort Mifflin, Pennsylvania, was a simple four-post design, with "side-boards connected by a mortise and tenon joint. Boards would have run the length of the bed to hold a double bed sack on each tier. Measuring five feet ten inches long and four feet wide, each level—or "crib," as it was called—was intended to accommodate two soldiers positioned with their head next to the feet of their bunkmate."[15] By 1875, single iron bunks were becoming the standard, as part of the effort to improve health.[16] Piling men on top of one another and squishing them together was one solution for fitting twice as many men into an inadequate dormitory space.

In May 1872, Post Surgeon Daniel Weisel described the two completed barracks:

> But two of the barracks are completed nor are they really finished. They are plastered inside but very badly and the greater part of the plaster has largely fallen off and no attempts made to repair the walls. The barracks are very untidy dirty and disorderly—they have earth floors which by want of proper attention are very dusty—and soil all articles of clothing in the barracks. The mess rooms and kitchens are not plastered, have earth floors and are equally as dirty and untidy as the barracks. Nor is the police as attended to as were formerly ... the walls of the other two barracks as those now occupied, were put up in 1868 and still so remain not being even closed in and have of course been much damaged by the weather. At one time seven companies were crowded in these two barracks giving each man not 100 cubic feet of airspace."[17]

Weisel's assessment was written near the end of his term at Fort Davis, and his words speak to his frustrations that commanding officer Colonel William Shafter had little concern for the well-being of his men.

Two years after Carelton's visit, in 1873, with an aggregate of 288 on post, as the two structures remained incomplete, then-commander Major Zenas Bliss reported,

> Barracks for enlisted men inadequate—without floor and very poorly ventilated—but three or four windows to each company quarters. . . . The quarters originally intended for two companies are now occupied by four. The men are much too crowded and the windows kept habitually closed. Company commanders have been directed to keep the windows wide open all times without except in the extremely cold and stormy weather.[18]

In November 1873, having returned to the command of the post, Colonel George Andrews forwarded a letter with an estimate for the cost of constructing a flat roof on the walls of "an unfinished company quarters to be used as a quartermaster's store house." He refers to the recent need to relocate men from the badly leaking post hospital to the barracks but makes no mention of the continued crowded conditions of quarters.[19] Nothing had changed since Bliss's observations a few months earlier, but different commanding officers clearly had varying opinions about what standards of living were appropriate for their soldiers.

The lack of sufficient housing was more than an inconvenience to the soldiers; in the scientific knowledge of the day, it was an active threat to their health and lives. Understandings of health at the dawn of the second half of the nineteenth century were entrenched in what is known as miasma theory. Miasmas, or the concentrations of noxious airs, were understood to be the source of diseases. Untreated sewage, standing water, trash piles, poorly lit areas, and areas with no ventilation (to disperse bad airs) caused disease. While the notion of a miasma may seem strange to us, this explanation for the cause of ill health was a solid interpretation of observations of the natural world available at the time. Some of the worst epidemics of diseases like cholera and yellow fever were found in the humid, swampy areas of the Deep South. Tuberculosis, or consumption as it was known, was a public health scourge that particularly plagued overcrowded housing in urban areas. Public health initiatives focused on improving sanitation and housing did mitigate some health problems. Likewise, the mid-nineteenth century saw the growth of health movements that gave greater consideration to diet and its relationship to health. Food reformers like Justus Von Liebig, Sylvester Graham, and John Harvey Kellogg changed the composition of the diet and promoted ways to prepare food that allowed the body to better utilize it. Dietary, personal, and public hygiene were the best tools available to combat the greatest health challenges of the mid- to late nineteenth century.[20]

The military's ability to maintain a strong, healthy fighting force necessitated a good diet, adequate access to clean air, and clean living conditions. At Fort Davis, 1867 and 1868 saw widespread outbreaks of scurvy and dysentery, illnesses related to sanitation and diet that were the leading causes of death among the enlisted men. On his arrival at the post in August 1868, then-assistant surgeon Weisel, a young and determined man of thirty, began a rigorous campaign of sanitation reform at Fort Davis. The archive of Fort Davis is peppered with documents dating from Weisel's tenure through May 1872 that attest to his attempts to improve the living circumstances of the men at the post. He developed recipes for preparing rations that drew on contemporary food science and nutrition, pushing for meats to be seared and then slow cooked to retain as much nutritional value as possible.[21] He was successful in decreasing the number of dysentery cases at the post and nearly eliminated scurvy through his attention to clean water sources and increasing access to fresh garden produce and "antiscorbutics" (what we would recognize as vitamin C) in the diet.[22]

Despite Weisel's efforts, by failing to provide "adequate space" for each soldier, the military was, according to standards of the time, threatening men's health and lives. Starting in 1875, with the publication of Circular No. 8, a proper military dormitory was recommended to provide five hundred cubic feet of air per man.[23] Circular No. 8 drew on post data from 1870 through 1874 and was intended to document hygiene at military posts and create new standardized guidelines. Post surgeons were asked to respond to surveys about troop housing, health, rations, and the general sanitation and health challenges. Among the information they were asked to provide was how much cubic footage of air was available in the troops' living spaces. What information was provided varied from post to post. Weisel, while no longer serving at Fort Davis, was responsible for summarizing the post. Weisel described the barracks as follows:

> East of and in a line parallel with, the officer's quarters, with a parade ground of 500 feet in width intervening, are located the barracks, two separated buildings, distant from each other 30 feet, built of adobe, plastered inside and out and ceiled, a wide covered porch extending entirely around. Each barrack is 186 feet long and 27 feet wide and contains two dormitories, separated by a passage-way of 27 by 12 feet which leads to a building, 86 by 27 feet, containing the mess-room, 50 by 24 feet, the kitchen, 20 by 24 feet, and the store-room, 10 by 24 feet. Each dormitory is 24 by 82 feet and 12 feet high containing 23,760 cubic feet of air-space. They are warmed by open fire places, and ventilated by large windows, four in the opposite sides of each room, and by a large ventilator in the ceiling, 20 by 4 feet. The men sleep upon iron bedsteads, having wooden slats. Five large and commodious sinks are placed 200 feet in rear of the quarters, and are kept well disinfected.[24]

Note that by 1875, the wooden double bunks previously used at the post had been replaced with iron ones. Weisel calculated that each dormitory had 23,760 cubic feet of air. Using his numbers, I calculate there to have been slightly less: 23,616 cubic feet. Weisel's numbers would result in a total of 95,040 cubic feet for the troops, whereas my number suggest a little less, 94,464 cubic feet. The average number of men varied at Fort Davis, with a high of 316 men at post in 1870-71 and a low of 145 in 1871-72, with 216 in 1872-73 and 204 in 1873-74. Recall Weisel's 1872 observation that at one point, seven companies were crammed into two barracks designed for a total of two companies. This suggests that in 1871-72, the men enjoyed a luxurious 651 cubic feet on average per man, and a less desirable 298 cubic feet per man in 1870-71. Since troops were moved in and out of the post throughout the year and at any given time a portion of troops could be on patrol or engaged in other off-post duties, these numbers should be thought of as a snapshot of a particular moment in time during each of those years.

How do these numbers compare with other forts in the Department of Texas, where so many Black troops were stationed? Fort Concho's post surgeon reported that barracks there, when companies were at full force, provided 368 cubic feet per man. Fort Bliss provided 500 cubic feet per man when at capacity. Fort Brown's surgeon estimated an average of 650 cubic feet per man. Fort Duncan, where Company E, Twenty-Fifth Infantry, was stationed prior to Fort Davis, also had two barracks. Their surgeon estimated that the infantry had an average of 542 cubic feet per man, whereas the cavalry had 463. At Davis, based on what we know of housing arrangements and relative numbers, cavalry men were likely to enjoy more breathing room than their infantry brothers. At Fort Duncan, the Twenty-Fifth Infantry band was reported to be living in a line of tents outside of barracks. While at Fort Davis, members of that same band, of which Martin Pedee was a member, were described as holing up in different spaces across the post in a quest for shelter.[25] Fort Quitman, where Company I, Ninth Cavalry, had been stationed prior to Fort Davis, had five hundred cubic feet per man, while Fort Stockton, the post closest to Davis in the east, had seven hundred cubic feet per man.[26] While certainly not the worst living conditions in the Department of Texas, which consistently seems to have been strained for housing, Fort Davis was also not among the best. Importantly, we have direct archival evidence that senior officers in the institution chose to not fund the completion of one much-needed barracks building and divert another to a different use—all while ensuring that the housing of white officers continued to be completed.

It was not until 1877 when Building 3 (now referred to as Historic Building-22 [HB-22] by the park service) was completed and occupied. It is this building, the third in the row of four planned barracks, where excavations under my direction were conducted in 2015. Although the building stood incomplete, the structure and its surrounds were in no way unoccupied. Two features found outside the barracks attest to men (and possibly their families) living outside of the barracks, and a discrete feature inside the building speaks to the ways men used unofficial post spaces to escape the routines and regiments of the military.

The Archaeology of Crowded Living at Fort Davis

Two archaeological cooking features were found during the 2015 excavations in the "courtyard" to the south of the mess hall and east of the southernmost dormitory of HB-22. This is the equivalent position relative to the barracks building as the tent seen in the 1871 photograph of the post, just in the yard of the unfinished barracks. The two cooking features date to slightly different times in the fort's occupation. The earlier feature was identified as a hearth and dates between 1869 and 1874. It survives as a ring of stones surrounding a circular burned area full of ash, charcoal, artifacts, and animal bone. Although at first glance, the feature appears to be an open campfire, excavations led by a team of Howard University researchers at Pine Springs, a cavalry subpost, found that men built campfires in holes to protect the flames from winds.[27] That is not the case for this feature, where the burning took place on what seems to have been a soil-fill surface. Fort Davis also enjoys high winds, and the fire's flames must have been protected in some way. The circumference of the hearth, as suggested by the ring of stones, was large enough to accommodate a Sibley stove, a commonly used conical-shaped military invention made popular in the Civil War. When one looks at the soil profile from the excavation, it is possible to see that the dirt that accumulated around the base of the rotting metal stove retained an image of the stove, clearly conical in shape.

The Sibley stove (and sometimes the accompanying tent) was a Civil War staple that found its way onto the frontier.[28] Sibley stoves were used both inside and outside tents, with iron pipe being used to vent the smoke. While the stoves are usually illustrated for use with Sibley tents (also conical), they were useful in any tent. What photos there are of tents at Fort Davis suggest that NCOs lived in the rectangular tents that typically housed officers, while privates lived in triangular shelter tents.

The highest density of artifacts in the area of the hearth were found surrounding the fire, with fewer materials recovered from the center of the feature. This would also suggest that the hearth feature was created as part of the use of a stove. A stove would serve as a burner for trash and as a heat source for cooking, but materials would have to be raked out of the feature as they accumulated, which would create a midden around the stove. That the trash was found associated with the hearth suggests that these materials were left as part of an abandonment event (i.e., when the tent was broken down, the stove and tent inhabitants moved elsewhere).

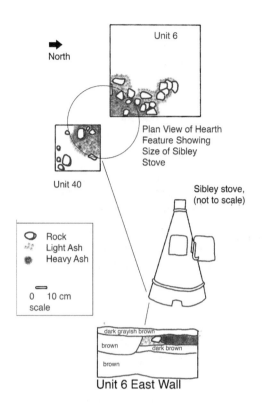

FIGURE 2.2. Vertical and horizontal views of hearth. When the archaeological traces of the hearth are compared to the known shape and dimensions of a Sibley stove, the interpretation of this feature as associated with such an appliance is supported. Illustration by the author.

So the hearth, although it is just one trace, suggests the presence of a bigger assemblage—a stove and a tent—sometime in the past. But when? Two artifacts recovered from the hearth feature suggest a very tight date range for its use: a .45 caliber bullet, 250 grain weight, was found at the top of the feature. These particular bullets were introduced in 1873 for use in the Colt single-action army revolver. Ordnance surveys for Fort Davis suggest that they were not distributed to enlisted cavalry men there until late 1874 but could have been available earlier as a personal sidearm.[29] To be conservative, it is reasonable to suggest that the hearth was abandoned no earlier than 1874. At the lowest depth of the feature was a brass .50-70 rifle casing (.50 caliber, accommodating 70 grains of black powder), produced between 1866 and 1873 and used for Springfield trapdoor rifles for 1866, 1868, and 1870. The ordnance surveys for Fort Davis first shows Springfield caliber .45 rifles used at the post in the second quarter of 1875.[30] All the items found in the hearth easily fall within a manufacture date of 1870 to 1875, with a number of artifacts not generally used past the mid-1870s. Thus, this feature seems to be related to the long periods of overcrowding experienced by the men at Fort Davis before the completion of the third barracks building and abandonment dating roughly to the period when married NCOs and laundresses were establishing non-tent housing elsewhere on the post.

A second cooking feature, a large ash deposit that included artifacts and animal bones, was found closer to the barracks but roughly in line with the hearth feature. The feature does not have the same kind of stone border as the hearth and seems to be a bed of ash containing burned material about ten to twelve inches deep and at least three-and-a-half feet wide. The soil in this feature had different concentrations of ash within it both horizontally and vertically, giving the impression that the pit had been dug through repeatedly, causing mixing in clumps. Beds of hot ash are left to smolder and are useful for slow cooking foods like beans or stews in covered cast iron pots. The pots can be embedded in the hot ash bed with additional ash shoveled on top to help cook the food. At least one frontier account also refers to cooking eggs by roasting them in the shell, buried in ash.[31]

During excavation, we took samples of the soil to later "flot" (flotation) in the lab. This is a process through which light fraction materials, typically organics, and heavy fraction elements, small artifacts and small bone and stone materials, are separated from the soil and analyzed. Flotation samples allow us to get a glimpse of the small evidence missed during excavation. In the case of the ash bed, eggshell was found throughout, suggesting that this was actively used as a cooking feature. Among the artifacts recovered were military objects and everyday trash.

Just as the hearth speaks to the development of canvas homes by troops who may not have had barracks space, the ash bed speaks to one of the ways men adjusted to limitations of post facilities.

The trash in the ash bed is different from that found around the hearth; different ceramic types and materials were found in the ashpit, suggesting that the ash source for this feature was not the other cooking feature. In other words, two different groups of people left these archaeological traces. Among the datable materials found in the ashpit are a .45-caliber casing of the type found in the hearth (and therefore dating from 1874 onward), two forage cap slides of the type used on the 1873 forage cap, a buckle from a drum sling that doesn't match the regulation sling introduced in 1885, a pepper-sauce bottle dating after 1870, and dark green or "black" glass bottle sherds, which are rarely found on sites after the 1870s. Importantly, neither of the cooking features found outside the HB-22 barracks contain any glass sherds that can be attributed to lager beers, which are ubiquitous on the post after their widespread availability in 1875.[32] Given the dates of these deposits as beginning sometime after 1870 and being abandoned during the 1870s, the troops most likely to have created these deposits are NCOs from Companies D, E, or G of the Twenty-Fifth Infantry, or from Company I, Ninth Cavalry. These possibilities will be discussed more in chapters 3 and 6.

A final deposit that deserves our consideration was found inside the partially built barracks, near the location of one of the interior fireplaces. My team excavated a unit against the interior wall to understand the construction sequence of the building from an archaeological perspective. We were able to find the edge of the foundation, the original surface, and the construction trench and footing. As we excavated, we also found areas that corresponded to slumping of adobe melt against the wall, presumably dating to the period when the building was unfinished, roofless, and melting. Melting adobe buildings create massive amounts of mud, and under one of these melt and rubble areas, the excavators found a concentration of artifacts that were deposited in the structure while the walls were standing but the building was not yet complete. This means that the materials necessarily were deposited between 1868, when construction stopped, and 1876, when construction resumed.

So how did these items come to be in the unfinished barracks? One possibility is that the empty buildings were used as dumping grounds. In the early twentieth century, many of the abandoned buildings at Fort Davis were used as places to dump trash, with thick deposits of garbage found during excavations by the National Park Service in barracks HB-20 and 21. In the case of dumps like that, the full range of domestic garbage is represented—cans, glass, tools, ceramics, metal, animal bones, abandoned construction materials, and so on. Two factors suggest that the materials are not part of dumping episodes. First, Assistant Surgeon Weisel was clear about identifying where trash deposits were and ensuring they were properly maintained with regular burning or liming, both of which leave archaeological traces. The dump located to the north of the barracks row that was discovered in 2009 seems to have been the main dump for the post referred to in Weisel's reports. Second, the materials from the deposit represent a narrow range of activities; there is a bit of charcoal suggesting a small fire, and the remains alcohol bottles. These materials speak to a small number of men (or men and women) sitting and drinking together, finding shelter and privacy against the tall walls of the unfinished barracks. Quiet spaces would have been valued on a post that had increasingly crowded barracks.

Private Henry Sappho, Company E, Twenty-Fifth Infantry, had been sitting on the steps of his company barracks close to the door of Sergeant Sample's room when he heard Mrs. Williams scream that Pedee was in her tent, an accusation that he doubted. "Here is Pedee in here in Sergeant Sample's room—there is somebody in here snoring it must be Pedee," Sappho said to Private James Wilson, Company E ,Twenty-Fifth Infantry, as he was entering the barracks. Sappho stayed on the steps for a few more minutes and retreated to his own bunk. He saw Private Stevenson enter the far end of the barracks by Sergeant Sample's quarters. Private Stevenson was none too happy to be knocking on the sergeant's room at such a late hour. He gently knocked and listened at the door. He heard someone sleeping, whom he presumed to be Pedee. Not wanting to draw the attention of the guard—and frankly, wanting to get back to bed—he took his knife and put it in the keyhole. His knife tip hit the key sitting in the other side of the lock. Satisfied that Pedee was asleep inside, he returned to the tent, assured Mrs. Williams that Pedee was inside asleep, and went back to bed.

FIGURE 2.3. North wall profile of Unit 5, showing where the materials evidencing use of the HB-22 building prior to completion were recovered. Illustration by the author.

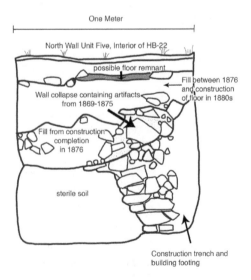

While the Black soldiers who interacted with Mrs. Williams that night seemed disinclined to believe her, the white officers who learned of the incident were more supportive. Pedee, who only learned of the "fracas" the next day, was quickly arrested, charged with "assault with intent to commit a rape to the prejudice of good order and military discipline," and scheduled for court-martial. The specifications against Pedee read like a Victorian melodrama:

[Martin Pedee] did feloniously enter the quarters occupied by Mrs. Annie Williams, when her husband was absent on guard, and in reply to the question put by Ms. Williams, as to who he [Pedee] was and what he wanted, did say, "I am John Williams" pretending to be her husband and did upon being recognized by the said Annie Williams, say "you know what I come for and if you have a mind to give it to me, it will be all right and if you don't I'll cut your darned throat" or words to that effect: and upon a refusal by the said Annie Williams to yield to his desires, did seize her by the throat and throw her down and attempt by force to accomplish his purpose, and did continue to assault and threaten the said Annie Williams until frightened away by her loud cries for help. This at Fort Davis on or about the night of the 9th August 1872."[33]

Excesses and Deprivations: The Entangled Courts-Martial of Martin Pedee and Frederick Kendall

Private Martin Pedee had never been court-martialed, neither during his Civil War service nor during his peacetime service. He first registered for the peacetime army on November 27, 1866, after being discharged from the Union Army in June. He was employed as a "boatman" in Norfolk, Virginia, at the time of his enlistment into the Fortieth Infantry, which would become the Twenty-Fifth after the merging of regiments by Congress in 1869.[34] Pedee, who also went by the name Pegee, had been born into enslavement in Anson County, North Carolina, in 1845. He was among the men who jumped at the opportunity to serve in the United States Colored Troops (USCT), enlisting in 1864. He had served in Company E of the Thirty-Fifth Regiment of US Colored Infantry, a regiment that saw combat action, first at Olustee and later at Honey Hill, South Carolina. The regiment lost four officers and forty-nine enlisted men in battle and another 151 enlisted men to disease.[35] Pegee, as he was then called, received a gunshot wound in his left arm November 30, 1864.[36]

Pedee had quickly reenlisted in 1869 at the expiration of service at Ship Island, Mississippi, signing up for a five-year term of service, and seemed settled into military life. His unit had begun their service in North Carolina and had moved to Mississippi and Louisiana before being sent west to Texas. Responding to a survey in 1870 asking captains of Twenty-Fifth Infantry companies to list examples of good soldiers, Captain David Schooley listed both Martin Pedee and John Sample as outstanding soldiers.[37] In Texas, the company served at Fort Duncan and Fort Clark, where, according to Mrs. Annie Williams's account, Pedee first became acquainted with his future wife.

Pedee's court-martial commenced on October 1, 1872, but not before more drama surrounded the proceedings. Standard Order No. 129 had named First Lieutenant Frederick Kendall, Twenty-Fifth Company E, as a member of the court-martial. However, on August 15, six days after the alleged Pedee incident, Kendall was charged with conduct to the prejudice of good order and military discipline and accused of having become "disgracefully and crazy drunk" at the post traders, failing to attend the parade of the guard, and showing up to roll call intoxicated.[38]

Kendall's court-martial had bearing on two cases to be tried during that session, Pedee's and that of Private Elijah Fillmore, Company G, Twenty-Fifth Infantry. In the case of Fillmore, Lieutenant Kendall was to have served as his counsel in the case, but when the case was convened on October 10, 1872, Private Fillmore was unable to draw on Kendall, who had legal problems of his own. Fillmore was accused of shooting to death Private George M. Dallas of the same company on May 5, 1872. According to witness testimony, Dallas had some sort of grievance with Fillmore, leading him to call the accused a "son of a bitch." Defense witnesses testified that Dallas had promised to kill Fillmore before he was off guard duty. Fillmore allegedly shot Dallas in the thigh outside the guard house, hitting the man's femoral artery. Fillmore was heard to say, "He cussed my mother and I will die for my mother." No one saw Fillmore take the shot, although as someone on guard duty, he was seen standing near Dallas holding a gun. His sergeant testified that when he took Fillmore's gun, it had not been fired.

Reading the testimony, it is clear that guilt or innocence would be highly dependent on how one responded to the testimony about the gun and whether one was inclined to believe Fillmore feared for his life. What most complicated this particular case was that Fillmore had already been acquitted by a civilian court in El Paso and returned to Fort Davis. The court-martial documents include an appeal stating that the military had no right to try him for murder under the Ninety-Ninth Article of War outside of wartime. The court-martial found him guilty, discharged him, and sentenced him to five years at a military prison. The sentence was ultimately reduced to two years.[39]

Kendall's offense happened after several officers gathered at the post trader's to enjoy a drink with a fellow officer visiting the post, one Major Albert B. Morrow of the Ninth Cavalry. Kendall apparently stayed at the post trader's and continued to drink after the party had ended. He stayed there, passing the night on a spare cot. Mrs. Kendall, noticing her husband's absence the following morning, showed a keen sense of awareness of the potential peril her husband faced and quickly went to the post surgeon to report him ill and have him excused from duty. This action ultimately saved the lieutenant from conviction. Meanwhile, as Kendall walked to roll call, none of the assembled failed to note that he approached from the opposite direction of his quarters. He completed roll call and then returned home, presumably to collapse in bed.[40]

Kendall will figure prominently in the pages to come, being the officer who led the first successful incarnation of the post school in 1873. He was a native of New Hampshire who served in the Fourth New Hampshire Infantry in the Civil War, earning a brevet rank of captain in 1864. On July 28, 1865, he was appointed captain of Company L, Eighth US Colored Heavy Artillery, and served until being discharged on February 10, 1866. He was appointed a second lieutenant in the Fortieth US Infantry on July 28, 1866, and was promoted to first lieutenant a year later. Kendall's family—his wife and three children—joined him at the post. His wife, Virginia Hutchinson Kendall, of New Hampshire, was the granddaughter of Jeb Hutchinson, who had formed the Hutchinson Family Singers, the wildly popular vocal group that toured in the antebellum period with the likes of Frederick Douglass, popularizing abolitionist and suffragist songs with their special brand of four-part harmony. It is interesting to ponder whether Virginia noted that both Douglass and her husband shared the names Frederick Augustus. The couple had married in 1864. One of the Hutchinson family singers would sing at Douglass's funeral in 1895.[41]

Service in the USCT was seen as a way to fast-track one's military career since the creation of the new units created new commissions. This was particularly attractive to men such as Kendall who had received field commissions during the Civil War rather than coming through a military institute like West Point. George A. Custer famously turned down a commission in the Black units, believing it beneath him. While there was a cynical and careerist motivation for too many of the officers in the Black regiments before and after the Civil War, there is some evidence that Kendall's decision was inspired by Black troops themselves: the Fourth Regiment New Hampshire Infantry served at both Fort Wagner and Chaffin's Farm, battles where Black troops definitively demonstrated their valor in 1863 and 1864. That said, Kendall did not have a perfect record during the Civil War, having been court-martialed in July 1862 after drinking too much at July Fourth celebrations and getting into a brawl with a man who called him "a son of a bitch." Like many of the soldiers he served with, he did not allow another man to insult his mother without a response. He was found not guilty. Drink and Kendall had a tumultuous relationship; in 1872, he noted that he had completely abstained from alcohol for the three years prior.[42]

Kendall's court-martial convened September 16, 1872. Kendall immediately objected to the presence of the post adjutant, Lieutenant Cyrus Gray, on the board since he was a material witness for the prosecution and connected to the collection of evidence. Further, Kendall stated, "I am morally certain that he is in no small degree prejudiced against me and interested in my conviction." Kendall represented himself during the proceedings, cross-examining prosecution witnesses and leading his defense. Like Sergeant Major Henderson, Kendall presented a long written statement for his defense rather than testifying. Written testimony ensured that no transcription errors would be made and that each argumentative point about the case could be clearly laid out.

The court-martial is fascinating given the alliances and discords it reveals about the Twenty-Fifth Infantry, particularly Company E. The prosecution called Cyrus Gray; Simon Chaney, a post trader; Captain Frank Bennett, Ninth Cavalry; Thomas Landers, acting assistant surgeon; and First Sergeant John Sample, Company E, Twenty-Fifth Infantry, the only Black man to testify against Kendall.[43] Perhaps now the connections between the Pedee and Kendall court-martials is more clear.

It was Sample who drew Kendall's greatest attacks during the trial. By 1872, Sample had an established military record of his own. Born enslaved in Virginia, he had joined the USCT 108 as the drum major. After the war, he joined the Fortieth Infantry, where he distinguished himself as a responsible soldier and NCO.[44] In March 1868, leading a group of fellow soldiers from Goldsborough to a court-martial detail in Raleigh, Sample and the men were treated in a disrespectful manner, with the Black men being barred from the mess hall while it was used by white soldiers and being granted sleeping quarters in the guard house. Sample wrote a passionate and skillful letter of protest that went up the chain of command. He emphasized in his letter that he sought not "equality," knowing full well the trigger that language represented. Instead, he demanded that the men deserved the treatment that was due them as soldiers. Endorsements on the letter include a comment supporting Sample as being as fine an officer as any white man.[45] Knowing this history, it was shocking to learn that Kendall attempted to tear down Sample as a "dishonest man."

Sample's testimony was no doubt damaging to Kendall's case. The first sergeant described Kendall's walk as wobbly and unsteady and evaluated him as having been drunk on duty. Kendall raised the possibility of witness tampering with his first question to Sample:

"Have you been influenced by any person to make the statement first given to the Court, if so, by whom?"

The court was cleared to debate whether the question could be asked, since no evidence had been presented to suggest that the witness had been influenced. The line of questioning was disallowed. Kendall persisted in this narrative throughout the trial. Sergeant Anthony Jackson, Company E, Twenty-Fifth, was called as a defense witness. Jackson testified that Kendall had not appeared drunk to him and that he had walked normally over the lumpy parade ground. Then, Jackson was asked about First Sergeant Sample's general reputation among his associates for "truth and veracity." After stating that he had known Sample for six years, Jackson stated, "Well Sir, I should pronounce it pretty bad," adding under additional questioning that he would not believe him under oath. "I have been with him ever since I've been in the service," he elaborated, "and I have known him to tell false on me and others." The court then challenged Jackson to answer what his understanding of an oath was. Jackson answered as follows: "I believe there is a God and when I hold up my hand and swear to tell the truth and don't do it, I think to be one of the greatest sins that can be done."

Sergeant John H. Martin, Company E, testified that Sample could not possibly have observed the first lieutenant during roll call as testified since the first sergeant stood with his back to Kendall. Martin, who testified that he had known Sample since 1867, also asserted that he was a noted liar and not to be trusted under oath. Likewise, Corporal Griffin Collins, Company E, Twenty-Fifth, was drawn as a witness solely to testify that he had served with Sample for five years and eight months and had found him to be dishonest.

The strategy of denigrating Sample broke down when Captain David Schooley was called to the stand. Schooley and Kendall had served together since 1866, and Schooley and the Kendalls had shared quarters at Fort Duncan. Kendall may have expected supportive testimony, but Schooley pointedly seemed unwilling to undermine his company's first sergeant,

"I have known him since January 1867. He was a private and a corporal until the 1st of March 1867, and since that time, with the exception of three months when he was out of the service, he has been First Sergeant of E companies of the 40th and 25th infantry. I have been in the command of these companies except for about five months. . . . His character has been good. Yes Sir, I would believe him under oath." Kendall pushed on Schooley, asking him to recall a time when Sample had lied or concealed the truth from him, clearly thinking of a specific example. Schooley responded after a court clearance, with the following account:

> I have no recollection but on one occasion that wasn't lying. I was once deceived by him, and that is all. I was ordered on a scout last November to one of the sub-posts and there were a number of pigs about the post, and I told the men and told the 1st Sergeant not to molest these pigs. In about one week afterwards, the owner of the pigs came along and asked me if I had seen any of them. I told him I had not for the last four days. I presumed he would find them about, as I had cautioned the men not to molest them. He went away and was gone about two hours. When he came back, he said he had seen one that was shot and had found the skin of another and told me if I would go with him, he would show them to me. I took the Sergeant with me. After coming back to the post, I made inquiries about it but could find no one for about four days that knew anything about it. A corporal of the company gave me the first information, all I think that he knew, and after questioning several other men of the company, I became satisfied that the First Sergeant was cognizant of some of the facts in the beginning."

In his closing statement, Kendall returned to the theme of Sample's dishonesty being in service of a commanding officer who disliked the accused in the case. Kendall wrote to the court, "It must be borne in mind that the witnesses for the defense have had to exercise more or less moral courage in testifying in behalf of the accused especially in the case of the Sergeants who are aware in who's name this 'persecution' is made." Kendall was ultimately found innocent of all charges against him, but his removal from court-martial duty had already been ordered. He would not sit in judgement of Martin Pedee. Was this the intent of the court-martial? Or was there some other history of dispute between Andrews and Kendall. Many events of the summer of 1872 become clearer from the archival record, but not this.

It is not surprising that Sample's one testified "lie" regarded the illegal acquisition of pigs by his troops. Hunger at Fort Davis seems to have been common among the troops, a reality admitted to by several post surgeons. One contributing factor was the isolation of the post and problems with military supply lines.[46] Food shipments could be delayed in transit, and when arrived, could be rancid. Compounding this problem, suppliers may not have shipped quality goods for the military. A letter of January 10, 1870, is not atypical:

> Of the 106 barrels of flour on hand, I found 18 barrels so damaged as to be entirely unfit for issue. The balance more or less caused by bugs, wet and from one to two years old, the barrels Champion Mills Extra St Louis MO is mostly unfit for issue. Hard Bread manufactured by Bels Miller and Co, New Orleans are inferior quality and unfit for issue. Also more or less damaged in transportation. Hard bread can be made at the post at lower rate probably than it can be sent from New Orleans. Pork, 75 barrels on hand and rancid, much of it light weight, some of the barrels including brine and salt with barrels only weighing 225 lbs. Two barrels of pickled beef tongue found. The pork not unusual, Packers name not legible, packed in Chicago, Illinois.[47]

Whether the US military ration was adequate for the dietary needs of the troops on the frontier became a debate between surgeons and top administration officials in the 1870s. As early as January 1869, Assistant Surgeon Weisel noted in his report, "Rations should be bigger since company savings are small and additional articles of diet cannot be procured.... One fact may be worth noting that colored troops consume more of their rations than white troops."[48] Circular No. 8 addressed this question in its report, drawing on feedback from posts about the adequacy of the ration and recent understandings of nutrition. The report made the following remarkable conclusion: men who were engaged in activities of great exertion required up to 40 ounces of water-free food to obtain adequate nutrition, and average activity required 30.92 ounces. In contrast, the military ration provided 24.79 ounces of food a day. Troops, said the report, were left to supplement their diet through hunting and fishing, selling back bacon, sugar, coffee, soap, candles, and vinegar rations to buy flour, by tending post gardens, and through direct contributions of salary by men.[49]

Given that enlisted men at Fort Davis were regularly detailed to extra work duties, including construction, tending the garden, and extra patrols, there should be no doubt that they were expending toward the higher energy levels. With so many of the men having been released from bondage before joining the military, they likely entered service in weakened health. It is no surprise, then, that eighteen enlisted men were buried at Fort Davis in 1868, the majority dying from the effects of dysentery and scurvy.[50] Hunger at Fort Davis was not ended by improvements suggested in Circular No. 8. In an 1879 questionnaire sent to post surgeons, Fort Davis's J. B Girard wrote of condition of rations at the fort:

> With regard to the colored troops with which I am serving at present, many of them during the past year preformed long marches and others have been employed in the arduous work of road making through rocky mountain passes. I have observed on their part an almost universal disposition to eat more than their regular allowance of food. Most of the men admitted in the post hospital unless affect with acute and serious disorders appear to suffer principally from hunger and to such an extent that even with the help of extra stores furnished by the hospital and the food not required by patients dangerously ill, it is practically impossible to save anything from the ration.[51]

The animal bones recovered from the two archaeological cooking features provide some insights into the ways men at Fort Davis sought to supplement the protein part of their ration. More identifiable specimens (60 of the 110 identified specimens) of animal bone were recovered from the hearth than the ashpit. Because of the relatively small assemblage size, interpretations drawn from these two deposits are best thought of as qualitative rather than quantitative, but still worthy of note.

The vast majority of the hearth specimens were from cow (*Bos taurus*), accounting for 45 percent of the identified materials. Deer species (white tailed deer and pronghorn, made up 11.7 percent of the identifiable species. Pig (1.7 percent) and goat (5 percent) were a smaller portion of the remains. Eggshell and one unidentified bird species were also represented. When one considers that cows are significantly bigger than the other species represented, it is clear that the majority of the meat in the diet was beef.

Among the beef bones recovered from the hearth was an articulated ulna and radius (a shank cut). These bones were found just outside the ring of the hearth and would have been perfect for the beef soups and stews that

Dr. Weisel, who was post surgeon until mid-1872, provided recipes for to the troops. As noted earlier, Weisel's writings demonstrated that not only was he versed in miasma-based sanitation discourses, but he was also up-to-date on the latest food science. His recipes, which he advised should be copied and kept by all the companies, were clearly influenced by the food science of German nutritionist Justus von Liebig, who argued that the greatest nutritional value of meat could be preserved through long, slow cooking. His Stewed Beef and Soup for Fifty Men called for sixty-five pints of water, thirty-five pounds of beef cut into four-pound pieces, mixed fresh vegetables, six pounds of barley or four and three-quarters pounds of rice, nine ounces of salt, three and a quarter pounds of flour, and half an ounce of pepper. The doctor called for the beef to be set on the fire and when it began to boil, for the cook to diminish the heat, let simmer gently for two hours and thirty minutes, add the flour mixed with more cold water, boil it all together for another half an hour, skim off the fat, remove the meat, and serve the meat and the soup separately. Regarding this recipe, Weisel noted, "Meat cooked this way is more nutritious." Weisel's recipes for Beef Stew for Fifty Men and Beef Soup for Fifty Men follow similar formulas.[52]

Weisel's instructions regarding cooking of meats is straight out of food science of the time: "Roasting should be slowly done, the meat must first be subjected to an intense heat and afterwards cooked very slowly."[53] The recovered shank would have been the kind of four-pound cut preferred by Weisel. The presence of large wild game in the form of pronghorn and deer speaks to the need to supplement the diet. Such animals were plentiful around the post, but the highly structured daily routine made hunting difficult. Men took the opportunity, when available on patrol, to hunt when game were encountered.

Small groups of men were regularly detailed away from the post to accompany supply trains to other posts or to guard stage stations. These remote and mainly boring details provided some opportunity to look for game. An example of a hunting trip gone awry happened in late August 1872. While stationed at El Muerto Springs, Private William Smith awoke early to gather wood and noticed a herd of deer. He rushed back to camp to grab his gun, woke Private William Johnson, and asked him to join him. The men rushed off after the deer and followed them for two hours before giving up and deciding to return to the station—at which point, they realized that they were lost. They wandered for eight days before coming upon the stage line, taking another wrong turn, northward toward Barilla Springs instead of to Post Davis, and were picked up by the superintendent of the stage line. The men claimed that they had only had some cactus and a rabbit to eat the whole time they were missing. The stage superintendent took the soldiers with him to Barilla Springs, fed them, and then took the two disheveled men back to Fort Davis on the stage. The men, described as being in "a wretched condition," were charged with desertion but acquitted due to the clear lack of intent, since they had left all their belongings hadn't bothered to take water or provisions with them. Instead, they were found guilty of "absence without leave" and forfeited one month of salary. The court noted that no other punishment was necessary given how the two had already suffered.[54]

The ashpit included twenty-two identifiable specimens. Unlike the materials from the hearth, the bone from this feature exhibited re-burning consistent with refuse disposal and perhaps the use of the ash as a cooking matrix. Pig, chicken, goat, cow, rabbit, deer, unidentified carnivore, and rodents were found. Cow, again, was the most abundant mammal species, accounting for 13.6 percent of the recovered specimens, whereas deer, sheep/goat, and pig each accounted for 9 percent of the assemblage. Bird species, represented by bone and egg shell, accounted for 18 percent of the specimens but clearly not the majority of the meat.

The heavy fraction of the flot material from the ashpit included examples of shot and was probably deposited in the remains of food that had been brought down by a rifle. At least 27 percent of the specimens recovered were from wild species, showing a continuing need to supplement the diet and perhaps greater opportunity to do so. Bird and rabbit would be easy to acquire around the post but do not provide the same kind of nutritional benefit as a deer or an antelope.

While Kendall may have attempted to condemn Sergeant Sample for failing to tell his captain about the fate of the pigs encountered on patrol, the archaeological and historical evidence suggests that the acquisition of additional foodstuffs, whether wild or questionably obtained domesticates, was a crucial component of enlisted men's diets. Fighting chronic hunger while being asked to preform strenuous labor, the decision to turn a blind eye to wrangling was beyond the simple moralities Kendell pushed in his court-martial defense.

Pedee's court-martial commenced on October 1, 1872. It quickly became apparent that Mrs. Williams's account of the night differed from the accounts provided by the prosecution witnesses but was clearly salacious enough to keep the attention of the court, which desired intimate details of the attack:

> Between 11 and 12 o'clock at night Martin Pedee came into my tent, I asked who he was, he replied he was my husband, John Williams, I told him that he was not and then he grabbed hold of me and said he was John Williams. Then I reached to get a knife and he said, "God damn you, I will cut your throat" then afterwards I got weak and he threw me on the bed and the knife fell out of my hand on the floor and he commenced to choke me—then he said that if I would give him what he came for, he would let me go, and I shook my head and meant no, I could not speak. He asked me if I would not report him if he would let me go. I told him no, I would not report him if he would let me go. He got off of me then and let me go. I cried out "Murder" when he let me go he then went out of the tent.

The judge advocate wanted to know if Pedee had attempted carnal relations, and if so, what caused him to stop. Mrs. Williams said that promising not to report him stopped the attack. She testified that she recognized him by his voice (apparently having recognized the oddness of telling Corporal McKenzie she recognized him by the feel of his head), which she knew from having come to know him at Fort Duncan and Fort Clark, stating that she had been "around the company for over two years—I have known him during all that time, he has been coming around my quarters during all this time."

Pedee asked only one question of Mrs. Williams, but it was a telling one: "Did you not some time before this, accuse Corporal Collins, Company C 25th infantry of entering your tent?"

She then testified it was at least fifteen minutes after screaming murder that Sergeant McKenzie had come to her tent.

Private Henry Sappho, who testified that Pedee was in his room at the time Mrs. Williams was accusing him of having just left her tent, and Captain David Schooley of the Twenty-Fifth were witnesses for the defense. Schooley's testimony was short but supportive, stating that he had known Pedee as an enlisted man in his company since December 1866 and that his character had been very good.

Private Pedee's statement in his defense was brief: "That night I was in my quarters asleep and did not know anything about this fracas until next morning after Reveille. I went to bed that night just as the drums beat taps."

There are notable absences in the list of witnesses. First Sergeant John

Sample, whose quarters were being used by Pedee, did not testify. Similarly, Corporal John Williams was not called, but given his role as a spouse to the accuser, this was appropriate.

Pedee was found guilty of the charge and was dishonorably discharged, to forfeit all pay and allowances that were or would become due him, except the just dues of the laundress, and to be confined at hard labor in such military prison as the reviewing authority may deem for the period of seven years.[55] On October 11, 1872, Adjutant of Texas Augur approved the proceedings and findings of the case of Musician Martin Pedee, but just as he had in Private Fillmore's case, he mitigated the sentence: "The sentence is mitigated to confinement at hard labor under charge of the guard at the station where his company may be serving for the period of one year, forfeiting to the US 12 dollars per month of his monthly pay for the same period and will be so executed."[56]

Housing and Rations as Necropolitical Assemblages

This court-martial outcome would anger Colonel Andrews, who a month and a half later would draft a letter demanding that Augur rethink his decision. Given the overcrowded and uncomfortable conditions of the Fort Davis guard house, Augur's mercy toward Pedee was not as generous as it could have been. Kendall was released from the considerably more comfortable conditions of his house arrest and promptly detailed with men of his company on road-construction duty away from post—exactly the labor that Post Surgeon Girard would use as an example of the kinds of arduous and demanding labor expected of Black infantry soldiers. Notably, road crews were typically led by NCOs, not commissioned officers. Post returns for the month of November 1872 show Kendall to be the only commissioned officer off post with a work detail. Perhaps Kendall was correct in thinking that his commanding officer disliked him.

While dislike of Kendall may have been personal, his attitude toward Pedee seems to have been categorical instead. Colonel Andrews presided over a number of courts-martial of Black soldiers besides the ones discussed here that required mitigations of sentences by the Department of Texas. Likewise, he is typically silent about the living conditions experienced by the enlisted men.

Achille Mbembe states, "Necropolitical power proceeds by a sort of inversion between life and death, as if life was merely death's medium. It ever seeks to abolish the distinction between means and ends."[57] We see in the ongoing failure of the military structure to listen to the pleas of doctors calling for better living conditions—be it housing, diet, access to sanitary living conditions, or appropriate workload—a passive commitment to allowing soldiers to fall sick, become disabled, starve, and die. Starvation and poor health were normalized. At the best of times, the biased behavior of some members of the military was corrected by other parts of the military structure, but not always. Circular No. 8 contains damning statistics about the comparative health of Black and white soldiers in the military. Death rates per thousand from 1870 to 1874 for white troops from consumption were 1.462 per thousand and 1.472 per thousand for other respiratory illnesses. Contrast this with Black troops, whose death rates were 2.47 per thousand and 3.162 per thousand from those same causes.[58] Crowded and poorly ventilated housing directly facilitates the spread of TB and other respiratory illnesses. Neglect could be, and was, fatal.

3

⪥≡◯⪤

PRIVATE STEVENSON'S
POCKETKNIFE AND
COMPANY K'S TUMBLER

Awakened from sleep by a cry of "Murder!," Private Joseph William Stevenson chose to grab not his trousers but his pocketknife.[1] By using his knife to establish that First Sergeant Sample's quarters were locked from the inside, Stevenson demonstrated the versatility of this small personal object. Frontier military life was characterized by constant movement—the drudgery of patrols and stage escorts off post, guard duty and other responsibilities on post, and at regular intervals, the complete relocation from one station to another. All one's belongings—personal and that of the company—had to be packed up and hauled away. Enlisted men, by default of the circumstances of their lives, had little ability to acquire many individual possessions beyond their military uniforms and equipage.[2]

So what were the personal items that Black soldiers held dear? What were the things they invested their salaries in? And what do they say about their lives and how they saw themselves as men and citizens? What do these objects tell us about the challenges they faced on the frontier? Documentary sources have little to say on the subject, making Private Stevenson's pocketknife a notable object. Court-martial records tell of objects that were popularly stolen—heavy military coats, revolvers, rifles, cash, food—or the items used offensively or in self-defense—guns, knives, objects of opportunity.[3] Archaeology provides a rare occasion to see everyday life beyond the constraints of the archival record.

The last third of the nineteenth century was characterized by an inordinate attention to "stuff," a circumstance that makes the period well beloved by archaeologists. During this time period, no matter their socioeconomic class,

Americans were highly self-conscious about the things they wore and used in and around their homes. The industrial revolution assured that large quantities of goods were available at a variety of price points. Improved transcontinental transportation assured that goods could find their way to the remotest regions of the country, even isolated Fort Davis. Etiquette and household management books explained proper modes of behavior and which material items were essential in a proper home. Proscriptive literature explained how domestics spaces like parlors could (and should) be decorated in ways that communicated one's character and personal history to visitors.[4]

The archaeological remains related to the enlisted men of Fort Davis date primarily between 1869 and before the end of Reconstruction in 1877. For the Black men stationed at Fort Davis, whatever hardships they faced, this was a time of guarded optimism. Enslavement had been ended, and Black men's contributions to the war effort were recognized and lauded by white northerners. Veterans groups dedicated to Black and white soldiers alike were forming. Black men were holding elected offices across the country, and constitutional amendments supporting freedom and citizenship rights were being ratified. Well-known Black activists like Frederick Douglass and Philip Alexander Bell continued to push for legislation to enforce the recently passed Thirteenth, Fourteenth, and Fifteenth Amendments. It was possible to cautiously imagine a future featuring integration and equality of the races and to participate in the material performances of manhood and civility that, as part of the continued efforts toward equality, would mark Black soldiers as worthy citizens.[5]

Black soldiers born free in northern cities would have been familiar with the material and behavioral tropes of American citizenship and gentility. They were important sources of information for men who may have spent their childhood and young manhood enslaved. Still, recently emancipated men would have some degree of familiarity with these modes of material communication.[6] As W. E. B. Du Bois noted, all people of color needed to view the world through a "double-consciousness"—the ability to navigate different systems of communicative behavior in a racialized world.[7] It is vital to consider the things that soldiers used in their day-to-day lives, particularly the things they acquired for themselves, outside of the equipage and uniforms required by the military service.

The materials considered in this chapter fall into three categories: standard military issue, things that were additionally acquired communally to be used within a regimental company, and those things attained by individuals for personal use. First, we explore additional considerations of the Black community of Fort Davis, the spaces they occupied, and what we know of their everyday lives.

The Men of Fort Davis

The 1866 military reorganization law established two Black cavalry (Ninth and Tenth Cavalries) and four infantry regiments (Thirty-Eighth, Thirty-Ninth, Fortieth, and Forty-First), representing the first time Black men were allowed to join the regular army. In 1869, the military was consolidated, with the number of regiments reduced from forty-five to twenty-five, and the four infantry units merged. The Twenty-Fourth was created out of the Thirty-Eighth and Forty-First and the Twenty-Fifth out of the Thirty-Ninth and Fortieth.[8] Post records identify which companies of which regiments served at any given

TABLE 3.1. *Regiments and Companies Stationed at Fort Davis between 1867 and 1878*

REGIMENT	COMPANY	DATES OF DEPLOYMENT AT FORT DAVIS
Twenty-Fourth	B	November 1869–May 1871
Infantry	F	June 1870–April 1872
Twenty-Fifth	A	July 1870–July 1871
Infantry	C	May 1872–July 1872
	D	November 1872–July 1876
	E	May 1872–May 1880
	G	July 1870–September 1875
	H	October 1875–July 1880
Ninth Cavalry	B	July 1870–March 1871
	C	January 1867–June 1871
	F	January 1867–June 1867; January 1869–February 1869
	H	July 1867–June 1868
	I	June 1871–April 1875
	K	June 1868–April 1871
Tenth Cavalry	H	May 1875–April 1885

time at Fort Davis. Prepared twice a month, these are valuable resources for a detailed, birds-eye-view understanding of the post community. At some point between 1867 and 1885, Fort Davis was home to every one of the Black regiments.

Trying to gather collective information about the men is challenging. Enlistment records note a man's place of birth, his age, his height, his hair, eye, and skin color, and his occupation at time of enlistment. Identifying a soldier's specific enlistment papers can be tricky. Several "John Allens" served at Fort Davis, and finding which John Allen is a particular John Allen is difficult. Misspellings and re-spellings of names were common, and pension records show that men often went by multiple names during their lifetimes.[9] Muster rolls do not list ages or places of birth, and the National Archive is generally reluctant to allow the originals circulate, directing researchers to Fold3 or ancestry databases accessible on site. Therefore, it is another public government record, the census, available only every ten years, that provides the best communal snapshot of the men of Fort Davis. The census is a problematic source, but it is the most accessible, and it ties particular people to particular posts and provides information on place of birth and age that can be triangulated with enlistment papers.

The 1870 census for Fort Davis, Presidio County, shows 285 Black soldiers living on post. Men were drawn from twenty-two different states (table 3.2), with the largest numbers coming from Kentucky (a major recruiting area for the Ninth Cavalry), and Virginia and Maryland, the result of heavy recruiting in the DC area. One man listed his birthplace as Bombay, another Jamaica, while two were from Canada. The vast majority of the men were between the ages of twenty and twenty-five, with few men in their thirties serving.[10]

This is a brief snapshot of the men who lived at Fort Davis in 1870; as early as 1872, most of these men would have moved on to other posts and new men would have arrived. The archaeological remains, therefore, represent things lost and discarded by men in constant motion. The artifacts represent those things considered essential (whether functionally or emotionally) by men who lived mainly on military schedules and itineraries. As you will see in photographs of artifacts here, the archaeological traces they left are small fragments, broken bits that are not impressive in and of themselves and look little like the whole objects they were part of. These men lived materially modest lives, but these small things are still crucial to study. They are traces of the soldiers' hopes, values, and needs.

TABLE 3.2. *Geographic Origins of Men at Fort Davis,*
1870 Census, Presidio County, Texas

COUNTRY	STATE OR CITY	NUMBER	SUBTOTAL
US: Union States	California	1	
	Connecticut	1	
	District of Columbia	3	
	Maine	1	
	Massachusetts	2	
	New Jersey	3	
	New York	6	
	Ohio	4	
	Pennsylvania	5	
	Rhode Island	1	
Subtotal			*27 (9.4%)*
US: Border States	Delaware	2	
	Maryland	27	
	Missouri	17	
	Kentucky	84	
Subtotal			*130 (45.5%)*
US: Confederate	Alabama	6	
States	Arkansas	3	
	Georgia	5	
	Louisiana	16	
	Mississippi	6	
	North Carolina	11	
	South Carolina	14	
	Tennessee	18	
	Texas	1	
	Virginia	46	
Subtotal			*126 (44.1%)*
Non US	Bombay, East India	1	
	Jamaica	1	
Subtotal			*2 (0.7%)*
Unknown		1	
Subtotal			*1 (.35%)*
TOTAL		286	286

The Things They Were Issued

While literacy is generally used to describe the ability to read written words, nineteenth-century social, cultural, economic, and political realms also required a heightened literacy in reading the material world. Military experience was extraordinarily proficient at developing this skill. The ability to read quickly the status of another man (rank, regiment, company, military branch) from a person's uniform and equipage was essential to successfully avoid conflict and ensure proper behavior. The artifacts from Fort Davis's barracks deposits vividly speak to the ways that the men simultaneously created a sense of community and individuality in an institution that most prized their labor.

For any soldier, his primary community was his company. For the infantry, after the reduction of the military, company size was limited to fifty men, whereas cavalry companies had a maximum strength of one hundred men.[11] These were the men who lived most closely together. They patrolled, slept, ate, and if required, fought together. When it was time to move to another post, they moved together.[12] The company also budgeted as a collective, sharing savings from economical use of rations or through regular salary contributions. Kept in the hands of the captain, these funds were used exclusively for the benefit of the company's men. Among other uses, company funds were used to buy specialty food items, to purchase "kitchen furniture" (ceramics, glassware, cutlery, etc.), and to build libraries.[13]

The men of a company built a large household together. The company fund allowed men to improve on the standard issue of the military but presented challenges as well. Less ethical captains could mishandle company funds, defrauding their men. A greater structural problem was one of history, or in the case of Black companies, the lack of it. Company funds, properly managed by captains, could grow large over time. Large company funds were a financial buffer that allowed troops to navigate through delays in supply trains, pay, or other shortages. For companies in the Black regiments, only formed in 1866, company funds (like the companies) were still new, fairly small, and vulnerable to being expended quickly. In addition, men consuming more of their rations had fewer rations to sell back for the company fund, yet another structural disadvantage. Therefore, the things that Black men acquired for their company represented a significant form of communal investment—a greater investment than similar purchases and investments by white troops. As in all aspects of the quest for citizenship, the costs were higher for Black men.

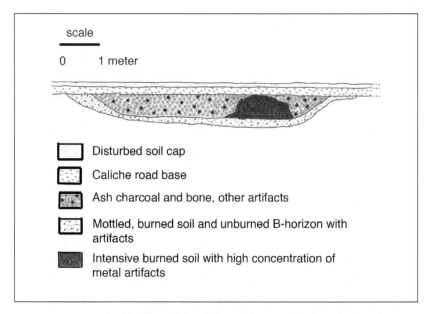

scale

0   1 meter

☐ Disturbed soil cap

☐ Caliche road base

☐ Ash charcoal and bone, other artifacts

☐ Mottled, burned soil and unburned B-horizon with artifacts

☐ Intensive burned soil with high concentration of metal artifacts

FIGURE 3.1. Profile of barracks' trash dump. Illustration by the author based on photographs and a profile prepared by archaeologist Timothy E. Roberts, Texas Parks and Wildlife Department's west Texas region cultural resources coordinator, and Fort Davis National Historic Site staff in 2009.

Company Gear, Company Investments

In 2009, the National Park Service discovered, quite by accident, a large dump deposit near the vicinity of the enlisted men's barracks.[14] Fortunately, park officials were able to call on a state archaeologist to oversee recording the deposit and recovering displaced artifacts. The deposit had two clearly delineated components: a generalized layer of garbage capped by another layer of burned trash (as indicated by a thick mixed layer of ash, charcoal, and heat-altered artifacts). A white leaching lens was visible throughout the deposit. This could be the product of natural calcification or of the depositing of quick lime, which was regularly used as a disinfectant around the post. A team of UC Berkeley students and I washed, cataloged, and analyzed the materials in 2013.

The burnt layer contained a thick layer of military equipage, most notably shoulder epaulettes, but also parts of canteens, buckles from harness and shoulder straps, uniform emblems such as Hardee eagles, regiment numbers, and company letters. Also mixed in that part of the deposit, but even more so in the deposit below it, are a range of ceramic, glass, metal, and some bone artifacts, also dating to the postwar military occupation. The deposit is a communal one, created over a relatively short period of time by several companies. All the identified materials are associated with enlisted personnel. Trash disposal by the officers seems to have been concentrated more densely around their quarters (Post Surgeon Weisel complained about the terrible police around the officer's dwellings).

One of the most useful artifacts for dating historical archaeological sites are ceramic manufacturing marks. By the mid-nineteenth century, manufacturers marked their ware with distinct designs and names, and careful research by ceramic historians allows for dating the uses of particular marks.[15] Six identifiable manufacturer's marks representing five different companies were found (table 3.3). One of the manufacturers represented, Powell and Bishop, a company from Burslem, one of the English Staffordshire pottery towns, began operations in 1867. Therefore, the deposit cannot date any earlier than 1867. This date also aligns with the reestablishment of Fort Davis. Looking at the seemingly wide range of dates for the pottery production, this information may appear of limited use for dating the deposits. However, archaeologists also use a tool called mean ceramic dating. Before the development of radiometric dating (such as radiocarbon), archaeologists used a range of techniques to develop relative chronologies for ancient societies. The most important of these is a technique called seriation, or ordering archaeological materials based on style or frequency. Mean ceramic dating is a form of frequency seriation. The technique is dependent on the presumption that every object has an introduction date, a period during which it reaches its peak popularity (or abundance), and a date at which it becomes obsolete.[16] Mean ceramic dating assumes that peak popularity comes midway between the introduction of an item and its disappearance. Using this logic, a W. Baker plate manufactured sometime between 1839 and 1893 could be expected to be most abundant in 1866. The mean ceramic date is the average of dates for the ceramics recovered. In theory, this date should be very close to the date the deposit was made.

The technique is clearly based on problematic assumptions. The technique assumes that any ceramic was most likely to break when it was most popular (and therefore, most abundant). But what if people were keeping their ceramics for a long time? The technique was developed at sites with short-term and well-documented use—mainly military and frontier sites—and dates derived from the archaeological assemblages came very close to the documented

TABLE 3.3. *Manufacturer Marks Recovered from the Barracks' Dump (dates drawn from Godden, 1964)*

MANUFACTURER	DATE RANGE	MEAN DATE (MID-RANGE OF MANUFACTURE)
"John Maddock and Son Burslem"	1855–1896	1875.5
"John Maddock & Son Burslem"	1855–1896	1875.5
"J & G Meakin"	1851–1890	1875.5
"Edwards and Son Dale Hall"	1851–1882	1866.5
"Powell and Bishop Hanley"	1867–1878	1872.5
"W. Baker"	1839–1893	1866
Mean Ceramic Date		*1871.9*

occupations. Testing of the technique since 1977 has established that mean ceramic dates are most useful for dating sites with short occupations and rapid occupation turnover, places like military sites.[17] Fort Davis, resettled in 1867 by troops who were part of recently established regiments (1866), is perfectly suited for this dating technique. The mean ceramic date for the deposit is 1871.9, which would suggest, if we were to consider the ceramic data only, that the barracks trash deposit was closed by the end of 1871. What other lines of evidence do we have for dating the deposit?

The military gear recovered from this deposit includes artifacts with ties to specific companies and regiments and items of particular styles, each with chronological implications. From the 1880s onward, when the military published clear manufacturing standards for uniform components, military-related artifacts are easily dated based on their style, manufacture and size.[18] This was not the case for the Civil War, and for men at Fort Davis during the late 1860s and 1870s, the recently ended war shaped much of their military experience.

The US military had contracted with multiple suppliers during the Civil War to meet the demand for uniforms and military equipment.[19] The use of multiple suppliers manifests in a variety of ways archaeologically. Not surprisingly, manufacturers consistently cut corners. While the rare preservation of these items prevents us from seeing, archaeologically, poor-quality cloth or garment construction, the short-changing of sizes to save materials is evident. For instance, military regulations specified that the general service coat buttons should be .875 inch in diameter and cuff buttons .5 inch, yet the coat buttons found at Fort Davis tended to be smaller, ranging between .78 and .79 inch. Archaeological work at Fort Bowie, Arizona, found coat buttons there ranged from .76 to .79 inch in diameter. On March 27, 1885, the military issued strict regulations regarding sizes and redesigned the embossed eagle decoration on the buttons. The Fort Davis buttons recovered from the dump, and all of the excavations around the HB-22 barracks were made prior to the 1885 regulations. They were of the "general service" style first introduced in 1854 and used throughout the Civil War.[20]

During Fort Davis's early occupation, the soldiers were likely to have worn Civil War period uniforms. The end of the war found the quartermaster department glutted with surplus, and though the fabrics and designs were inappropriate for frontier life, the army continued to draw from stockpiled goods throughout the 1870s, and in the case of some goods, well into the 1880s.[21] In 1872, the military adopted a new uniform, with manufacturing of garments undertaken by the army in Philadelphia; Jeffersonville, Indiana; and San Francisco. Inmates at the military prison in Leavenworth produced shoes, brooms, and barracks chairs. Contractors produced some clothing and equipage including headgear, furniture, camps gear, flags, and fabric, with new standards for these uniforms published in 1877.[22]

For our purposes, the presence of large numbers of epaulettes found in the dump is significant. Epaulettes, also called "scales," were worn on the shoulders, and in military lore, they were supposed to protect the cavalry men's shoulders from saber cuts. Each epaulette had a long strap made of seven ribbed scales, terminating in a circular disk worn on the shoulder. The epaulettes recovered from the feature were manufactured of brass and iron. The epaulettes for men holding the rank of private featured a disk with a four-inch diameter, those for NCOs was four and a half inches in diameter. A third epaulette form used by military bands and hospital officials apparently features rivets on the strap, but none of these were recovered at Fort Davis. Epaulettes had to be kept polished as part of the dress uniform and attached to the shoulders by thin brass straps that passed through staples sewn onto the dress coat shoulders. A turnkey at the end of the strap near the neck was used to secure the scale as well.[23] Fragments of enough epaulettes were recovered from the trash pit sample to equip the shoulders of twenty-five privates and five NCOs—in effect, half a company's worth of scales.

Soldiers hated epaulettes. As early as the Civil War, soldiers were trying to lose their scales. Civil War captain Anson Mills was reprimanded for ordering his sergeant to throw his company's chest of epaulettes into the sink (privy).[24] During frontier service, Mills reported that with less oversight, soldiers were quick to discard useless pieces of equipment and uniforms. In 1872, epaulettes were deemed no longer a required part of the military uniform. Fort Davis records show that the Department of Texas was not waiting to discard epaulettes. Letters sent from post commander Andrew Sheridan between February 27, 1871, and April 28, 1871, detail the destruction by fire of materials from the post hospital, Company F, Twenty-Fourth Infantry; Companies A and G, Twenty-Fifth Infantry; and Company K, Ninth Cavalry (table 3.4). Included in these burning episodes were fourteen pairs of sergeant scales and ninety-five pairs of private scales. The trash deposit's burn layer is likely related to one or more of these burning episodes but certainly not later than 1872, when scales were rendered obsolete. This means that the materials deposited under the burn layer had to predate the period 1871–1872. None of the materials suggest a clear antebellum depositional date; therefore, we can state that use of the dumpsite corresponds to the period following the rebuilding of the post in 1867.

The possibility that this deposit is related to the recorded discard of materials in mid-1871 requires further consideration. Table 3.4 shows materials discarded by each company and how many of each article were identifiable in the artifact assemblage. The cap regiment numbers and company letters are the most useful for identifying which companies contributed to the dump. These brass artifacts would have been attached to the front of the forage cap, with the regiment number mounted above a bugle (infantry) or crossed swords (cavalry) insignia, with the company letter below. On a dress helmet, the numbers and letters would be mounted above and below a Hardee eagle (objects also listed as destroyed and recovered from the deposit).

The Company K, Ninth Cavalry, contributions to the deposit seem very clear, with cap letters and number 9s and letter Ks being recovered, as well as a number of crossed-sword emblems. The number of bugle insignias found in the dump shows a clear infantry trash presence as well, but the 8s and 3s made little sense to me until I wrote them in numerical order: 3 and 8. The Twenty-Fourth Infantry was formed from the Thirty-Eighth and Forty-First Infantry units during the 1869 reduction of the military. It would not be surprising, therefore, if materials dumped from the Twenty-Fourth Infantry included outdated regiment numbers and even company letters. The last

TABLE 3.4. *Materials Recorded as Destroyed and Discarded at Fort Davis versus Those Things Recovered from the Sample of the Archaeological Trash Pit*

OBJECT DESTROYED	COMPANY F, Twenty-Fourth Infantry, February 27, 1871	COMPANY G, Twenty-Fifth Infantry, March 9, 1871	COMPANY A, Twenty-Fifth Infantry, April 28, 1871	COMPANY K, Ninth Cavalry, April 28, 1871	# FOUND IN PIT
Cap letters	48	0	0	100	7 (D, E, K)
Cap numbers	81	50		92	13 (3, 8, 9)
Cap bugles	61	0	0	0	17
Crossed sabers	0	0	0	130	13
Eagles (dress helmets)	46				20
Sergeant scales	8	0	0	6	Minimum of 5 pairs
Corporal scales	0	0	0	46*	
Private Scales	49	0	0	0	31.5 pairs private scales
First sergeant sashes	2	0	0	0	
Single bedsacks	5	90	15	0	
Knapsacks	62	106	68		
Haversack	69	90	60	0	37 haversack buckles
Canteens and straps	42	129	50	45	Minimum 15 canteens
Ax halves	8	21	5	0	
picks	0	0	5	0	
shovel			1	0	
Hatchett handle	0	29	0	0	
Camp hatchett	0	0	2	0	
Camp kettles	0	4	0	0	
Mess cans	0	10	0	1	1 mess can
Shelter tents	0	40	30	0	
Shelter poles	0	40	0	0	
Wall tent	0	1	0	0	
Wall tent fly		1			
Tent pins	0	192	54	0	
Single mosquito bars	0	11	87	0	
Double mosquito bars	0	1	0	0	
Guard report book	0	1	0	0	
Snare heads	3	5	5	0	
Drum head buttons	0	5	5	0	
Bugler cords	0	2	0	0	
Bugle emp	0	0	0	1	
Trumpet cord	0	0	0	1	

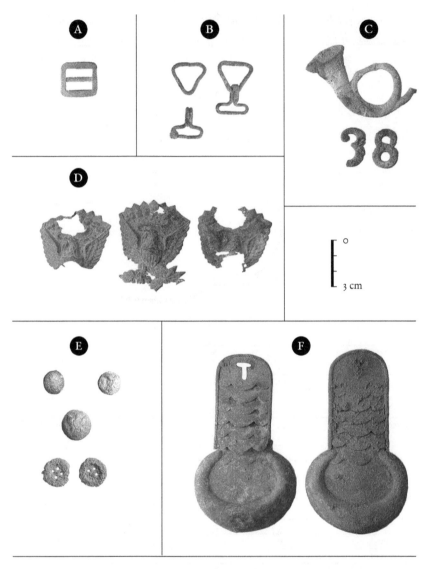

FIGURE 3.2. Examples of military uniform artifacts recovered at Fort Davis.
A. Brass cap strap slide. B. Brass knapsack hooks. C. Examples of brass cap bugle (infantry)
insignia and regiment numbers. D. Brass Hardee eagles from dress helmets.
E. Top, brass cuff-sized buttons; middle, brass coat-sized button; bottom, trouser buttons.
F. Brass epaulets. Photographs by the author.

company of the Twenty-Fourth Infantry left Fort Davis in April 1872. The only regiment number found outside of the dump during excavations was the recovery of a broken partial number that unfortunately could fit as a fragment of an 8 or a 5 from the hearth behind the barracks. Companies D and E of the Twenty-Fifth Infantry served at Fort Davis starting in May and August 1872 and could have also contributed cap letters to the dump deposit. What is clear from this alphabet soup of company letters is that the materials found in the dump seem to have been deposited within a narrow time frame given when particular troops were stationed at Fort Davis. Certainly, there is strong evidence that at least some of the materials from the deposit were discarded and burned between February and April 1871. The materials below this discard and burn layer, then, by stratigraphic necessity, must predate those events. Together with excavated materials found in other deposits, these artifacts provide insights into the personal and communal priorities of the enlisted men of Fort Davis.

Personal items

The archival record reveals few details of the soldiers' personal material lives. Court-martial transcripts do note some men keeping belongings in small boxes or trunks, but more often, items are described as stashed in knapsacks or at the head of one's bunk, but they provide little additional information.[25]

A maudlin set of documents that seemed to promise more information is the "Bimonthly Returns and Inventories of the Effects of Deceased Soldiers."[26] This paperwork, which consisted of a checklist, was completed by the captain of deceased soldier's company. Articles on the checklist included "hats, Caps, Forage Caps, Great Coats, Uniform Jackets, Flannel sack coats, blouses, stable frocks, fatigue overalls, pairs trowsers [sic], pairs flannel drawers, pairs cotton drawers, flannel shirts, cotton shirts, pairs boots, pairs shoes, pairs socks, blankets, haversacks, knapsacks, and money." Space was available to add other entries. The top part of the form asks for several details about the individual and his death, most of which would have been available from the man's enlistment papers: which company and regiment he served in, rank, name of captain, where and when he enlisted, age, height, complexion, eye and hair color, occupation when enrolled in the military, and finally, cause and place of death. The forms, like many other things used in the postwar military, seem to have been designed for use in the Civil War, with references to "volunteers."

These records are not complete nor consistently available across time, but it was possible to find records for the six men from the Twenty-Fifth Infantry who died at Fort Davis in 1872 and several years afterward. Musician Eli Smallgood and Privates George Brown, Sanford Kinney, Edward Smith, Henry Butcher, and George Wallace died in 1872. None of the men was described as owning any personnel effects. There are several possible explanations for this circumstance: the paperwork may not have been taken seriously, and the post adjutant and commanding officer may have just regularly signed off on incomplete documents. Another factor may be that because each man died in the post hospital, some of the men might have had time to ask a bunkie or NCO to handle the disposition of their property in case of their death. Musician Eli Smallgood and Privates George Brown, Sandford Kinney, Edward Smith, and Henry Butcher were sick for some days before death, giving them opportunity to ask someone to distribute their belongings. Private George Wallace, however, died in the post hospital shortly after being shot in the thigh and would not have had that chance. There is, of course, another explanation: perhaps these men owned no more than the clothing they were buried in.

Private Henry Butcher was aged forty-one at the time of his death from dysentery, July 15, 1872, and had served since December 1869. His paperwork was filled in by First Lieutenant Jacob Paulus. Paulus tried to ignore blanks about enrollment of volunteers, leaving them unfilled. J. W. Patterson, captain of Company G, Twenty-Fifth Infantry, used red ink to scratch out the irrelevant blanks and wrote "enlisted" over every instance of "enrolled." Certainly, the officers of Fort Davis seemed attentive to the top part of the form. A comparison with forms from nearby Fort Stockton reveals that some privates were recorded as having personal belongings. Private Allen Leck, of Company F, Twenty-Fifth Infantry, died in the post hospital there, leaving behind a cap, a great coat, two uniform coats, four trousers, flannel drawers, boots, gloves, and a pistol, as well as $23.20 in notes. In contrast, another private from Company K, Twenty-Fifth Infantry, had no effects and a hastily filled out form.

To further examine whether incomplete record keeping was a factor in the apparent materially impoverished condition of the men who died in 1872, other available records for Twenty-Fifth Infantry deaths at Fort Davis extending to 1878 were reviewed. This provided a sample of six other men's records: Sergeant Anthony Jackson, Corporals Richard Robinson and Abram Jackson, Principal Musician Charles Hill, and Privates George Wilson and James

Lusk. Corporal Abram Jackson was reported killed off post and his "effects were buried with him by the men who killed him," suggesting that he had few other belongings. Hill, Wilson, and Lusk were recorded as having no effects.

In contrast, Corporal Richard Robinson, who was murdered in his bed in 1878, and Sergeant Anthony Jackson, a long-serving member of the Company E, Twenty-Fifth Infantry, who died in the post hospital, were described as having personal effects. As NCOs, these men would have been paid slightly more than enlisted men, and as men who had long-served, they would have had time to acquire more things. That said, the non-uniform goods listed are minimal.

Jackson, who died in 1875, had towels, Berlin gloves, a necktie, two packages of smoking tobacco, sheets, two towels, a pocket book, and three dollars currency. Captain David Schooley, who had served with Jackson for nearly nine years, filled out the paperwork in a careful hand. Captain M. L. Courtney of Company H, Twenty-Fifth Infantry, took similar care over Corporal Robinson's effects. Robinson's non-uniform effects were scissors, a feather pillow, a comb and brush, towels, handkerchiefs, and razors. These items speak to small luxuries that would have made frontier service more comfortable—improved bedding and personal hygiene items. The archaeological record reinforces these scant inventories. In crowded quarters, anything too ostentatious would have drawn attention, so little extravagances, be it tobacco, liquor, or hygiene items, were acquired. The archaeological deposits from Fort Davis include small numbers of items that were likely to be individually owned, but before those are considered, there is one rather unique archival source that provides insight into what things were valued by one of the Fort Davis men.

Included in the successful pension application of Lucinda Jackson, the widow of Sergeant Anthony Jackson, are several letters from her husband.[27] The letters submitted with the successful application date mainly to the Sergeant Jackson's service east of the Mississippi, with only one letter from Fort Duncan, Texas, surviving. Still, these letters provide some insights, in Jackson's own words, into the things he valued. I have chosen to transcribe Jackson's spelling and grammar as he used it. Lucretia was not literate, and these letters would have been read to her. I found that reading the letters gives a sense of Jackson's speaking voice. For men who had so much of their voices edited from the archive, I did not want to contribute to that silencing.

The letters and the witness affidavits describing the Jacksons' marriage reveal a man with a romantic streak who loved and missed his immediate and extended family and felt a deep commitment to supporting his wife and children (see chapter 6). His letters are notably filled with giving more than wanting, with particular attention to assuring Lucretia that she would receive his pay.

From Goldsboro, North Carolina, April 21, 1868, he wrote, "I will send you money so that you can dress my little boyes [recently born twins] before I come home. I want them to look sweet when I come home. You never told me how they look, I wont to sea them very bad." In March 1869, now in Smithville, he wrote, "I can't say when we will be pade of again on the account of us moving about as we doe now from place to place." On November 23, 1869, he wrote, "We will be pade of in a few days then I will send you my money as soon as I get pade of. . . . Give my love to my little boys an learn them to fear God as well as yourself." In the last letter included in the pension request, sent September 12, 1870, from Fort Duncan, Texas, he wrote, "I sent 12 dollars in my last letter. . . . I have a peace of Gold to send to Anthony but it is too heavy to send in a letter." In addition to money and letters, he apparently also sent a photograph. Writing from Ship Island, Mississippi, on November 9, 1869, he queried, "I sent you my picture with first Sargents stripes. You never told me whell you gotten it or not."

More than anything else, Jackson asked for letters from his family. On September 20, 1867, he wrote, "Give my love to all of the family and tell them thay must rite to me soon." In his November 23, 1869, letter, he chided Lucinda "My dear hit has been a long time since I has heard from home." When he received letters, he was thrilled. On April 21, 1868, he wrote, "My dear I received your most kind and wellcom letter, which came to hand today and I wore more than glad to hear from you and to hear you are well at this time."

When he asked for material things, he asked for paper and stamps, citing that both were hard to come by. He also asked for pictures of his wife and son (one of the twins tragically died as an infant). Things of greatest sentimental value seem to have been left at home with his wife and children. When the pension investigator asked for proof of the couple's marriage date, she retrieved a book where Jackson had inscribed, "Alexandria VA, Dec the 25th, 1862, I Anthony Jackson ware married to Lucindey." The statement was recorded halfway through a book that Lucinda stated Anthony had purchased shortly after the death of Abraham Lincoln. The book was Justus Keefer's *Slavery, It's Sin, Moral Effects, and Certain Death* (1864), a poem that lauded the necessary and divinely mandated end of enslavement. Its stanzas may also have provided inspiration for military service for Jackson:

As an instrument in the hands of God,
You will have to bear a less heavy load.
A slave! A soldier! Who cannot discern
The Contrast? And with a heart that
Must burn for Freedom—Freedom for himself and race—
Nothing less can remove this foul disgrace.[28]

Jackson had not enlisted in the USCT during the Civil War but had worked in a military depot in Washington, DC. It was there that he encountered Reverend Gladstone, the man who performed Anthony and Lucinda's wedding ceremony. Gladstone reportedly also ran a school for former slaves where Jackson learned to read and write.[29] Jackson's letters home demonstrate how obligations afar shaped military experience for some Black men. While enlisted men were supposed to be single at the time of their enlistment, pension records demonstrate that it was not unusual for married men to enlist anyway, keeping marriages quiet.[30] Men also had parents, grandparents, siblings, and other loved ones who both provided support to and needed support from their soldiering loved ones.

Archaeological Evidence of Personal Belongings

The archaeological record supplements and complements the meager archival one, giving some additional insights to the kinds of things men chose to spend their wages on. Not surprisingly, most of those things were consumables—liquor, tobacco, food condiments, medicines, and toiletries. Again, just as indicated by Jackson's letters, most of the items speak to small amenities rather than large purchases.

Liquor, once part of the military ration, by the postbellum period had to be obtained by purchase from the post trader or elsewhere. Writing in 1877, the Twenty-Fifth Infantry's chaplain, George G. Mullins, described the alcohol consumption of the troops at Fort Davis: "There is no such thing as utter drunkenness, and the small quantity of ardent spirits consumed could not be pronounced a serious evil, were it not frontier and Texas whiskey. . . . The officer and soldier should be restrained by an iron hand from ever visiting the low dram shops and gaming dens that surround a military post."[31]

Liquor-related artifacts that were found on the post grounds would presumably be those things that were consumed (or at least their consumption finished) on the fort grounds, thus leading to their deposition. While alcoholic beverages were available off post, the amount of liquor consumption represented on post is fairly modest given the number of men. If the archaeological deposits dating from around 1869–1877 are considered collectively, a minimum of fifty-two beverage containers are represented, of which four are likely to have contained non-alcoholic mineral waters. The remainder of the assemblage—eleven imported single-serving beer bottles, eleven wine and champagne bottles, six bitters bottles, three single-person flasks (probably refillable) and seventeen other alcoholic beverage containers—hardly seems excessive. Courts-martial reveal that some men clearly struggled with at least bouts of intoxication, but the archaeological record suggests little evidence of rampant drinking on the post.[32] The porters and stouts contained in the imported beer bottles would have had nutritional value for malnourished men. Bitters and brandy were associated with medicinal uses and were not just consumed for alcoholic content.

One of the more memorably named products, Udolpho Wolfe's Aromatic Schnapps, was a gin touted for its health benefits, particularly for regulating digestive and urinary tract disorders. At least three examples of this gin were found associated with the enlisted men's barracks. While the product helpfully shows the blurry line that separated medicine from alcohol in the nineteenth century, it also speaks to important ties between the Twenty-Fifth Infantry and Louisiana. Before Fort Davis, the only place I had ever encountered Udolpho Wolfe's Schnapps was at the Civil War battle site of Port Hudson, Louisiana. Udolpho Wolfe was an alcohol importer who had a presence in New Orleans as early as 1859, importing madeira and other wines and brandies, as well as his gin. The Twenty-Fifth Infantry was founded in New Orleans, and heavy recruiting was undertaken in Louisiana. Advertisements for the product can be found in the *Daily Dallas Herald* through 1876, but not in places closer to Fort Davis.[33]

The small number of beer bottles is notable since beer is usually ubiquitous on frontier posts. This is an artifact of chronology. The year 1872 marks a momentous occasion in American brewing history: the year that Adolphus Busch perfected pasteurization of lager beers. Lagers were introduced to the US in the 1840s, and by 1860, they had claimed half the beer trade. These light, effervescent beers were fragile and could not travel far before becoming stale and flat. Pasteurization provided a means to ensure lagers' shelf life for bottling

FIGURE 3.3. Examples of alcohol containers recovered at Fort Davis. A. Base of olive glass liquor bottle. B. Udolpho Wolfe's Schnapp's bottle fragments. C. Top of champagne bottle. Photographs by the author.

and sales further afield. For Busch, with his factory in St. Louis, this was very desirable.[34] In 1872, the bottle manufacturing industry offered few bottles that could withstand the pressure created by the beer's carbonation. After early experiments with German mineral waters, an American manufacturer developed a form that became known as the export beer bottle. By the mid-1870s, export beer bottles covered the West, having been happily emptied by thirsty soldiers. From the late 1870s through the mid-1880s, households occupied by several noncommissioned officers and their laundress wives at Fort Davis demonstrate an overwhelming preference for lagers. Katrina Eichner argued that in addition to the appealing taste of lagers, African American consumers may have also appreciated the clearly patriotic design of Busch's label, which featured a bald eagle and a large letter A.[35] The clear lack of lager beer bottles recovered from in and around the HB-22 barracks suggests that none of the discrete deposits discussed in this work were created much past 1873 or 1874.

Lager beer bottle sherds are represented in the yard scatter around the building but not in the other deposits.

The recovery of three flasks from the site suggests that some men chose to discretely carry a small supply of alcohol with them, either while on duty or off (it would have been tempting to take a warming nip of alcohol during late-night and early-morning guard patrols). One of the flasks was a generic glass design and was probably discarded after being emptied of its original contents. The other two, however, are more ornate and distinctive (see figure 3.5). The only truly personalized ceramic recovered from the barracks was a molded yellowware flask mouthpiece. A review of museum collections show that these objects could be quite elaborate and often took the form of figural bottles. From the small sherd found in the ashpit, it is impossible to know what the original form was. It is not unusual on archaeological sites to recover objects that had been clearly curated for long periods of time, even after being damaged. Continued use demonstrates that the value of the object to the user is not completely lost as a result of the damage, and the lack of any other sherds from this object may suggest that it continued to be used after it was chipped. A cork would still have fit snugly in the remaining neck of the flask. The last flask recovered was aqua glass with an ornate floral-embossed pattern. Refillable flasks of the type found near the barracks, whether glass or ceramic, were produced in England and the US most commonly between the 1840s and 1870s.[36] Flasks could easily be carried on the person, and if distinctly decorated, they would have been instantly recognizable as the property of a particular person, making theft more difficult.

As a native of Virginia, it is not surprising that Sergeant Jackson's final effects included tobacco, and he hardly would have been alone. How tobacco was consumed would have had regional and historical resonances for the men. On the frontier, many Black and white enlisted men widely adopted the Mexican practice of smoking cigarillos (cigarettes wrapped in tobacco leaves rather than paper). It is not surprising, then, that only four tobacco pipes were represented in the deposits.[37] The decision to use a pipe would have been a distinctive performance among a group that favored other forms of smoking. Two of the three pipes were redware elbow pipes of the kind manufactured in the Ohio River Valley and the American South. These were cheaply obtained, sometimes being included free in a pouch of tobacco, and were used with a reed stem. Both of the elbow pipes had blackened interiors showing long-term use. The third pipe, made of ball clay, also required a separate stem and was represented only by the part of the pipe where the stem would be inserted. The ornate style of what remains of the pipe is in keeping with the beautiful figural pipes made by companies like the Gambier Company of France. These were distinctive and beautiful pipes, and like the yellowware whiskey flask, the small single piece recovered suggests the pipe was still used after being damaged.

While the stem fragment is too small to make a definite identification, it is identical in shape and angle to the stem used on Gambier's most popular (and regularly copied) "Jacob pipe," which featured a bearded man with a wrapped head, sometimes explicitly labeled as "Jacob" of the Old Testament. There are several reasons it would be interesting if this were a Jacob pipe. The complexion of Jacob, as a result of leaching of tobacco juices from the tobacco bowl, would darken with use, in essence changing from a white to a brown man, something that may have been appealing to Black men. But more importantly, Jacob was the subject of the spiritual "Climbing Jacob's Ladder," which spoke to the perils and sorrows enslaved people would face on the way to freedom (or heaven). The lyrics explicitly have the singer self-identify as "Soldiers of the Cross." This merging of religious and military imagery, as well as the powerful associations with the struggle for freedom, would make the Jacob pipe potentially appealing to Black soldiers.

Unfortunately, we cannot know if this particular piece was from a Jacob pipe, but the possibility is tantalizing. The fourth pipe is represented by a wind guard, a brass cover that fit on the top of a pipe to keep wind from extinguishing one's fire. In the sometimes high winds of Fort Davis, this would have been useful. Wind guards were available on pipes by the 1850s.[38]

Other personal items played a role in personal grooming and health care: two rubber hair combs, several toiletries, and a bone-handled pocketknife. Toiletries included remains of a liquid dentifrice and a cologne bottle. The combs were made of vulcanized rubber and of a generic form. The pocketknife was no longer than three inches and would have been easily carried on one's person. The bone was carved to look like antler, a popular style even today.[39] In 1873, Commanding Officer Zenas Bliss would ban the possession of pocketknives out of fear that the soldiers would use them in fights against civilians.

A final pair of personal items worth consideration is a four-centimeter length of brass chain recovered from the ashpit and a glass intaglio recovered from inside the unfinished barracks. The chain is gold-washed interlinked brass loops making a kind of basket-weave pattern that is 8 mm at its greatest width. Chasing is visible on the horizontal links. Chains such as these were

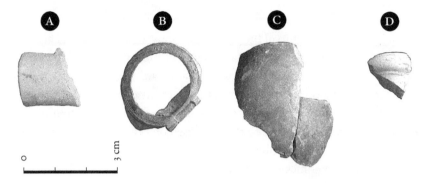

FIGURE 3.4. Tobacco pipe fragments. A. Redware ceramic pipe stem. B. Brass pipe wind guard. C. Redware pipe bowl fragments (different from A.). D. Ball clay pipe stem. Photographs by the author.

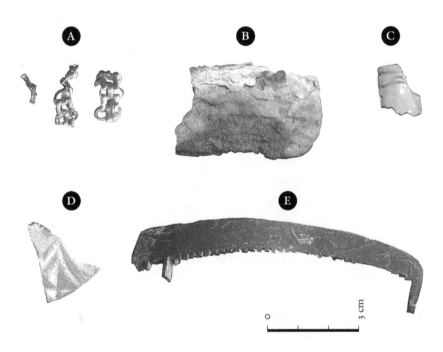

FIGURE 3.5. Examples of personal items. A. Fragments of gold-washed brass watch chain. B. Fragment of bone-handled pocket knife (see brass screw in upper right hand top). C. Yellowware flask mouth. D. Glass flask panel. E. Rubber hair comb. Photographs by the author.

still advertised as watch chains in the Sears Roebuck and Montgomery Ward catalogs of the 1880s and 1890s, providing excellent examples of how this poor broken object may have appeared before being broken and deposited in a fire.[40]

Pocket watches were important elements of proper manly dress, and in formal portraits, soldiers can often be seen wearing them. Watches were available in a range of prices, and while pricey, they were generally affordable. Imagine, in particular, the freedoms conveyed to a watch's owner. Military time in the 1870s was regulated by bugle calls dictating where and when soldiers had to be. Access to a watch allowed a person to monitor *their* time relative to military time and would have been valuable to anyone attempting to inject some liberty into their schedule. For NCOs, who had to manage their time and company time, a watch was a worthwhile investment. The glass intaglio, which would have dangled as the end of a watch fob, depicts the profile of a classical figure (see chapter 6). We should also consider that a watch chain and fob could be worn on a man without a watch being attached. It is therefore an artifact that could fully communicate all dimensions of masculine citizenship as a thing unto itself.

The archaeological record largely complements the portrait of personal possessions roughly sketched from other sources. Enlisted men seem to have had few personal possessions other than a few indulgences, be these in alcohol or tobacco consumption, paper and ink, small personal grooming items like razors, combs or toiletries, utilitarian pocket knives, or more rarely, larger investments that spoke to manly gentility and accomplishment. While men may not have spent a great deal of money on personal items, when it came to purchasing goods as a group for their company, they were more extravagant.

Kitchen "Furniture"

Standard issue for a soldier's mess kit was a canteen, a tin cup, a mess can, and an iron spoon. Only after 1891 did the quartermaster's department begin to supply ceramics. Yet glassware, bone-handled cutlery, and ceramics were recovered from every deposit associated Black soldiers at Fort Davis. Despite the limited nature of collection and excavation, a minimum of thirty-three distinct ceramic table wares and bath wares were recovered from the barracks trash dump/fire pit, and a minimum of twenty ceramic vessels were found in the 2015 excavations. While this may not seem like a large number of vessels

TABLE 3.5. *Summary of Tableware and*
Bathware Associated with Enlisted Men's Barracks

VESSEL FORM	MINIMUM NUMBER REPRESENTED	PERCENT OF TOTAL FOR SUB-ASSEMBLAGE
Enlisted Men's Dump (1869–1872)		
Plates	7	21.8
Bowls	5	15.6
Teacups/Mugs	6	18.8
Saucers	2	6.3
Pitchers	4	12.5
Serving vessels (e.g., platters and tureens)	4	12.5
Wash basins	1	3.1
Chamber pots	3	9.4
Hearth (associated with tent occupation 1872–1874)		
Plates	4	36.4
Bowls	3	27.3
Teacups	3	27.3
Mugs	1	9.1
Ashpit (associated with tent occupation 1874–1876)		
Plates	1	25
Platter	1	25
Teacups	2	50

for the number of men who served at Fort Davis, these are just the vessels that were broken and discarded over a short period of time and equal the number of alcoholic beverage containers recovered for the same period (table 3.5).

United States Government Circular No. 8, on post health, contained a lament regarding what was referred to as mess furniture. "The mess-furniture of a company is provided from the company fund, and some companies have a very good supply, in which they take much pride."[41] It was recommended that the military should instead provide plates, knives, and forks for the men so company funds could instead be spent on food. This brief comment demonstrates that the soldiers saw these artifacts as doing important work for them and their companies. The enlisted men at Fort Davis seem to have taken pride in building their company's mess furniture. A fragment of a commissary record from 1871 from the fort provides some evidence of how companies funded and acquired goods (table 3.6).

During five months of 1871, the commissary shows companies of the Twenty-Fourth and Twenty-Fifth Infantries and the Ninth Cavalry selling coffee rations and purchasing tin plates and cups and forks and knives, as well as washbasins. There were many ways companies could acquire ceramics. Diaries of military women like Alice Grierson, wife of Benjamin Grierson, commander of the Tenth Cavalry who arrived at Fort Davis in 1880, describes officers' families needing to downsize their households when moving posts and abandoning tableware or selling them to those left behind.[42] Merchants in town could have provided opportunities to buy table wares. Further, just because something was broken at Fort Davis doesn't mean it was acquired there. Companies outlived their members and over time grew large assemblages of communally owned goods. In addition to table wares, a number of companies came to feature well-known libraries, which were seen as valuable assets of the post. In August 1871, Company A, Twenty-Fifth Infantry, which was leaving the post, argued with the post commander about the division of books of the post library, which the company had contributed to. The post commander refused to divide the books, claiming that to do so would decimate the post library and offering instead to repay the company the value of the books.[43]

Recall the dietary deprivations suffered by the enlisted men, nutritional shortages that led them to supplement their diet with wild food stuffs and to poach cattle and pigs from local farmers. Despite hunger, the men still decided to allocate valuable company resources toward the purchase of table wares. These were not frivolous purchases; this was an act of decorating done with serious intent.

So what work was being done by these table wares? In the last half of the nineteenth century, the virtue of manliness, even martial manhood, was associated with the trappings of gentility—skills in rhetoric, the martial arts, music, chivalrous gentlemanly behavior, godliness, and educated and cultured appreciation of the arts and the natural world. Frontier military officers were seen by many as the perfect embodiment of civilized manliness—enacting civilized behaviors while also engaged in the project of enforcing settler colonialism—defenders of the so-called boundaries of civilization.[44] It was within these discourses that Black men situated their performances of martial citizenship. For them, at stake was not merely a recognition of gentility; citizenship

TABLE 3.6. *Purchases by Regimental Companies Listed in 1871*
Post Trader Fragment (FODA-TRADER)

DATE	COMPANY MAKING PURCHASE	GOOD ACQUIRED OR TRADED
February 25	Company A, Twenty-Fourth Infantry	2 ½ dozen tin plates, 2 ½ dozen tin cups, 5 sets knives and forks
February 13	Company B, Twenty-Fourth Infantry	Credit for 35 lbs. coffee
February 15	Company B, Twenty-Fourth Infantry	4 sets knives and forks
February 25	Company B, Twenty-Fourth Infantry	Postage
April 10	Company C, Twenty-Fourth Infantry	2 papers shoe polish
May 5	Company F, Twenty-Fourth Infantry	1 book
February 25	Company G, Twenty-Fifth Infantry	2 ½ dozen tin plates, 2 ½ dozen tin cups, 5 sets knives and forks
March 25	Company G, Twenty-Fifth Infantry	38 lbs. coffee
April 10	Company G, Twenty-Fifth Infantry	15 ½ lbs. coffee
April 24	Company G, Twenty-Fifth Infantry	Credit 51 lbs. coffee
April 25	Company G, Twenty-Fifth Infantry	3 brooms, 1 bottle ink
April 15	Company B, Ninth Cavalry	8 sets knives and forks, 4 sets knives and forks
May 3	Company B, Ninth Cavalry	1 chest lock
May 5	Company B, Ninth Cavalry	1 pair scissors
May 11	Company B, Ninth Cavalry	Credit 31 ½ lbs. coffee
May 12	Company B, Ninth Cavalry	2 ½ dozen quart cups
April 25	Company C, Ninth Cavalry	2 padlocks, paper tacks
May 1	Company C, Ninth Cavalry	83 lbs. coffee
March 7	Company K, Ninth Cavalry	1 dozen tin cups, 1 frying pan
March 9	Company K, Ninth Cavalry	By orders, 98 rations (in preparation for patrol)

DATE	COMPANY MAKING PURCHASE	GOOD ACQUIRED OR TRADED
March 12	Company K, Ninth Cavalry	4 padlocks
March 12	Company K, Ninth Cavalry	94 rations
April 13	Company K, Ninth Cavalry	½ dozen wash basins
April 15	Company K, Ninth Cavalry	2 papers shoe polish,
		4 sets knives and forks,
		4 sets knives and forks,
		7 dozen tin plates,
		6 dozen tin cups
April 29	Company K, Ninth Cavalry	Credit 73 lbs. coffee
May 2	Company K, Ninth Cavalry	82 lbs. coffee
May 10	Company K, Ninth Cavalry	Credit 67 lbs. coffee

rights themselves were at stake. If to be a citizen was tied to genteel martial manhood, demonstrating their membership in that elite group was essential.

Enslavement had significantly limited or denied for African American men the opportunity to define and preform manliness to their own community standards. The random and arbitrary separation of couples and families that resulted from sale or inheritance, combined with the inability of enslaved people to enter into legally recognized marriage relationships, served to render the future of every personal relationship uncertain. Whereas patriarchal authority over one's family was a defining feature of white manhood—and therefore citizenship—enslavement denied a similar role for Black men. Men raised in enslavement came from households that may or may not have included biological kin and where gender relations between men and women were more often more egalitarian, an expression of the tremendous physical demands that manual labor placed on both sexes. Men who had lived as freedmen before their military service had also lived under the threat of separation from loved ones through illegal seizure and enslavement and within extended kinship networks that included free and enslaved people. Emancipation of all Black men provided an opportunity to imagine, and when possible to create, intimate relationships—between kin, with loving partners, with friends—in ways distinct from those during enslavement. These realities, of both experience and hope, meant that Black men brought a flexibility and creativity to building relationships with one another and with their community.[45]

The 1860s and 1870s was marked by Black families navigating freedom and exploring, debating, and experimenting with new labor and household arrangements as men and women negotiated with one another and their communities what they could be. Legally marrying was a priority for many new and long-term couples, whereas others sought to explore other models of intimacy. Many households strove to remove women from the workplace outside of the home, where sexual violence and other abuse was so common, and to work toward building nuclear families with male providers. Others refused to embrace white demands for respectability and built other kinds of families and households. Within the period of flux, the twenty-something-year-old soldiers of Fort Davis were members of that generation of men trying to figure out what kind of men they wanted to be.[46]

Black men also fought stereotypes of them that had been nurtured and entrenched over centuries in white supremacist narratives. Black feminist scholarship has advocated understanding the historical construction of gender as experienced at the intersection of race, class, and sexual identity.[47] Enduring stereotypes of African American men (and women) used to justify enslavement continued to circulate labor in white supremacist narratives and portrayed Black men alternately as sexually depraved and dangerous brutes, emasculated old men, or ridiculous and clownish man-children. Scholars of Black masculinity have looked at the contradictory positions held by Black men, occupying spaces that were simultaneously hypermasculine and effeminate or juvenilized, or as Tommy Curry has described it, the genre of the "man-not," a less-than-human who embodied the phobias and caricatures of white supremacy that naturalize why it is and has been historically so easy for the deaths of Black men and boys to be accepted within society. In other words, enforcement of the "man-not" narrative of Black manhood is a necropolitical tool of the state.[48]

These caricatures and phobias circulated within the military—often malignantly, sometimes benignly—by well-meaning officers, but always with the same affect: to render Black soldiers as less-then-men. Captain Higginson, who led Black troops in the Civil War, often described the men as having a childlike innocence that drove their desire to be good soldiers.[49] The most notorious stereotype of Black men was that of the Black rapist. In a November 21, 1872, letter to Brigadier General Augur, Department of Texas assistant adjutant, protesting the mitigation of Martin Pedee's attempted rape conviction,

Colonel George Andrews managed to draw on both the Black rapist and the Black child stereotypes:

> It is now two years since I commenced my service with colored troops and during that time attempts similar to the one related above [purported attempted rape] have been made upon the officer's quarters at Forts Duncan, Stockton and Davis, and I think McKavett and Concho. While stationed at Fort Clark five such attempts were reported to me. . . . Under such circumstances it is not surprising that officers are reluctant to leave their families for any purpose after dark and that detached service becomes a positive cruelty and these feelings are shared by the best of the enlisted married men and I have had them come to me and with tears rolling down their cheeks, beg permission to remain in garrison while others took the detail for detached service."[50]

Higginson also used the image of crying soldiers to emphasize their childishness and innocence. For Higginson, who was advocating for widescale enlistment of Black troops into the Union Army, the childlike nature of his soldiers was intended to reassure those who feared the prospect of arming men who might retaliate against their white enslavers. Andrews seems to have deployed the trope here to a different end. Men who are really children could not be expected to take on the full responsibilities of citizenship, nor could they be seen as equal. In combining the image of crying children and sexual brutes, Andrews paints a portrait of Fort Davis as a failed experiment in Black soldiering. It is worth noting that historians have not been able to find evidence of any such a rash of attempted rapes sweeping across the military bases of west Texas (see chapter 7 for further discussion). These were the attitudes of white officers confronted on a daily basis by the Black soldiers of Fort Davis.

The performance of table etiquette was an essential component of manly gentility. The selection of primarily plain white ceramics seen in the fort assemblages was not simply a function of cost. Matching white tableware was popular in middle-class homes to denote the sacred simplicity of domestic life, while expensive and highly decorated tea ware was used to negotiate status by middle-class women during social teas. In addition, the simple embossed designs, several of which featured floral elements, also spoke to the growing influence of the aesthetic movement in decorative arts. Regina Blaszczyk, a design historian, has noted that while most cultural historians have emphasized the role of the aesthetic movement among the upper and middle classes, they have failed to adequately recognize the wide-ranging nature of the late nineteenth-century "art-craze" and its "democratization of genteel living." She emphasizes that men were part of this consumer drive, decorating banks, law offices, and club houses as self-consciously as women decorated domestic spaces.[51] The soldiers' selection of simple, plain tableware, including service vessels like tureens, platters, and pitchers, served to create a sense of family among the men of a company, and dining from tableware rather than from mess cans elevated meal time to a communal event as well. Ceramics held powerful messages about respectability, faith, family, and beauty, and Black soldiers were eager to show their embrace of these values. Through the purchase of ceramics and other table wares, the men literally transformed eating from the experience of men shoveling food with spoons from cans into their mouths into a shared ritualized experience of community. The powerful statement made by the use of ceramics is only increased when it is remembered that these objects were used by men living in overcrowded barracks and tents. When treated like animals, the soldiers acted like men.

While the majority of the ceramics from Fort Davis's barracks were plain, several distinct embossed patterns (raised decorations creating a white-on-white look to the wares) were found, and these deserve attention as well. A number of the seemingly plain plates are actually identifiable by their rim shape as the specific pattern "Union," a design first registered by T. and R. Boote of Staffordshire in 1856. Given the number of Civil War veterans among the soldiers of Fort Davis, the selection of a pattern with this name does not seem arbitrary.[52]

Also harking back to a shared military memory is a serving bowl decorated with a molded fleur-de-lis pattern. The fleur-de-lis was found in French religious and secular contexts by the late medieval period where it simultaneously indicated saintly attributes of the Virgin Mary, Trinity, Royalty, and purity.[53] The fleur-de-lis was a potent symbol in a number of contexts for Black soldiers and is not commonly seen as a ceramic pattern. It has not been possible to identify the manufacturer of this ceramic, however, and it is possibly of French manufacture. Nonetheless, by the mid-nineteenth century, this was a well-recognized symbol in the French coast of the American South, stretching from Mobile, Alabama, to Galveston, Texas.

Louisiana held multiple resonances for Black soldiers. It was at Port Hudson where in 1863, Butler's Louisiana Native Guards stormed the heavily defended,

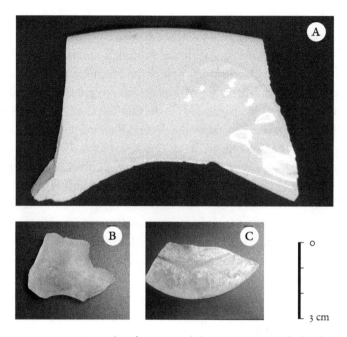

FIGURE 3.6. Examples of ceramic and glass wares: A. Rim of Lily of
the Valley semi-vitrified ceramic sherd. B. Part of body of Honeycomb
pattern pressed-glass goblet. C. Pressed-glass foot of stemware vessel.
Photographs by the author.

higher, Confederate position. Several hundred Black soldiers died in what was
an impossible task, yet their bravery against insurmountable odds convinced
Union generals that formerly enslaved people would fight for their own freedom. The Louisiana Native Guard were the only troops in the Civil War who
fought under Black officers. Their captain, Andre Cailloux, a formerly enslaved
man who had negotiated his freedom, was particularly heralded for his bravery
as he led six siege attempts against the confederate fortifications before being
mortally wounded. He was widely discussed as an inspiration to Black troops
and commemorated following the war and to the present.[54] In recent protests
surrounding the removal of the statue of General Lee from Lee Circle in New
Orleans, newspaper photographs revealed signs proclaiming Cailloux a hero
deserving a statue instead. The pride felt toward Louisiana's Black soldiers in
the fight to free themselves in the nineteenth century was profound and enduring. New Orleans and Baton Rouge were important recruiting centers for

the Black regiments, and the Twenty-Fifth Regiment, born of the Thirty-Ninth and Fortieth Infantry Regiments, was organized in New Orleans.

Closely related to the fleur-de-lis are multiple examples of another pattern, lily of the valley, which was widely popular and manufactured by a number of companies. Like fleur-de-lis, lily of the valley has religious connotations and is widely cited in the Bible, particularly in the Old Testament "Song of Solomon." In folklore, the flower represents the Second Coming of Christ or denotes a better future. The blossoms are reputed to have bloomed from the tears shed by Mary when Jesus was on the cross. For Victorians obsessed with sentimental icons of motherhood, lilies of the valley were a popularly reproduced image. For Black soldiers, the hope for a better future was a collective ambition. Multiple potteries manufactured the pattern, including a number of companies whose manufacturer's marks were recovered from the post deposits.[55]

Glassware patterns identified from the site include honeycomb, which marked communal work spirit and industry—a worthy set of values for soldiers working together—and paneled tumblers that evoked the popular molded gothic ceramic pattern that signified the sacred nature of domestic life.[56] In selecting communal tableware, the men were attentive to the practices of using things to tell stories about themselves. These were stories intended for different publics. In their barracks, the men of Fort Davis put on elaborate dances and Christmas balls open to the broader post and civilian communities. White commissioned officers, their families, and the post commander were expected to make appearances at these events. While slightly later than the period represented by the archaeological materials, an 1883 account from parties hosted by the Tenth Cavalry includes descriptions of "table cloth covered tables, an abundance of food and goblets of eggnog at Company B's party, while Company K provided an equally abundant repost for visitors, with one guest observing special silvery that was marked with the company letter and regiment number of the 10th."[57]

In the 1960s, when barracks building HB-20 was excavated by the National Park Service, they found an example of a Company K, Tenth Cavalry, monogrammed plate. This plate was manufactured by Ott and Brewer of Trenton, New Jersey, most likely in the period between 1863 and 1880. Trenton was one of the centers of the ornamental pottery decorating industry that emerged with the aesthetic period. Plain stock ceramics were personalized for groups, creating truly unique pieces of art. Regimental decorated ware, like this example, were used by several white regimental companies, with examples recovered

FIGURE 3.7. Company K, Tenth Cavalry plate, recovered in 1960s from HB-20, curated at Fort Davis National Historic Site. The painted edge of the plate was a deep red color, and the hand-painted center regiment and company emblem seems to have been matching red with gold embellishments (the over-glazed painted decoration has now mainly washed away from years in the earth). The plate was manufactured by Ott and Brewer in Trenton, New Jersey, and probably decorated in that same city. Photograph by the author.

from the San Francisco Presidio, California, and Fort Concho, Texas.[58] Marking in this way served to reinforce that these were not just any kind of domestic space, but a uniquely and specifically male space—a brotherhood so to speak.

Given that the troops hosted balls and receptions, some of the food containers found in the communal dump may reflect company purchases. A mustard barrel, multiple pepper-sauce bottles, pickle and preserve bottles and food jars may represent attempts to improve the flavor of rations to suit a company's tastes or may have been elements used in the preparation of special celebratory foods.

Shared possessions needed securing, particularly when living in over-crowded and easily accessible barracks or tents, as evidenced from a padlock recovered from the ashpit. Given that men seem to have individually owned few personal items, it seems likely that the padlock protected communal resources. The Ninth Cavalry is recorded in the partial post ledger as purchasing multiple padlocks with company funds. With large numbers of their men sent on patrol away from the post for extended periods of time, it would have been necessary to protect the property of the company. Marking tableware and silverware could also help reduce chances of theft of mess furniture, but it wasn't necessarily enough of a deterrent. A gothic-shaped flint-glass tumbler base was recovered near the post commander's house in 2009. The gothic-styled tumbler matches sherds recovered from the barracks area and has engraved on its base a cursive K, seemingly etched into the glass with a pocketknife. As commissioned officers visited enlisted men's barracks as guests, but not

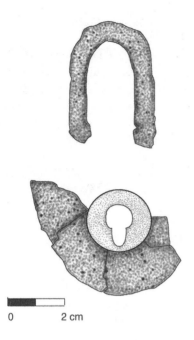

FIGURE 3.8. Padlock recovered from ashpit feature, near HB-23. Illustration by the author.

0   2 cm

vice versa, it seems likely that this object was taken from the barracks at some point and that it was originally the property of Company K, Ninth or Tenth Cavalry; both companies served at Fort Davis.

Troops mobilized communal purchasing power to change the materiality of their dining and entertaining experiences. Other communal purchases, like periodical subscriptions, books for the company library, and postage and paper for correspondence encouraged the development of other kinds of behavior that would be recognized as appropriate to men of a certain status. Importantly, for Black troops, much of the performance of manliness was communally based and was distinct from the emphasis on individuality favored in white constructions of manliness. This communal spirit is seen not only in the form of group purchases, but also in political actions, such as the drafting and signing of group petitions when their rights were violated or in writing to advocate for fellow soldiers. As seen in the archaeological record, this is not to say that men did not value their individuality, but rather that they expressed it in small ways. The majority of their investments were in their shared community, and as such, they demonstrate a commitment to racial uplift.

4

SERGEANT HEWEY'S STICK

By early March 1875, Sergeant John Hewey had become too cocky. When he slipped out of post, violating his doctor-ordered confinement to quarters, he headed to Chihuahua and picked a fight with the Richies, a Mexican family. Hewey kicked Manuel, the family's young son, and stole a basket containing a bag and two teacups from the house. He taunted the Richies, stating that because he had such an excellent reputation with his superior officers, he was untouchable.[1] It was not without reason that Hewey felt smug. He *had* been untouchable.

Hewey joined the military in 1886, at an estimated age of twenty. He was recruited at Braschear City (now Morgan City), Louisiana. The Atchafalaya basin town had two Union- force forts in the town, where the Ninety-Third Regiment USCI served in 1864–1865. Their presence may have shaped the young Hewey, a carpenter who identified as a native of New Orleans. When he joined the cavalry, he was described as a twenty-year-old who was five feet five inches tall; when he reenlisted at Fort Davis five years later, he was five nine.[2]

Such height changes are not unusual between enlistments, suggesting two non-conflicting possibilities: that the military was regularly enlisting men young enough to still be growing; and that access to a steady diet improved Black men's baseline health. As difficult as circumstances for soldiers could be, military life was a vast improvement over enslavement. Veteran William Branch, who served at Fort Davis in the early 1870s, succinctly observed, "I'd rather be in the army than be a plantation slave."[3]

Hewey was court-martialed first in August 1872 and again in 1874. In both cases, he escaped punishment. But what Hewey hadn't anticipated that March day was that commissioned officers learned that he had falsified testimony in another court-martial, accusing two privates in his company of resisting his authority. Some officers saw this as akin to accusing the men of mutiny. Hewey's testimony had convicted the men. His foray off base provided angered officers the means to charge him with assault and theft against a civilian and to tack on specifications about his false testimony.[4] Hewey's run as a trusted NCO was over. The post returns for late April and June 1875, just after his court-martial, show him "sick" in the hospital at Fort Davis and as being discharged on disability with a surgeon's certificate at the end of July. Somehow, Hewey avoided a dishonorable discharge and left eligible to request a military pension.[5]

⋆⇒◯⇐⋆

Hewey's schemes, fights, and foibles illustrate the complex terrains navigated by soldiers. Strict temporal and spatial controls of military life disciplined soldier's bodies. From the call of the bugle at day's start to the last notes of taps, days were strictly scheduled. With enlistments lasting three or five years, the military's control over one's time could seem never ending. Spaces of the military reservation and access to the spaces beyond were equally rigorously policed. Military control extended to the most mundane details of life—which clothing to wear, which personal items you could possess—and the most intimate: permission to marry.

The oppressive, monotonous, and boring routines of military life drove many men to desert the frontier army. Statistics clearly show that white soldiers deserted in much greater numbers than Black soldiers. Several reasons have been cited for these differences, including that desertions for white soldiers corresponded with strong economies; men who had the opportunity to earn significantly more as civilians had good reason to desert. While commissioned positions were out of reach, NCO ranks provided a higher salary and the opportunity to develop leadership skills, seldom were such opportunities available in civilian life. While a man's position as an NCO was vulnerable to the whims of commissioned officers, many men built comfortable careers over multiple enlistments.[6]

Troops could face extreme racism within the military, but the institution had structures for review and a chain of command for making complaints. Civilian life had no such protections, particularly in the South. While life in the military included structures, practices, and policies that contributed more to illness and even death for Black men than their white counterparts, the dangers of military service could not compare with the increasing racial injustice that characterized civilian existence for Black communities in the American South and in major cities.[7]

Some historians have suggested that being Black in largely non-Black western areas made Black men who deserted more conspicuous. This argument is not without merit. In March 1868, deserters Buck Taylor (Company I, Ninth Cavalry) and Spencer Lewis (Company C, Ninth Cavalry) were arrested by civil authorities who described them as "negroes under suspicion of being deserters."[8] Other scholars have posited that lower desertion rates suggest that Black men were more satisfied with military life than were white men.

As argued here, for many Black men, citizenship and service were interconnected. This was especially true for Civil War veterans who entered the peacetime army. These men had been involved in bringing about the demise of enslavement. That was only the first part of the struggle for full access to citizenship rights and equality. Military service provided a continued means to demonstrate Black men's claims on martial manhood and to stake a place in the country's manifest destiny. Le'Trice Donaldson has made a parallel argument, stating that military service became a space that created "race men"—a community of men dedicated to racial uplift through their service and afterward, in the ways they engaged within their communities, building schools and fighting for social justice.[9] While much of Donaldson's study focuses on periods later than discussed here, the same influences shaped many of the men at Fort Davis.

This aspect of Black service was not unnoticed by some white men serving with them. Writing in 1877, George Mullins, chaplain of the Twenty-Fifth Infantry, described the men posted at Fort Davis as follows:

> Our men have really had to learn "arts military" under trying difficulties. However, such as they are, the most ambitious officers might well be proud of the command. The ambition to be all that soldiers should be in not confined to a few of these sons of an unfortunate race. They are possessed of the notion that the colored people of the whole country are more or less affected by their conduct in the Army . . . . The Chaplain is sometimes touched by evidence of their manly anxiety to be well thought of at Army Headquarters and throughout the States.[10]

While the discussion of the Black regulars at Fort Davis thus far has centered around post life, in this chapter we will also venture further from the confines of the post. After further consideration of the post grounds, we will discuss the interactions between civilian and military populations in the area immediately around the post, and finally, the more far-flung travels from the post that soldiers engaged in as part of their duties. This chapter concerns the ways that military structures controlled and disciplined the soldiering body and the ways soldiers navigated around or ignored these obstacles to improve everyday living.

Human Allies and Obstacles within the Post

The primary obstacle confronted were the prejudices of commissioned officers, particularly those who occupied structurally unavoidable positions—commanding officers, adjutants, company captains, post chaplains, and post surgeons. Men in these positions could ameliorate or exasperate the conditions of service. Since the archaeological record speaks to a brief period of the post's history, instead of considering abstract placeholders for different positions, it is possible to discuss the specificities of different men and their actions during the period from1869 to 1875.

NONCOMMISSIONED OFFICERS

NCOs were the mediators between commissioned officers and privates, and they occupied a powerful space in military life. NCOs could have their own biases. Regimental officers during the organization of the Black units sought men with educational backgrounds to take on the necessary accounting and record keeping. Recruiting efforts in the North targeted free-born men to take on these positions. There was color bias in this process, with mixed-race men seen as having more desirable personal attributes than darker-skinned men and being preferentially selected as NCOs. Vast differences in background, and in some instances, colorist privilege, could influence the relationships between NCOs and the men they led, the majority of whom had been born into enslavement. During a fight with Private James Wilson, Sergeant Collins called the man "a son of a whore" and a "pimp." Collins, based on military correspondence during the Civil War, was raised in a nuclear family on a farm that provisioned the Union Army during the war. His father was described as "nearly white." One wonders what biases toward formerly enslaved people may have shaped this insult.[11] NCOs who abused power were not unknown, and they were frequently complained about even after service. William Watkins, a veteran from Fort Davis (and a housemate of previously quoted John Branch), expressed anger about Sergeant Jeff Walker, who he claimed had made-up charges against him, leading to discharge without a character reference. Since there was no court-martial, Watkins could not defend himself.[12] NCOs also appear in court-martial cases testifying in support of privates in their company, and men like First Sergeant John Sample, who turned a blind eye to poaching by hungry soldiers, supported their men in a variety of ways.

How important an NCO became in the lives of a company was in part related to how consistently men remained in those ranks. Some of the companies, such as Company E of the Twenty-Fifth, had great stability among their NCOs. John Sample, Anthony Jackson, John Martin, and Griffin Collins were long-serving NCOs who had been with the Fortieth Infantry and then the Twenty-Fifth. In contrast, Hewey's company, Company I, Ninth Cavalry, had little stability, and seemingly little discipline. NCOs typically appear in courts-martial as witnesses, and based on a consideration of NCOs in courts-martial, there was a great deal of turnover in these positions, with only a few men seemingly appearing repeatedly, one of whom was Sergeant John Hewey.

COMMISSIONED OFFICERS

Commissioned officers played an important though more distant role in the day-to-day affairs of camp life. Not all the officers were pleased to receive commissions in Black units. Others saw better opportunities for advancement, and few were motivated by ambitions for promoting equality.[13] Fort Davis's officers included men with strong abolitionist credentials. Lieutenant James J. Birney, Ninth Cavalry, was grandson of James Gillespie Birney, an Alabama planter turned abolitionist who sold (but did not emancipate) his enslaved people and wrote widely read abolitionist tracks. To be an abolitionist was not necessarily to be an advocate for equality and citizenship; the elder Birney advocated for gradual emancipation and recolonization to Africa.[14]

The younger Birney was the officer who argued with Sergeant Major Henderson, leading to the latter's court-martial (chapter 1). Testimony demonstrates that Birney resented any tone of voice that suggested disapproval from an NCO. Birney thought little of his troops' abilities, writing, "A year's service with the Negro troops has taught me they are not reliable in positions of trust . . . it is utterly impossible to detail a soldier as a clerk in this or other departures [of civilian employees]; three is not an average of two to a company who can sign their own names legally."[15] Yet there is no evidence that Birney or any officer at this time advocated for or worked to develop a post school.

Captain David Schooley, Company E, Twenty-Fifth Infantry, had sought a transfer to a white company shortly after receiving his commission but from all evidence was extremely supportive of the troops and finished his military career with the Twenty-Fifth Infantry.[16] Schooley regularly testified on behalf of his men, even to the extent of asserting their good character, as during the court-martial of Lieutenant Kendall, which required him to disagree under oath with fellow commissioned officers.

In contrast, Lieutenant Cyrus Gray, who served as post adjutant, had little respect for Black soldiers. A vivid example is a conflict between First Sergeant Joseph Chapman (Company G, Twenty-Fifth Infantry) and Gray. In Gray's telling, Chapman had reported on December 9, 1872, that he was unable to fill his guard detail, being short a man. Gray stated the Chapman could not provide a satisfactory accounting of his men and became agitated, at which point Gray ordered him arrested. Chapman refused and Gray had him escorted to the guard house. Military policy stated that NCOs would be put under house arrest—in the barracks—not placed in the guard house. This was parallel to the privilege of house arrest enjoyed by commissioned officers.[17] Sergeant Major William F. King of the Twenty-Fifth Infantry was called as a prosecution witness, but his testimony supported Chapman. By King's account, Gray began to curse Chapman, who politely and without anger asked him not to do so. This request prompted the arrest. Second Lieutenant Wallace Tear of the Company G, Twenty-Fifth Infantry, testified that he had known Chapman since 1867 and that his character was excellent. Chapman provided his written statement and account of the incident:

> The morning before this affair occurred, my written detail called for three privates for guard, at guard mount I furnished thee privates and one more for supernumerary and at inspection of the guard the Adjutant rejected one man of Company E 25th Infantry and took my supernumerary to fill his place so that I actually furnished four privates for guard instead of three as the detail called for. When I was trying to account for the men I had forgotten that I had furnished four privates for guard instead of three the day before and I told the Adjutant that I had no men for detail. I had no wrong intention. Since the Adjutant gave me no time to account for the men before he commenced to curse me and I became very much excited and said to him, "Don't curse at me. I don't curse at anybody and I don't like to have you curse at me."

Then he ordered me to arrest in my quarters and as I started and before I could get out of the office he said he would put me under guard."[18]

Chapman then followed a rhetorical pattern evidenced in Henderson's defense statement: he recounted having served three years in the military during the war and having joined the peacetime army in 1866, being promoted to the rank of noncommissioned officer in 1867. He also asked that the court consider the indignity that he had already endured as a result of his arrest:

> I respectfully ask the court to take into consideration the fact that ever since this affair occurred I have been kept in confinement in the guard house with deserters and convicts as if I were the worst fellow in the world. The right of being placed under arrest in my quarters was denied me as if I were a danger-ous character to be loose in the garrison. This seems to have been an attempt to crush me before my trial. Were the charges all true there would be no justi-fication of my treatment. I am even brought by a sentinel before the court.

In Chapman's statement, we see the ways that soldiers could assert their enti-tlement to the privileges of their rank and assert the military's responsibility to treat them equally. Notably, after the reading of the statement, Lieutenant Wallace Tear was recalled to testify as to the veracity of the accused being escorted by a sentinel to the trial. This was confirmed. While Chapman was convicted, Brigadier General C. C. Augur, the same man who mitigated Private Martin Pedee's rape conviction, completely remitted Chapman's sentence.[19] Chapman retired from the military in 1893, having served his entire career in the role, in his words, "of duty sergeant."[20]

Gray had conflicts with other NCOs. In August 1873, Private Charles South-erner resisted arrest while on guard duty. He grabbed a rifle, threatened oth-ers, and fired several shots toward officer's row. Sergeant Jonas Cox rushed to assist his guard and passed Gray, who hearing the commotion, had come out of the commissary. In his testimony, Gray claimed he ordered Sergeant Cox to take the prisoner under arrest, "either dead or alive," and Cox had disobeyed. Multiple witnesses testified that the men of the guard were shaken by the shooting and had not consistently responded to commands, and by all appearances, Sergeant Cox was following Gray's orders. The incident ended when an unarmed Cox approached Southerner and convinced him to turn over his gun and submit to arrest. It is hard to come to any reading of the event that does not make the sergeant's actions appear heroic and lifesaving. No one else testified to hearing Gray order the man be shot dead. Cox, in his written defense, stated that he had not heard that order but added, "If I had shot this man Southerner, there would have been a mutiny in the garrison. It was my aim to take him and did try to take him." Cox was found guilty, but his punishment was remitted in consideration of four of five members of his court-martial asking for lenience. Cox returned to service, reduced in rank but saved from loss of pay and freedom.[21]

Gray seems to have been a man who resented his service in a Black regiment. Major Zenas Bliss, post commander during Chapman's and Cox's trials, in his memoir of military service, recalled an event that may provide some context for the man's seeming racial bias. Bliss recalled that at Jackson Barracks, Louisiana,

> There was but one officer's child in the garrison ... a little girl about eighteen months old, the daughter of Lt. Gray ... he had a Negress about fifteen years old as a nurse. One morning Mrs. Gray was engaged in the back part of the house and came into the parlor and saw the babe lying on the floor on its face and thought it was asleep. She picked it up and found it was dead, blood coming from its mouth. It was soon discovered that the child had been shot in the mouth, killing it instantly."[22]

The death was first blamed on a young officer who had been in the parlor that day and had dropped a small cartridge on the floor. The child was thought to have bitten and exploded the cartridge. Gray examined his own pistol, which had been left on the mantel, found that one of the chambers had been discharged, and accused the nurse of shooting the child. After first denying involvement and being threatened with hanging, the nurse confessed. Not realizing that the gun was loaded, she had picked it up and discharged it, accidently killing the child. She was never prosecuted.[23]

POST COMMANDERS

Post commanding officers showed support for their troops based on their degree of willingness to fight for allocation of resources for the them, on their defense of troops during conflicts with civilian populations, or through the way they ran the post. Special and general orders about post policy provide some insight into post climate under particular leadership.

Wesley Merritt commanded the post for only fourteen months; the next five commanding officers led for one to three months each. Merritt was an 1860 graduate of West Point who had built his reputation (and his brevet rank) through valor in battle. He came to Fort Davis with no post management experience, which perhaps explains the cost overruns he accumulated in rebuilding the post.[24] Colonel Edward Hatch led the post for thirteen months following the departure of Merritt and was himself replaced by Lieutenant Colonel William Shafter of the Twenty-Fourth Infantry Company, who served at Fort Davis from May 1871 to May 1872, collectively. He was only on post for eight of those months, spending the rest of the time leading patrols. Shafter regularly clashed with Post Surgeon Weisel, who thought the commanding officer had little concern for the police of the garrison. Despite having led a Black unit during the Civil War, Shafter had little respect for his Black soldiers, and it was upon his return to Fort Davis in 1881 that Lieutenant Henry O. Flipper, the first Black graduate of West Point, then stationed with the Tenth Cavalry at Fort Davis, began to experience the administrative persecution that led to his court-martial and removal from the military.[25]

Colonel George Andrews began a period of leadership stability when he took command of the post in May 1872, staying until the mortal illness of his first wife led him to take a leave of absence in March 1873. Andrews returned in September 1874 and continued to lead the base until April 1876. In the interim, Major Zenas Bliss, the only officer to serve at Fort Davis before and after the war, took command from March 1873 to April 1874, and Captain David Van Valzah briefly led between April and September 1874. Between 1869 and 1876, eleven different men commanded the post.[26]

Orders made by commanding officers could strongly shape how men lived in the garrison spaces. For instance, Standard Order No. 27 of 1870 pronounced several ways that soldier's bodies would be disciplined. "All enlisted men ordered to not cross the parade ground" except by proper roads, and no enlisted men were allowed on front porches of officers' quarters. While the first part of the order was clearly intended to help maintain the police of the fort (the parade ground was described in 1872 as uneven and filled with clumpy grass), the last part of the order seems to have anticipated Jim Crow laws that pushed Black persons to the rear entrances of buildings. This order especially effected NCOs, who were conduits between privates and commissioned officers. For men like First Sergeant Chapman and others trying to assert their earned right to respectful treatment, this order meant that NCOs, when needing to approach their officers' quarters, had to do so like enslaved men, from the back porch.[27]

In 1873, Commanding Officer Bliss released an order that "prohibited carrying personal weapons, especially knives, razor, sling shot, and pistols."[28] Bliss's order may have been motivated by incidents such as a fight that took place at the Creek in early January 1873, at the house of Archer Smith. Smith, a former soldier who had married a local woman and settled in the area, was one of a number of men who hosted dances or balls at their homes for soldiers and the local community. There was typically an entrance fee and liquor sold. A group of as many as twelve soldiers from Company E, Twenty-Fifth Infantry were described as having stolen an overcoat from a civilian, who was attacked with a razor and beaten by a group of soldiers when he tried to retrieve it. Privates Henry Jenkins and John Jacobs were the only men in the group identified and court-martialed.[29]

While limiting violence between soldiers and civilians was probably one goal of the order, there were other implications. Pocketknives were useful tools. They would have been used in food preparation and consumption, personal hygiene, and any number of routine activities. Using them to harm others was one use, certainly; however, a blade could be used in self-defense. When moving across civilian spaces, this was a concern.

Orders like these enforced discipline and contributed to the police of the post but also served to re-inscribe rights among men on the post based on status. In west Texas garrisons that were exclusively staffed with Black enlisted men and white officers, like Fort Davis (1867–1880), the effect was a racialized caste system. With Black men barred from commissions, these institutional practices became naturalized structures of inequity concretized in the system. For Black men quietly working to assert their rights to citizenship and equality, these orders were grave obstacles.

CHAPLAINS

Chaplains were inconsistent players in post politics. In the late nineteenth century, influential Black men like Colonel Allen Allensworth and Theophilus Gould Steward would come to occupy some of these positions and create enduring legacies in education and social uplift.[30] Military chaplains were most highly represented in the Black regiments, with one assigned to each regiment. The first two chaplains at Fort Davis spent little time on post and had little impact on the men's lives. In addition to religious instruction, chaplains were expected to run the post school.

Manuel Gonzalez, chaplain of the Ninth Cavalry, was first assigned to Fort Davis in November 1869 but was "on duty at regimental headquarters" at Fort Concho until June 1870, when he is described as being "on leave." October 1870 found him "on route to the post," and he finally arrived in November 1870. By May 1871, Gonzalez was on leave serving as a witness in a civil case, and although back on the post by the end of June, he was transferred to Fort Stockton on November 18, 1871.

Chaplain David Barr was a man who wrestled with the demons of addiction. He was quietly removed from service as a result of his struggles with alcoholism and a tendency to public intoxication. The post records have little say about him. He arrived with the Twenty-Fifth Infantry on May 26, 1872, but the August 1872 post return lists him as "Sick since August 31, 1872, in arrest since August 8th." He doesn't appear in another return.[31] An August 4, 1872, letter from Andrews to Barr demands an explanation for his absence from the funeral and burial service of recruit Edward Smith of the Twenty-Fifth Infantry, who had died in the post hospital the day before.[32] This seems to be the event that precipitated his removal.

It was with the arrival of Chaplain George Mullins in 1875 that the post finally had a chaplain with passion for his vocation. Mullins was first posted at Fort Davis in 1875, and his first reports about the troops were less than flattering. He complained of intoxication, whoring, and gambling. He shortly thereafter had "a change of heart" and is often lauded in the historiography as being a primary force in first developing the post's education for Black troops. It is clear that Mullins was outstanding at self-promotion, but that criticism aside, his observations do capture the idealistic aspects of military service.[33] While he promoted the men as a collective, Mullins does not seem to have known them as individuals. In his chaplain reports, he kept an accounting of marriages and deaths, and he attempted to say a few words about the deceased. In May 1875, he made the following notation for Sergeant Anthony Jackson:

Died in the hospital at Fort Davis, early in the morning, May 30, 1875 AD Sergeant Anthony Jackson of Company E 25th regiment Infantry. His home was in Aldie, Virginia. He was a good soldier but member of no church. He was sick only a few days—suffering agony from inflammation of the bowels and was not conscious for several hours before death came to his relief. He was buried with solemn military and religious services in the post graveyard at sunset of May 20th and his grave is marked and recorded as No. 44."[34]

Letters to his wife demonstrate that Jackson had a deep religious faith, something the chaplain apparently did not know. The presence of a motivated chaplain had both positive and negative effects for the enlisted men. On the one hand, Mullins demonstrated enthusiasm for his role in providing educational opportunities, but on the other, he was much more concerned about policing the moral health of the post, which had implications for men's recreational activities.

POST SURGEON

Dr. Daniel Weisel has already been introduced. He represents the highest ideal for a post surgeon, committed to decreasing risk of disease among the troops and attentive to the dietary and habitation needs of the men. His records include accounts of his attending dinners with the troops and evaluating the quality and preparation of the meals. Dr. Weisel's immediate successor was Thomas Landers, who held the role of acting assistant surgeon. In November 1872, Captain C. L. De Graw joined the post in the role of post surgeon, with Landers continuing on as acting assistant surgeon.[35] De Graw seems to have used the excuse of the poor state of the post hospital to beg off of particular duties (such as autopsies) when it suited him. As discussed in chapter 2, he did advocate for improving the soldier's rations and argued that the work load of the Black soldiers was a consistently heavy one, with a high caloric expenditure. None of the post surgeons at Fort Davis seems to have been inept or intentionally negligent.

Temporal and Spatial Control in the Post

People were not the only controlling influences in the post. The temporal geographies of the post were also very structured (table 4.1).[36] From 4:50 a.m. until taps at 9:00 p.m., much of the day was accounted for. Not included in this schedule is the extra duty that men pulled doing post construction projects (earning them thirty cents extra pay a day), or the constant demands of guard duty.[37] Schedules were tweaked constantly, with men hearing of changes through Standard Orders. Most men faced a full day of fatigue and

TABLE 4.1. *Example of Daily Schedule,*
from General Order No. 11, May 30, 1872
(NMRA 66-783(7675)-3, FODA)

ACTIVITY	TIME
First call reveille	4:40 a.m.
Reveille	5:00 a.m.
Stable and police call	5:10 a.m.
Breakfast call	6:10 a.m.
Sick call	6:30 a.m.
Fatigue call	7:30 a.m.
First call for guard mount	7:50 a.m.
Guard mount	8:00 a.m.
First call for drill	8:20 a.m.
Drill call and band practice (except Saturdays), cavalry mounted Mondays, Wednesdays, and Fridays	8:30 a.m.
Recall from drill	9:30 a.m.
Water call	10:00 a.m.
Recall from fatigue	11:30 a.m.
Orderly call	11:45 a.m.
Dinner call	12:00 M.
Fatigue call	1:00 p.m.
First call for drill	3:20 p.m.
Drill call (except for Saturdays, infantry only)	3:30 p.m.
Stable Call	3:30 p.m.
Recall from Drill and Stable	5:00 p.m.
Retreat and Parade	Sunset
Tattoo	8:30 p.m.
Taps	9:00 p.m.
Sunday morning Inspection invariably in being marching orders	8:00 a.m.
Church Call	10:00 a.m.

drill or work in the hospital (as orderlies), the quartermaster department, the stables, or work off post doing construction, tending the post garden, acting as escorts, manning stage stops, or working in the pinery. General Order 22, from October 1870, stated that drill would take place each day except Saturday and Sunday. In 1870, cavalry men were exempted from afternoon drill, under the logic that they had to be ready to respond if there were need for their services off base.[38] Guard duty was particularly onerous duty, since it cut into one's limited sleep time.

Within these temporal controls, men pushed where they could on the schedule to benefit themselves, but in doing so, they ran the risk of running afoul of military rules. Guard duty cut into off-the-clock time for soldiers and also created a landscape of checkpoints necessary to navigate when soldiers were living outside military schedules. Sentinel stations were numbered, and in testimony, witnesses will sometimes provide both the number of the station they were guarding and the location. Station 1 was the guard house, located on the south side of the parade ground, immediately north of the sutler and about three hundred feet to the west of the quartermaster's office and storehouses. Station 2 was in front of the quartermaster's storehouse. The bakery and commissary store were also in this immediate area. Part of the duties for this guard station was to check on the multiple locks that secured the storehouse.[39] Station 6 was described as corresponding to the cavalry stables, which were immediately north of the quartermaster's office and to the east of the completed company barracks (HB-20 and 21), separated from the barracks by a road.[40]

The other stations are a bit trickier to locate because of the ambiguity of maps and descriptions, but I am fairly confident of my interpretations. Station 3 was described in the court-martial of Private Alfred Taylor as both "the commissary" by a private and more explicitly as the "commissary storehouse" by the corporal of the guard. The commissary store is shown to be in the same immediate complex as the quartermaster store, but an 1872 map shows a second commissary storehouse on the northeastern edge of the parade grounds. Greene describes the commissary storehouse to the south of the parade ground as being surrounded by water barrels to protect the stores from fire, thus it seems likely that station 3 was the building located near the bakery. This means that there would have been a substantial guard presence near the guard house.[41]

Station 4 was in the quartermaster's stable area, located directly north of the cavalry stables. Forage storage, the blacksmith's workshop, and a lumber pile were located in this work complex.[42]

While most of the guard stations seem to be concentrated on the eastern edge of the post (the side not protected by rock cliffs), station 5 corresponded to the commanding officers' stables and lower magazine and was identified from the court-martial of Jordan Hudson, who stole Commanding Officer Bliss's revolver from under a seat in his carriage. This area was located in hospital canyon, to the west of the commanding officer's quarters, where the

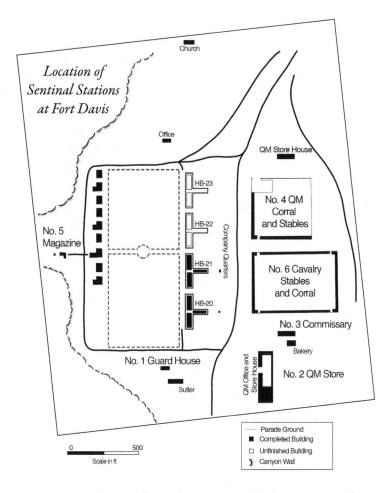

FIGURE 4.1. Location of sentinel stations at Fort Davis, as reconstructed from court-martial Testimony. Illustration by the author.

structures of the first fort occupation are clustered. One 1872 map also shows a magazine in this area. This fits with testimony from the Martin Pedee rape trial, where one witness, who was at the flag post, heard the scream of "Murder!" and thought at first it had come from the sentinel at station 5.[43]

If we think of the sentries as serving a defensive border guarding entry to the post, then it is clear that any soldiers returning to post would consider how much attention they wanted to draw. A favored route back to the barracks from forays off post was to cut between the two sets of stables. This route would have had the greatest potential of avoiding sentries (who were overseeing a large area, and based on court-martial records, had many places to shelter for a nap). The barracks buildings obscured the view shed of this area from the officer's quarters or the sutler's (where officers went to drink). The empty barracks do not seem to have been patrolled to any extent, making them excellent refuges on post as well.

Being seen or not seen at particular moments had a strategic element to it. It is worth considering again the use of space around HB-23. Test excavations were undertaken in the rear of the building on either side of the mess hall. I had expected that we would find each of these open areas utilized by the men, as evidenced by scatters of materials. Instead, we found almost no artifacts on the northern side of the empty barracks but evidence of heavy use in the space to the south. This use of the space does not date to the occupation of the barracks but to before its completion. The southern side of the barracks adjoined the northern side of barracks HB-22, which was occupied. The tall adobe walls of the finished barracks and the unfinished barracks next to it created a semiprivate courtyard for the troops who had a limited-view shed from the officer's quarters across the parade ground. Using the area behind the unfinished barracks as an extension of the occupied barracks yard also made it easier to move in and out of the unfinished barracks. Who were the most likely users of this area given the dates of the deposits? Company E, Twenty-Fifth Infantry.

Some historians have argued that the military was not a racist institution, merely an institution that had racists in it.[44] This characterization makes institutional and structural features of our social world seem distinct and independent of day-to-day life. Instead, we can see how specific individuals in particular roles at given times had real impacts on post life—sometimes with deadly or lifesaving outcomes. Brigadier General Augur, in his role of overseeing court-martial outcomes, was an important person who protected soldiers from the worst impulses of court-martial juries. At the post level, NCOs, commissioned officers, chaplains, and post surgeons could serve as important allies or oppressors. Soldiers thought through the spaces of the post, moving across them in ways that promised to avoid the worst possible interactions and oversights.

Visiting Town

To the west and north of the post reservation was undeveloped land and the volcanic spines of Sleeping Lion formation of the canyon walls that enclosed the post. Mr. Buchoz, who briefly had authorization to be a post trader, had a house on this part of the post grounds. His building was later absorbed by the fort and was used as the temporary church and school building in 1872-73. The post hospital was planned to be in this area, but those plans never came to fruition, and it stayed instead in the canyon.[45]

Immediately south of the post, on the other side of the mountain ridge, was a small settlement of mainly white-owned businesses and farmsteads, known as Fort Davis. Lonn Taylor attributes the strange layout of the modern town of Fort Davis to the competing interests of several landholders—the Keeseys and two distinct and unrelated families of Murphies—who attempted to control the layout and development of the town to their own interests, and while this has clearly left an enduring impact on the landscape, it ignores the ways that race also shaped the town's development.[46]

Today, Fort Davis is bisected by State Highway 118/17. Route 17 follows the old stage route and goes south from Fort Davis to the town of Marfa, and in

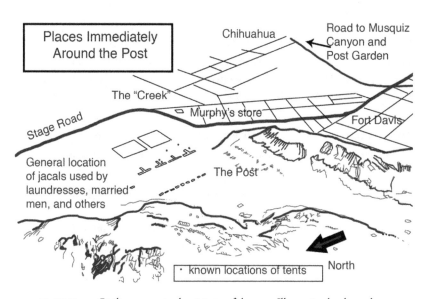

FIGURE 4.2. Civilian spaces in the vicinity of the post. Illustration by the author.

the northeasterly direction winds through Wild Rose Pass up to Toyah Creek and Balmorhea. Through town, the road serves as a line of racial segregation, with Mexican-descended populations mainly settled to the east of the road and the white populations on the west side.

The Creek and Chihuahua were east-side settlements and the most contentious areas near the post, with Murphy's store serving as the gateway. Daniel Murphy, a storekeeper and post trader since the earliest days of the post, had a popular store immediately to the southeast of the post, the same side of the overland trail as the post. Soldiers regularly passed by Murphy's on their way in and out of post, and as a result, Murphy's house figures in a number of to-dos around the post; one could both play billiards in the store (in a dedicated billiard room) and buy liquor.

If one continued southeast from Murphy's store, one would come to a seasonal wash of Limpia Creek, whose collection of households with brothels, dance halls, and saloons to serve the soldiers was nicknamed the Creek. Former soldiers and their families owned a number of these businesses. The Creek, typically described as being about a half mile from the post (which seems to have meant the parade ground, not the post boundary), appears to have been closer than the settlement of Chihuahua, which was described as a mile from the post. Through time, spatial boundaries separated the two areas blurred, but courts-martial do regularly distinguish between the two areas. In November 1871, Samuel McKinney skipped out on guard duty to go to the Creek, and in September of that same year, Private Richard Thompson (Company I, Ninth Cavalry) left his guard at the cavalry corral to head to Chihuahua.[47]

By the 1880s, the name Creek seems to have fallen out of use, and Chihuahua describes all the settlements on the Mexican side of the post. This area was increasingly home to former soldiers who decided to build lives in Texas. Among these were Archer Smith, who married a local woman and became an important local citizen, his name showing up in country records as a juror. In 1884, Lieutenant John Bigelow of the Tenth Cavalry recounted visiting the Smith house for Christmas celebrations, a far more respectable gathering than the fight recorded there ten years earlier.[48]

John Allen, a Black man who is likely to have been one of many John Allens to serve at Fort Davis, set up a saloon that was in operation by at least 1873. Black-owned businesses potentially provided safer recreational spaces for off-duty soldiers, but this was not always the case. A disgruntled Allen wrote to Andrews in January 1875, complaining about rowdy soldiers: "On the night of January 23, 1875, four soldiers of Co I 9th cavalry came to my house drunk and disorderly raised considerable disturbance without any cause of provocation on my part." He named Corporal Daniel Grigsby and Privates Richard Roper, Squire Bartley, and Moses Digous as the culprits who threw stones at him and broke his door down.[49]

Richard Roper, trumpeter for Company I, Ninth Cavalry, was no saint. He was court-martialed in 1872 for being so intoxicated that he could not perform his duties and upon his conviction was given a sentence of seven days confinement on a bread and water diet.[50] Lieutenant W. W. Tyler (Ninth Cavalry) was charged with investigating the Allen incident. He found:

> The complaintant [sic] made the first belligerent demonstrations by shooting at Roper. Corporal Grigsby states he took a pistol from Allen as he was about to fire a second shot. Bartlett claimed only to have taken a razor from him (Allen) with which he was making good effort to carve Roper. While Roper says he only knocked Allen down after he (Allen) had shot at him. All the parties agree in saying that the door of Allen's house was broken down while other men were attempting to force him into his house and stop the fight. The affair seems to have originated in Roper taking away from Allen's house some female whom he had brought there for the dance to some other house. Allen had followed Roper who in turn followed Allen back to the house where the shooting occurred.

Tyler concluded his report on a pragmatic note, stating, "Making liberal allowances for the truth of all the statements." Allen had brought the problems on himself, noting that he did not give the appearance of an orderly, respectable citizen. "If the men were drunk and disorderly—and no doubt they were—he sold them the rum and ought to suffer the consequences of keeping a disorderly house."[51]

The military and civilian population lived entangled lives, economically and socially, and citizens can be found making their way across the post in the company of soldiers at different times. It is mainly in court-martial testimony where these interactions come to light.

Given that soldiers were most likely to encounter difficulties when off base, it is not surprising that social events on the post were permitted, including dances. Alcohol was still present at these events, and apart from the Christmas balls described by officers and their families, the archival record notes these events only when something goes wrong. In December 1878, Twenty-Fifth

Infantry Chaplain Mullins expressed irritation that the church building was proposed as a location for a dance: "Understanding that it is the intention to use the Post Chapel on Wednesday evenings for Hops and social parties, constrained by serious conscientious considerations, I wish to put upon permanent record that as an ordained ministry of the Church of Christ and as Chaplain in charge at this Post, I do solemnly protest against the use of our chapel building for any other than religious and educational purposes."[52] Whether the social events went forward is not recorded. The idea to use the post church may be related to ongoing challenges with overcrowding in the barracks and a sincere desire to limit opportunities for conflicts between civilians and soldiers.

A particularly notable fray grew out of a barracks' party in April, 1874. This event led to Sergeant Hewey's second court-martial—for biting off the ear of Private Griffin Collins (formerly Corporal Collins, since demoted) during a fight. A barracks party hosted by Hewey (a party that Hewey emphasized had been approved by the commanding officer and company officers) caused the row. Visitors were charged a dollar to come in and drink (and dance). By Hewey's account, Collins had come to the party drunk, continued to drink, but refused to pay. Collins was kicked out of the party and allowed to return only after promising to behave and later pay the entrance fee. The following morning, Collins and Hewey met in the post bakery. Collins asserted that he had no intention of paying the fee after all. Push literally came to shove, and during the tussle, witnesses saw Hewey with Collins's ear between his teeth, and several witnesses heard Collins shout out, asking Hewey to stop biting his ear. The court confirmed through visual inspection that indeed, a part, but not all, of Collins's ear was missing. Hewey claimed to have sort of "fallen into the ear" during the tussle and to have accidently pulled part of it off with his fingers while trying to maintain his balance.[53]

Collins, after a number of years holding the rank of corporal, had some difficulties after the Kendall court-martial in August 1872, when he was still an NCO. In May 1873, a case alluded to earlier in this chapter, Collins got involved in a dispute with a private in his company over a small sum of money. While two men were changing uniforms to go on guard duty, one of them, Private Wilson, left six dollars on his bunk. He was holding the money for a man confined in the guard house. Collins scooped it up, and when he was asked to return the money, he returned only four dollars. When challenged, he swore at Wilson, telling him he was a "son of a bitch" whose mother was "a goddamned whore." Wilson "snapped" his gun twice at Collins, who then called him the N-word, grabbed a shovel, and said he would kill Wilson.

Captain David Schooley and Lieutenant Frederick Kendall were both called by the defense as character witnesses. Their word choices are interesting. Schooley stated that he had known Collins since January 1867, saying that "I consider him one of the most sensible non-commissioned officers I have in my company—intelligent and faithful to duty. The greatest objection I have to him is that he will get a little drunk every once and a while." Kendall testified that he had known Griffin since February 1867 and that "I consider him one of the most sensible non-commissioned officers I have in my company—intelligent and faithful to duty."[54] The court found him guilty but only sentenced him to forfeit a month of salary. The adjutant for Texas approved the sentence but commented that it was very light for the kind of offense committed. When Collins was reduced in rank is unknown, but by 1874, when Hewey removed part of his ear, Collins was no longer a corporal. Hewey was found guilty of taking off a part of Collins's ear and sentenced to lose a portion of his salary for three months without a loss of rank.

Far from the Post

Fort Davis patrolled a large portion of west Texas, with Fort Stockton 87 miles to the east and Quitman 143 miles to the west. As early as 1869, troops could be found stationed far from post. In May 1869, Dr. Weisel was sent to inspect the post's pinery and troops at the stage stations of El Muerto and Barrel Springs.[55] Barrel Springs is twenty-one miles to the west of Fort Davis (between modern Fort Davis and the town of Valentine), while El Muerto is a similar distance from the post, slightly to the northwest.[56] Continuing northwest on the Butterfield stage route was Van Horn Wells, on the way to Fort Quitman. Each of these stage stops was an important location for providing water and fodder for stage teams. Troops were regularly stationed to guard other water holes: Barilla (also called Varilla) Springs was located ten or so miles to the northeast of Fort Davis, and Leon Holes and Toyah Creek were further to the northeast on the way to Fort Stockton. Men traveled seventy-six miles south to the Rio Grande border town of Del Norte, now known as Presidio, which borders the Mexican town of Ojinaga.

While the scouting missions often involved commissioned officers as leaders, escorting and guarding stations was often done by a small number of

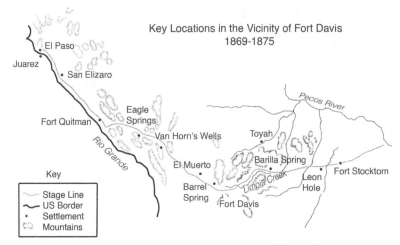

FIGURE 4.3. Stages stops, posts, and substations regularly patrolled by soldiers from Fort Davis, after Ely, *The Texas Frontier*, 272, map 6. Illustration by the author.

privates under the command of an NCO. A November 1869 escort consisting of Corporal Robert Giles and three privates from the Ninth Cavalry to Fort Stockton was a typical assignment. The men escorted the government supply train, rested one day, and then returned to the post.[57]

Life in these stations was different from life on post, perhaps most notably in the relative lack of oversight that the men enjoyed when stationed off post. The account of Privates Smith and Wilson getting themselves lost and wandering the countryside while detailed at El Muerto in 1872 shows this contrast well. That is not to say that life was relaxing on these details. The military, settlers, and stages were drawing on water sources long used by native peoples, both those with long histories in the area and those who cut through the vicinity during travels between reservations and Mexico. Jumanos, Lipan Apaches, Warm Springs Apache, and Mescalero Apache were indigenous groups recorded living or passing through the area during Fort Davis's occupation. Likewise, roads were regularly used by Mexican guerillas who stole stock from the stations and held up coaches.[58] Patrols also required the movement of provisions and arms over long distances and loading and unloading of cargo. In the summer of 1872, Private Courtney Sullivan was part of a patrol to Del Norte. While lifting heavy boxes of arms, he suffered a severe hernia that affected him the rest of his life. Sergeant Chapman remembered the incident in 1913 and that Sullivan had been medically discharged, helping Sullivan earn his pension.[59]

Native American and Black Regulars' Interactions

Soldiers far from post, whether part of larger patrols or small groups escorting or guarding stage stations, ran the risk of hostile engagements. Least likely to be engaged, however, were native peoples. By the time troops at Fort Davis were aware of incursions, Indian groups had moved elsewhere. An 1871 report of a patrol by Fort Davis Commanding Officer William Shafter offers a typical scenario:

> The scouts left the post October 5 and returned November 5, 1871 having scouted a distance of 500 miles. The most of the country scouted through south of Pena Blanca [sic] was entirely unknown to the guides or to anyone at the post as it had not been visited by troops for twenty years. About seventy miles south east of Pena Blanca we struck a moving stream of living water and about fifteen miles further down found several deserted Indian villages, some of them definitely inhabited in June and July last.[60]

Utley, in his study of Fort Davis, noted that the period 1871–1875 represented a period of relative peace between native peoples and the Texas posts, with the Mescalero Apache mainly remaining at Fort Stanton. It was after 1876 that conflicts rose in numbers again.[61] This is not to deny a native presence at the post or the surrounding areas. The town's earliest inhabitants included missionized Indians who merged into the general farming community after the secularization of the Texas Missions in 1794. Attacks in Musquiz Canyon and at the Point of Rocks, not far from the fort, happened fairly regularly, and archaeological surface remains suggest an ongoing native presence during the fort period at Point of Rocks. Native peoples also came to the Fort as military personnel, captives, and guests. Pueblo Indian Scouts came to Fort Davis to be equipped, and Black Seminole Scouts stayed for brief times while traveling from one post to another.[62]

Still, much of the period represented archaeologically at Fort Davis corresponds to a period with relatively few armed engagements with native peoples. American Indians were a presence on the broader landscape surrounding the post, even if they were rarely seen and even more rarely found within the boundaries of the post reservation. Still, men who served in Fort Davis in the

FIGURE 4.4. Photograph of William Branch (foreground) and William Watkins (background), 1937, outside their San Antonio residence. Portraits of African American ex-slaves from the Works Progress Administration Federal Writers' Project slave narratives collections. Digital id ppmsc 01096, hdl.loc.gov/loc.pnp/ppmsc.01096.

1870s remembered encounters with native peoples. William Branch told his interviewer, "Then we were ordered to Fort Davis and we are in the mountains now. Climb, climb all day and the Indians give us a fit ev'ry day. We kills some Indians and they kill some soldiers. At Fort Davis I join the colored Indian Scouts."[63] His housemate and fellow Fort Davis veteran, William Watkins, echoed that he, too, joined the colored Indian scouts at Fort Davis, and he reported encountering Cheyenne Indians who were seven feet tall."[64] Clearly, the memories of the men were subject to one another's reinforcement. But they also demonstrate how through time, the story of military engagement and interactions with indigenous peoples were important elements of remembering frontier service. Notably, while neither man appears to have been a member of the Black Seminole scouts, they would have served with these men both before and during their service at Fort Davis.

Native scouts were regularly employed on the frontier by the military for patrols through undocumented terrain. It was the Black Seminole—or Seminole-Negro Indian Scouts, as they were called by the US military—who were most familiar to companies stationed at Fort Davis. Descendants of self-liberated enslaved people and Seminole Indians, the Black Seminoles, under the leadership of Chiefs Wild Cat and John Horse, crossed into Mexico, settling on the border between 1849 and 1850. In 1857, the Seminole Indians in the group returned to the US, but those who identified strongly as descendants of formerly enslaved people stayed in Mexico. In 1870, Chiefs John Horse and John Kibbitts and scattered bands of several hundred people were settled along the US-Mexican border. Captain Frank Perry, serving under Captain Bliss at Fort Duncan, visited Chief John Horse's settlement at Nacimiento, Mexico, and extended the offer to join the US military as scouts.[65] In his autobiography, Bliss recalled 150 Seminole Indian-Negroes coming from Mexico, camping near the post, and being provided rations by the military: "The Seminole-Negro Indians who came over to Fort Duncan and enlisted were under the command of an old Negro named John Kibbetts [*sic*]. He was made a sergeant, and his son Bob a corporal."[66] In Bliss's memory, the Black Seminoles "had all the habits of the Indians."[67]

The Black Seminole scouts have a fascinating history over the eleven years of their existence. For the present story, it is the time at Fort Duncan, where activities were mainly limited to recruiting and training, that is relevant. When the Black Seminole troops came to Fort Duncan, Company E, Twenty-Fifth Infantry, was stationed at the post and would have interacted and engaged with the new scouts. The troops met with some of the scouts again in August 1874, when seven to nine scouts stayed several days at the post while in route to Fort Clark. In the deposits at Fort Davis, there may be material evidence of the enduring legacy of these interactions.

Among the artifacts recovered from the area of the barracks were thirty-six culturally modified stone tools. Chert accounted for most of the artifacts, while quartzite, amber, basalt, quartz/fulgarite, and a single piece of obsidian were also recovered. It is not uncommon for lithics to be found associated with military forts. Often, however, these objects are often dismissed as intrusions from prehistoric sites.[68] This interpretation is not unwarranted given that many posts, like Fort Davis, were founded on the sites of long-occupied Indian villages. Fort Davis was the location of a series of pre-fort occupations, including a possible Apache rancheria that surveyors in the 1850s encountered and described as recently abandoned on Limpia Creek.[69]

While there are prehistoric sites identified and recorded at Fort Davis, none corresponds to the location of HB-22. The largest concentration (six

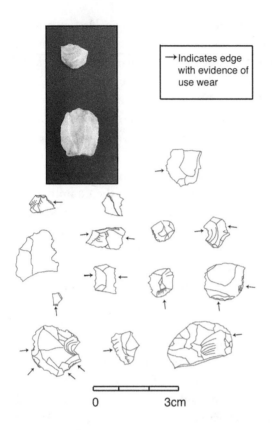

FIGURE 4.5. Examples of flaked stone found at the barracks. Photograph shows nature of the stone, on line drawings. Arrows indicate edges that showed use. Despite being small, these were heavily used tools, with even the broken biface (lower right corner) being used as a scraper edge. Photograph and illustration by the author.

→ Indicates edge with evidence of use wear

0   3cm

of the thirty-three) of stone tools were found in a unit to the north of the barracks' kitchen, an area otherwise devoid of artifacts, while the remainder were found scattered across other units in association with historic materials. Five of the remaining twenty-seven flakes were found in association with the faunal remains deposited outside the 1873 hearth fire and three were found in the ashpit. The remaining thirteen flakes were recovered from inside the barracks structure. Smaller objects, like debitage (the small flakes removed when finishing or sharpening a stone tool), recovered from the heavy fraction of flot samples could have easily been contained in the adobe bricks of the building and would then have nothing to do with the post occupation. Some of these objects surely could have been curated. Soldiers were trained to look for "Indian signs" while on scout, to locate and identify evidence of recent native occupations. Any of the objects found could have been recovered and brought back to post in this way. If this were the case, it is interesting that the men chose to curate stone scrapers, preforms, and angular shatter exclusively rather than iron arrow heads or stone bifaces. Only one of the lithic artifacts appears to have been a fragment of a biface, an artifact recovered from the washhouse of the barracks building.

Lithic production is a reduction process, during which the toolmaker systematically removes flakes from a core. A properly prepared core can produce multiple flakes that can be used for expedient cutting or scraping. Flakes are classified as to whether they have evidence of a stone's exterior (cortex) or not. A primary flake has one face that is cortical material, signifying that it was removed early in the preparation of the core. A secondary flake has some cortex showing, typically at the base, whereas tertiary flakes have no cortex visible and have been removed from a prepared core. While debitage includes a wide range of other knapping waste, most of the debitage from the site were small flakes of stone removed during the production of a tool from a flake or when resharpening the edge of a blade or scraper. Noticeably missing from Fort Davis is any amount of shatter or primary (cortical) flakes. This suggests that whoever left these lithics was traveling light, carrying some prepared cores to make flake tools for expedient scraping and cutting. If these were deposited in pre-fort times, the composition of the assemblage (albeit a very small assemblage) would suggest short-term resource exploitation, not a village occupation, as was recorded at Fort Davis.[70]

Knapping was not an unknown skill among the soldiers, for a number of glass sherds that had been modified into scrapers and cutting edges were recovered from the barracks' deposits. Such tools are well documented on African American sites throughout the South.[71]

Perhaps, then, these objects were made and used by Black soldiers. Working glass is significantly different from the physics of working stone, particularly cherts, which can be difficult. The removal of flakes from a prepared core would be significantly easier than fashioning a core from a chert nodule. It is easy to imagine this kind of knowledge and simple cores being exchanged between the Black Seminole scouts and other Black troops at Forts Clark and Duncan or perhaps while visiting Fort Davis.

But why would such knowledge or objects be valuable to the soldiers at Fort Davis? It is worth considering again Zenas Bliss's Standard Order of 1873 banning possession of razors and knives. While broken glass would be easily recognizable as a potential weapon, a simple stone flake would be less ostentatious and could easily be carried on one's person. Terrance Weik has undertaken significant long-term research on Black Seminole and African/ Native American relations in other parts of the country, and his research suggests that such technology and idea sharing were common.[72] If archaeological investigations are undertaken at Posts Clark and Duncan, it would be intriguing to learn whether there is evidence of the exchange of lithic or other indigenous technologies there.

Considering Further: Troops and Civilians

Soldiers faced threats from the civilians they were to protect, either in the form of a failure to meet their obligations to soldiers or outright violence. In exchange for protection, the stage operators were to provide soldiers transportation back to post. In early 1871, Shafter wrote to an agent for the El Paso Mail line, stating that his men had been refused a ride by stage drivers from Leon Hole and had likewise been refused the ability to stay at the station and had not been furnished rations. He stated that men were provided rations to last until the first return stage, and "if they are not brought back are obliged to get their rations by their wits." He then stated, "They must be properly treated. They should either be fed by the [stage] company or allowed facilities at the stations for cooking their own rations, a decent place to stay while at the station and invariably brought back by first return stage."[73]

A letter written by an upset Sergeant John Moore, Company D, Twenty-Fifth Infantry, who was in charge of the detached troops, described a particularly disastrous encounter at Barilla Station in November 1873, where a physically and verbally abusive stage driver was killed by one of the escorts. Moore described the situation:

> When the stage first drove up to the station Private Charles Stern went to help to take the mules from the stage and the driver did say to him 'you Black Son of A Bitch do you want to fight and the reply was from Stewart no and at this he left Stewart and went after [Frank] Tall and was killed by him. The driver followed Tall from the Stage which was 32 steps from the detachments quarters and Fire in the door at Tall was killed by the shot which Tall fire at him.

Moore relayed that a passenger on the stage saw the driver strike Tall twice in the face and saw Tall kill the driver after being shot at himself. Moore had the presence of mind to list witnesses, including George Mackley, the station keeper, but couldn't get the name of the passenger.[74] Tall must have been seen as justified in shooting the man in self-defense. He shows up in 1875 as a witness in another case, still clearly with Company D, Twenty-Fifth Infantry.[75]

As seen by the fight at Archer Smith's house, violence between civilians and soldiers was instigated on both sides. Soldiers took advantage of their role as representatives of the government as a means of self-protection from some racially motivated violence. Wearing the blue uniform in public made a particular statement of authority. The general lack of evidence of civilian clothing among the barracks' trash deposit emphasizes both the costliness of clothing and also the symbolic power of the uniform. Still, there were men who abused their power, creating horrible optics for the troops. In January 1871, members of Company K, Ninth Infantry, were sent by officers to track down two stolen spencer carbines. Sergeant Henry Browler led the party into what was described as the "Mexican quarters" and entered each of the houses looking for the gun. Calvin Robinson (a self-described peddler who was a witness the following year to the fight between William Donaldson and Old Man Cotton) was mentioned as someone who might know the whereabouts of the weapon. The troops found Robinson standing in the Mexican quarter near the home of John and Laura Tonsell, one of the Black families who stayed in the area after the end of service, where he was living. When Robinson said he knew nothing, he was dragged to an area called "the rocks" (most likely the ridge of exposed rock at the southern boundary of the post, below the sutler), where the sergeant's interrogation of the man included putting a noose around Robinson's neck and raising him so he was on his toes. Both civilian and soldier witnesses disputed how much harm was done to Robinson, with the general opinion being that he exaggerated the abuse he received. A private named John Allen (perhaps the man who later owned the saloon?) was credited with stopping the interrogation.

Browler was dishonorably discharged and sent to Fort Jackson, Louisiana, to serve five years at hard labor.[76] What is remarkable about this case is that Robinson, based on all available records, was a white man, though one who admittedly had a bad reputation around town, as witness testimony confirms. Testimony revealed that the search was largely undertaken on the orders of the company lieutenant, who also testified to Browler's excellent character. Still, both this and the Cotton case (chapter 1), both of which involved Black men inflicting violence on white civilians, did not result in the kinds of extrajudicial justice seen at this time in other parts of Texas. While the military worked within a racialized caste structure in which challenging white authority was always punished in court-martial sentencing, ethnoracial hierarchies among the civilian frontier population were not so rigid and were situated in the intersection between class, race, gender, and reputation.

To end this discussion, I return to the storied career of Sergeant John Hewey. This incident, which was the basis for the sergeant's first court-martial, illustrates the complicated ways soldiers and civilians crossed back and forth across garrison boundaries and the equally complicated interplay of people, places, and things through which men read these encounters. On the night of August 22, 1872, a disagreement between Hewey, a woman, and several privates after an off-post dance threatened to turn violent on post grounds. Sergeant Hewey, Private Adam Hall (band, Twenty-Fifth Infantry), laundress Annie Carter, and citizen Felix Johnson had been attending a dance at the house of Daniel Murphy.

This particular night, Annie Carter boasted that she had danced every dance but refused to dance with Sergeant Hewey, upsetting him. Hewey left the dance by 1 a.m., according to Carter, to get his carbine. In their account, Hewey jumped out at them from a bush by the blacksmith shop, threatened them, and fired a pistol in their direction at close range. Corporal Squire Jackson, Company G, Twenty-Fifth Infantry, heard the gunfire, which he believed had come from the direction of Mr. Murphy's, and went to investigate. People at the dance stated that Sergeant Hewey had fired the shot. When he neared the corner of the corral, Jackson heard a woman saying, "Get away from me with that revolver." Jackson found Adam Hall, Annie Carter, and Felix Johnson, who told him that Hewey had a pistol and intended to shoot Carter and Hall. Corporal Jackson tried to arrest Hewey at the quartermaster's corral, but Hewey ignored him. Jackson got reinforcements and arrested Hewey. Jackson testified that Hewey had a pistol in his hand when he first saw him but not when he was arrested.

Hewey claimed in his defense statement that he had been gambling with citizen Willis Owens and Creed Harris all night at a place between where the old haystack had been and the Creek. Owens testified that Hewey, Creed Harris (a post employee), and he were walking to the garrison when they heard a shot over toward Mr. Buchoz's old house (about two hundred yards from the gambling house). Hewey, according to Harris and Owens, left them at the blacksmith shop to go through the corral while they continued to the Company I, Ninth Cavalry, barracks.

Owens and Harris testified that Hewey had nothing in his hands and was wearing his fatigue uniform and cap (suggesting that he could be read as being on duty). Also called by the defense were two men who had been stationed guarding the corrals: Corporal Daniel Tallifero, and Private Albert Dennis, both of Company I, Ninth Cavalry. Clearly coached, each man testified that when he entered the corral, Hewey was carrying a stick, not a gun. When asked to describe the stick, each man independently described the stick as "a little larger than my sabre scabbard and about half as long as my sabre." Tallifero, a corporal since May 1872, also testified that he picked up the stick to examine it after Hewey had thrown it down. Tallifero testified that he looked at the stick on the ground for about fifteen minutes before walking over to examine it, and when questioned, he declared that he had kept his eyes on the stick for the whole time. It is hard to know whether the corporal's testimony speaks to his willingness to stick by a story no matter how ludicrous or underscores exactly how boring guard duty was.

Captain Bennett described Hewey as a good and reliable soldier whom he had known since 1871 and stated that the sergeant had turned in his pistol to the company's first sergeant over a month ago and therefore was not believed to have access to a weapon. Second Lieutenant J. H. McDonald testified that he believed Hewey to be the best NCO of the company.

Hewey was found guilty. In an extraordinary display of unity between officers who often squabbled, Colonel Andrews, Captain Patterson (Twenty-Fifth Infantry), Captain Bennett (Ninth Cavalry), First Lieutenant Kendall, and First Lieutenant Sanborn signed a letter requesting leniency: "In consideration of the previous good character of the prisoner, as shown by the evidence and in consideration of the questionable character of a part of the evidence for the prosecution." Auger remitted the sentence.[77]

Hewey was likely no innocent party, but he had learned to navigate the court-martial system with great aplomb, drawing on the same strategies employed by commissioned officers. He won the cases against him not by proving himself innocent but by demonstrating that he had the allegiances of the men he served with. The case demonstrates the complicated ways that civilians and soldiers and civilian and military spaces were not so easily kept separated.

5

⤝⟫⊙⟪⤞

PRIVATE JOHNSON'S
LETTERS

By the time he was writing his third letter to Secretary of War Belknap, Private Lemuel Johnson, Company F, Twenty-Fourth Infantry, was clearly frustrated. He was no longer employing polite niceties, such as the emphatic insertion of "sir" into sentences as he had in his first letter. Instead, he expressed exasperation at the lack of response to his earlier missives:

> I have the honor of writing you a few lines to inform you that I had written to you the 13th of this month and also the 12th of last month (1872) and I have not yet received any answer from you . . . will you please write and inform me whether you ever received a letter from a prisoner written at Fort Davis, Texas. . . . I think that our letters are broken open before they leave Davis.[1].

Johnson was writing on behalf of himself and three other men who had been convicted together of deserting the military. A factor in the case was that when the men were confronted by a scout of cavalrymen, they reportedly fired on them and resisted capture.

Johnson explained to the secretary of war that the group had only deserted because of the unjust treatment of their (unnamed) first sergeant. Johnson explicitly noted that he was not "treated as a man in his company." Complaints against the company first sergeant were made by each of the men during their court-martial but were not taken seriously by the court. Further, he explained, the men were armed because they were in a land full of wild animals and Indians; their firing on the cavalry had been the reaction of scared men who had not recognized who was coming upon them. Johnson was not requesting a pardon but asking that the men be transferred from Fort Davis, where they were enduring harsh circumstances and were chained together with only a foot of space, to the federal prison at Baton Rouge, where they were supposed to serve their sentence. Considering Dr. Weisel's reports that Fort Davis's guardhouse often had less than fifty cubic feet of air per man available due to overcrowding, the request for transfer was not surprising.[2]

While the contemporary reader may smile at the idea of a private convicted of desertion demanding a timely response from the country's secretary of war, it is important to see the letters as the important artifacts they are. The existence of these letters powerfully contradicts the idea that Black regulars left no first-hand accounts and that they must be understood through the eyes of their commanding officers.[3] Equally important, the letters demonstrate that literacy was seen as a necessary tool in asserting one's citizenship rights. An arrest accompanied by a clear statement of one's alleged crimes, a fair trial, and sentencing with a clearly defined punishment—these were rights intrinsic to US citizenship. Convicted and sentenced, the men had a right to begin the terms of those sentences rather than languishing in a fort guardhouse. The repeated attempts to gain a response from the secretary of war were the actions of a man demanding to be treated as a citizen.

The ability to write, to communicate one's thoughts and experiences beyond the range of one's voice, is a dangerous tool in the hands of oppressed and marginalized people. It was, after all, the published slave narratives, such as those accounts by Solomon Northrup, Linda Brent, Frederick Douglass, Sojourner Truth, and others that fueled the Abolitionist movement. Strong and righteous voices detailing their lives in bondage, even if couched in the niceties of nineteenth-century language, revealed the physical, moral, and emotional horrors of enslavement.[4] Accompanied by photography, another medium that allowed images to travel beyond the scope of the eye, first-hand accounts of enslavement resisted ambivalent responses.

While this chapter is foremost about education and the crucial role of literacy and writing for Black soldiers making claims to citizenship, the kinds of documents created by Black soldiers must be examined further.

Central to this discussion is also consideration of how these artifacts were created and the archaeological evidence of the artifacts used to create documents. The military promised an education to Black soldiers. At Fort Davis, efforts to fulfill this promise were sporadic and inconsistent until the mid-1870s. When offered schooling, the men at Fort Davis embraced the opportunity enthusiastically. Like Private Johnson, men recognized the protection of their rights and demanded that they be able to represent themselves remotely. That ability to cast oneself across space and time through one's words makes documents especially powerful objects, giving them an attribute of animacy that Mel Chen has termed "liveness."[5] Black regulars were fully aware of the liveness possessed by documents.

Sergeant Anthony Jackson was clearly aware of his letters' "liveness." He wrote regularly to his wife, knowing that being unable to read herself, she would always be accompanied by someone else who would be there to share his words. When he sent words of comfort after the death of their infant son, it must have been a consolation to know someone was with her physically in her grief. Yet he also understood the potential intimacy lost in their arrangement, and he encouraged her, if she wanted, to learn to read and write. Jackson understood the power of documents, and it is fitting that years after his death, Lucy's pension application was approved based on his letters demonstrating that she was "his dear wife." Even after death, the liveness of his letters allowed him to continue to provide for his wife.[6]

The Materiality of Words

Historical archaeology developed by advocating for its ability to write alternate histories, histories focused on the otherwise under-studied pasts of under-documented communities. Those early anthropological studies presumed a dearth, if not a complete lack, of first-hand archival records related to some populations.[7] Methods were developed for analyses of materials that would compensate for a lack of materials. In all things, the written word was presumed to be the better source of accurate or detailed information about the past, so archaeology had to try harder to compensate.

Some archaeologists insisted that historical archaeology was stronger when it recognized its role as handmaiden to history, simply filling in gaps in a pre-existing historiography.[8] There is a fundamental problem with the separation of word and thing as somehow distinct objects. Archaeologists define an artifact as something human-made and portable. Words are arbitrary things, carried in the minds and mouths of speakers, hitting the eardrums of listeners as physical sound waves. Words can be inscribed through human-made tools (or directly with fingers and hands and toes) into a material form. In written form, words are matter layered on matter.

Similarly, the word cannot be separated from the material on which it is inscribed, and its value is often entangled with the material of its delivery—a constitution handwritten on parchment, a wedding invitation engraved on quality card, a dissertation typed on linen, a grocery list scribbled on scrap paper, a text on a phone. All materials of transmission shape the way the written word is consumed. This reading of textual sources within the context of their materiality is not new; the Ten Commandments, after all, are said to have been inscribed in stone. If authority is performed through both materiality and communicative media, then documents, whether in the national archive, a published newspaper, a local courthouse, or a family album, must be seen as artifacts.

Archaeology is the study of time-place-human-thing interactions. Things are studied for their form and function, their manufacture and their use, and ultimately for their deposition.[9] It is useful to think about these aspects of documents as well, when using them to understand past social relationships.

Why were things written to particular people in particular ways? The reader will have already encountered my practice of contextualizing documents and words in similar ways to archaeological objects. For me, there is no difference; each of these assemblages of objects are artifacts that need to be understood according to their provenience and associations with other things. And just as I have attempted to design archaeological excavation strategies that would provide evidence of daily life, interpreting different material lines against one another, I have approached my time in the archive in the same way, identifying and studying the documents in a rhizomatic way, looking for interconnections between documents that emerge not from classification systems through which they are organized, but attempting to following these objects' travels organically and without concern for smoothing the narrative that emerges from them.[10] Conveying the inherent messiness of human relationships and the traces left of that messiness, is my goal.

Hearing Black Soldiers' Silences

As I began my archival research into the Black regulars, I was inclined to believe the narrative that Black-authored documents were few. Fort Davis is a well-studied post, with some of the foremost western military historians having worked at or written on the site.[11] The lack of first-hand documents related to archaeological sites' occupants is not unusual, nor is it unique to African

American sites. The average person leaves little archival trace. Few people wrote journals. When family papers are kept, the letters and correspondence in those collections are typically the letters a person receives, not the ones a person has sent. I planned to mine what I could from court-martial and hospital records, to comb the Work Progress Administration ex-slave narratives for accounts by former soldiers, and to hunt down stories that were preserved in period newspapers and journals and interviews that had been conducted by scholars such as Don Rickey.[12] I quickly found that the archival silence of the Black regulars had been greatly exaggerated.

The first documents I discovered among the National Archive Records authored by Black regulars were reports from the 1880s written by noncommissioned officers in charge of Fort Davis outposts or substations. These letters, directed to their commanding officers, post adjutants, or quartermasters, detailed events and actions of men they commanded and civilians who visited the subposts.[13] While these were administrative documents, one gains a sense of the men who wrote them. Corporal J. F. Ukkerd, Company A, Twenty-Fourth Infantry, who wrote letters while leading a detachment at Barilla Springs in August 1880, was particularly notable for his dignified alteration of the traditional military sign off, "Your obedient servant." With a beautiful script signature, he signed his letters "Most respectfully" or "Your obedient Soldier." Clearly, he had no problem with obedience and order, but he was no one's servant, a term that had often been used as a masking descriptive synonym for enslaved persons. Corporal Ukkerd's time at Barilla Springs corresponded with a particularly tense period between stage drivers and the soldiers, with drivers attempting to force soldiers to do menial or dangerous labor. In an August 1880 letter, he notes that stage drivers were "refusing to take any escort either to Fort Davis or to Leon Station when they have any passengers unless the get orders to do so from the stage company superintendent." Following Ukkerd's report, the stage company was reprimanded by the commanding officer of Fort Davis.[14]

I found letters protesting treatment at the hands of officers or asking for lenience for oneself or a comrade. Other letters were composed by anonymous writers or groups directly to the secretary of war as formal petitions demanding equal treatment to white soldiers. Unfortunately, it was the policy of the secretary of war's office to investigate only those petitions that were signed.[15] A particularly moving letter was written to the adjutant general of the Department of Texas on February 10, 1876. The soldier, Jonathon Billings, a private in Company H, Tenth Cavalry, begins the letter as if he were advocating for a fellow soldier, relaying that the soldier is about to be discharged on a medical complaint but he is concerned that the officers are using an old resolved health issue to force his departure. He writes, "And as he has considered the army his Home, it wald seem hard for them to put him outdoors, and from those he has been with for years, and after he has served in the army without breaking his Oath and no mark he is ashamed of now sir, I pray to your Honor for me, for I am that soldier."[16] Billings's pleas were not heard, and on March 19, 1876, he was discharged from Fort Davis on disability.[17]

I studied court-martials for the period from 1869 to 1875 at Fort Davis originally to learn what details of fort life could be gleaned from witness testimony. In addition to the voices of Black regulars being recorded in trial transcripts, I also found a number of enlisted men who, like officers being court-martialed, instead of submitting themselves to the stresses of testifying, submitted handwritten and signed statements in their defense. Court-martial files sometimes provided another unexpected form of Black-authored letters. Enclosed in some of the files were letters written by incarcerated soldiers, as Private Lemuel Johnson did. These letters provide important insights into how soldiers understood their rights as humans within the structures of the military and the nation's necropolitical agenda.

Pension records are another space where soldiers tell their own stories. Because the pension process required soldiers who had used different names throughout their lives to prove their identity and provide evidence of their injuries, their friends and loved ones were also called on for statements. Here is insight into the ways men were seen and remembered by others and hints of the relationships that were maintained or lost after the service. The pension process was brutal, requiring proof of service during particular campaigns. It was easier for men who had also served in the Civil War to earn pensions for that service rather than for service in the regular military.[18] Black men were particularly susceptible to administrative bullying and abuse. The pension experience of Private Sullivan Courtney, encountered in the last chapter, provides evidence of the many abuses soldiers endured.

Courtney, despite having been discharged on a certificate of disability, did not apply immediately for a pension, an omission that raised suspicions with the pension bureau. He claimed that his papers had been stolen from him shortly after he left the service. Officers in the Twenty-Fifth Infantry, writing in response to a survey about reenlistment problems in 1870, noted that men with a "good character" discharge had great earning potential in the civilian world.[19] Discharge papers could lead to good earnings, or in the case of a medical discharge, the opportunity to falsely apply for a pension. Upon discharge, Courtney had his final statement sent to New Orleans, thinking he would return to the place where he had enlisted. Instead, he took several jobs in Texas. For his first pension interview, a storeowner misled Courtney and told him that the police were looking for him. Instead of taking the interview, he hid. When asked during the second interview why he had avoided the first, he quite reasonably stated that even though he had done nothing wrong, he was afraid of the police. Like many soldiers, Courtney enlisted the help of an agent to shepherd his application through the pension process. That agent argued that Courtney was not intelligent enough to operate without a guardianship. A Texas judge appointed a guardian, and Courtney later sent letters to the pension bureau stating that the guardian had stolen his money. In one man's heartbreak, the worst abuses and failures of the pension system are illustrated, with the particular racialized threats faced by men of color underscored.[20]

Had Courtney been literate (his documents are all signed with his mark), he could have overseen the process and advocated for himself. Instead, a man with a remarkable memory for details of his early life and an astute understanding of racial politics in the nineteenth-century US, was ripe for victimization. Unfortunately for Courtney, during the time of his enlistment, the military had failed in its promise to provide Black soldiers with a basic education.

During the Civil War, when self-emancipated people fled to the Union lines, they set about educating themselves, with the help of one another and Black soldiers. As a result, the US military recognized the necessity of setting up schools for formerly enslaved people. Anthony Jackson worked for a military depot in Washington, DC, after fleeing from a plantation in Virginia with his uncle and gained an education from a school set up by a northern chaplain serving in the garrison. He was writing letters to his wife from North Carolina and other posts as early as 1867.[21]

In the book *Self-Taught*, Heather Andrea Williams demonstrates that rates of literacy among enslaved people has been greatly underestimated by historians and that there is ample evidence of enslaved people teaching themselves and one another to read.[22] The eloquence of First Sergeant John Sample's written arguments regarding the proper treatment of his troops suggests that he may have learned to read and write earlier than the commencement of his military service. Though they predate his service at Fort Davis, these letters demand attention.

In February 1868, while stationed in Goldsborough, North Carolina, Sample was assigned to escort a guard of six soldiers to testify at a general court-martial being held at Camp Rupel, at Raleigh, North Carolina. Arriving at the post, Sample and his men were ordered to sleep in a room used as a prison during the day, and they were required to take their rations and eat after the white troops. Upon return to his post on March 10, Sample wrote a letter of protest on March 16, 1868, describing what the soldiers experienced and demanding that such behavior be eliminated in the future. The letter is written in a clear and distinctive hand, with few if any spelling and grammatical errors, a rarity in any mid-nineteenth-century handwritten prose. He described his quartering experience as follows:

> We were sent to Company F 8th infantry for rations and quarters. In the evening the First Sergeant of the above named company gave me a note to the sergeant of the guard saying that he could not provide me quarters but the Sergeant of the Guard would do so, a place filled with filth and vermin where the garrison prisoners were kept through the day was pointed out to me as my quarters. Being a First Sergeant of my company and having a faint idea of decency and cleanliness I left the disgusting hole with the determination to procure quarters at my own expense which I succeeded in doing in a day or two. I would have to say that the excuse made by the 1st Sergeant of Company F 8th infantry that he was unable to furnish me quarters is false for he provided fifteen cavalry men with quarters who applied to him after.[23]

Sample described the messing as no better, being both segregated temporally, under-provisioned, and subjected to "scurrilous remarks." He ended the letter with the following statement:

> Now I ask not nor expect social equality with the white man but I am a soldier in the service of the United States and only ask for what is provided by law for troops. I am not surprised at receiving taunts from some of the enlisted men but in the service as many of them are from the scum of society, prejudiced, ignorant, low and vulgar, but am astonished that such doings are not corrected when made known to their officers.

He states a hope that by describing the situation, such events will not happen in the future.[24] While Sample's anger emerges at points, his is a careful letter.

He seems to nod to white supremacy in his statement that he is not asking for social equality, but he is actually making a much more powerful demand: equal treatment with white men based on his and his men's status as soldiers, and on his own achieved status as a first sergeant in the service. He is making a plea to the notions of martial citizenship and echoing demands that shaped the fight for equal pay engaged in by Black men serving in the military during the Civil War. His dismissiveness toward the enlisted men of the white Eighth Infantry unit makes it clear that he does not see them as his social equals.

Sample's letter was forwarded by his company, post adjutant, and regimental officers up the chain of command, asking for an investigation. Captain David Schooley first wrote an endorsement on the letter on March 16 and simply forwarding the letter, then adding on March 17 a note stating, "I have reason to believe the statements made here are true. The Sergeant though clean and neat in his personal habits, I do not think is overly fastidious." Schooley had been to the Raleigh Post on March 9 to retrieve his troops and encountered the first sergeant of the Eighth Infantry during his stay.[25] On April 1, 1868, Brevet Brigadier General Colonel Edward Hinks, commander of the post of Goldsboro, added his endorsement, forwarding the correspondence for investigation. He wrote that if the evil described was found, it must be removed, noting, "It is no discredit to some officers whom I have observed in the service to say that Sergeant Sample is the equal in real truth, efficiency, and in personal deportment, and I know of no regulations which permits an invidious distinction to be made against any soldier in the army. Men causally at this Post are treated as the rest of the Garrison and it is respectfully submitted that it is not overmuch to demand the same from other posts."[26]

The officers at Camp Rupel were asked to respond to the charges made in Sample's letter. Henry Sanford, company clerk of Company F, Eighth Infantry, argued in his response that to his "knowledge" and observation, no one insulted the men. He stated that Sample and his men arrived without bedding and could not be accommodated. Sanford expressed surprise at Sample's letter, saying he had expressed no unhappiness while at the post. The letter conveniently forgets the chain of command issues that would have made it difficult for Sample to complain to a superior officer in a different company.[27]

It is the letter from the first sergeant of Company F, Eighth Infantry, that supports (probably unintentionally) Sample's account of events. Hill stated that only seventeen bunks were completed at the new camp, providing four sleeping spots a piece for a total of sixty-six men. Double-berthed bunk beds, with two men sleeping in the bottom bunk and two in the top, were common in the frontier military, including at Fort Davis. Likewise, when camping, men would be expected to make bedrolls out of two blankets and would sleep bundled together either under the sky or in two-man tents.[28]

Hill noted that the cavalrymen described by Sample as usurping the sleeping spots of the Fortieth Infantry men were provided berths by sleeping in the bunks vacated by men on guard duty. Sample was traveling in a group of seven men, a group half the size of the cavalry group that was accommodated. Hill provided a detailed description of how quarter furnishing worked, trying to make it seem that the cavalry arrived slightly earlier, thus the assigning of the bunks to them over Sample's men was fair. But he undermined his account of fair treatment by adding, "Surely it would not be expected that negroes even if they be soldiers should sleep in the same bunks as white men."[29]

Regarding "messing," Hill complained that Sample and his men kept irregular hours (Sample argues that it was due to the court-martial, but if they were quartered off post as his letter suggests, this would have also affected schedules) and were denied their meals only if, in his estimation, they were unreasonably late. He argues that the later seating for the Black men was necessitated by the recent breakage of a number of bowls, leaving only forty for sixty-six men, which required that some men eat later. He also stated that the men were rationed all their bread in the morning, and the Black men ate all theirs earlier in the day and expected more.[30] The men at the post used the materiality of bunks and bowls to support their racism.

Post doctors regularly noted that Black troops required full rations to sustain themselves. The regular un-supplemented ration for Company F, Eighth Infantry, was inadequate for the Black soldiers. Compounded with the likelihood that they did suffer smaller portions as a result of being fed last, we see how institutionalized practices in the military combined with personal racism on the part of individuals combined to create inequities in provisioning with enduring health consequences for Black soldiers. Sample and his men were stationed at the post from February 28 to March 10, a long time—nearly two weeks—to go hungry. The events at Raleigh explains why Sergeant Sample was a man who turned a blind eye when his men rustled a stray pig for themselves, an incident alluded to in Lieutenant Kendall's 1872 court-martial.[31]

Sample's willingness to make an argument for equal treatment of Black soldiers echoes arguments made by Black soldiers during the Civil War, when the troops of the Fifty-Forth and Fifty-Fifth Massachusetts Infantry famously refused to take pay rather than accept lower wages than white soldiers.[32] It also demonstrates that he understood the pen to be a crucial tool in the quest for citizenship rights. In this context, the failure of many posts to commit to developing post schools with any consistency can be seen as a means of subverting Black men's attempts to participate fully as citizens. It was not unusual for white officers in the Black regiments to complain about the uneducated state of many of their troops or to suggest that many formerly enslaved people were ignorant and superstitious as part of their nature rather than the circumstances in which they had been condemned.[33]

In 1869, when the first three-year term of service finished, the Twenty-Fifth Infantry found that massive numbers of men failed to reenlist. Company captains were asked to provide explanations detailing why they thought soldiers had not reenlisted. While many of the captains noted the undesirability of stations like isolated Jackson Barracks and Fort St. Phillipe, located across from one another near the mouth of the Mississippi, the forts were constantly prone to flooding, alligators, and worst of all, clouds of mosquitos. Officers also blamed the high wages commanded by good workers in civilian life or took the opportunity to complain about the quality of the soldiers and to comment on what they saw as the "nature" of the average southern Black man.[34] Notably, George L. Choesy, captain in the Twenty-Fifth, was one of the few officers who observed that post conditions contributed to men's reluctance to reenlist, observing explicitly that men stationed at St. Phillipe did not have access to the post library, which was housed at Fort Jackson, across the Mississippi River. This comment speaks to the soldiers' interest in reading and pursuing educational uplift, a topic not addressed in any of the other letters.[35]

What kinds of volumes were in the post library? An 1872 notation in Weisel's May 1872 inspection notes mentions that the post library had four hundred volumes, "all standard works of history, romance and fiction."[36] An 1881 list shows a range of daily, weekly, and monthly newspapers and magazines being received at the post, with daily papers including the *New York Herald Daily*, *St. Louis Globe*, *Chicago Times*, *New York Graphic*, *San Antonio Express*, *Houston Post*, *Boston Herald*, and *Philadelphia Inquirer*. Weekly publications were the *Washington Sunday Herald*, *Army and Navy Register*, *Frank Leslie's Illustrated Newpaper*, *Harper's Weekly*, *London Graphic*, and the *Nation*. Monthly publications included *United Service*, *Appleton Journal*, *Harpers Monthly*, *North American Review*, *Scribner's Monthly*, and *Popular Science*.[37] How far back in the post's history these papers were subscribed to is unknown, but there are scattered references to newspapers and other journals being subscribed to by the post library. The ones listed here include the major papers of the post–Civil War US and were likely subscribed to in the 1870s as well.

Officers rarely mention the reading activities of the Black soldiers, even though their own letters and journals are filled with references to their own reading activities. A rare exception to this is an intriguing 1878 entry in the journal of Lieutenant John Bigelow of the Tenth Cavalry, made while stationed at the small outpost of Peña Blanca, Texas:

> At inspection of quarters I saw a couple of books in Corporal Bowman's tent . . . one was the New Testament and the other, Grecian Mythology. I do not know whether the two books represent a difference of faith between Bowman and his tentmate or whether they are the text books to the study of which they direct their unbiased and unprejudiced minds in making a comparison of ancient with modern religion.[38]

Despite the obvious sarcasm in Bigelow's remark, it is worth noting that Bowman, now a sergeant, and Bigelow both served at Fort Davis in the 1880s.[39] That the Bible and a book on Greek mythology would be of interest is not surprising. The aesthetic movement, which shaped the kinds of decorative materials and kitchen furniture selected by companies, was informed by each of these sources (chapter 3). It is worth emphasizing that while an education allowed men to express their thoughts in writing, reading also allowed them to engage with broader worlds and to build the cultural capital that was part of genteel manliness. For enlisted men new to reading, the proscriptions of tone, form, and style needed to be learned, not just to survive in the military but to situate themselves within proper modes of polite manhood. Reading helped develop those skills as much as writing did. Communication was a particular kind of manly performance.

Letters written by enlisted men, both to loved ones and as part of official correspondence, demonstrate attempts to conform to particular stylistic etiquette of both military and genteel culture. Sergeant Anthony Jackson's letters to his wife offer a rare opportunity to see how manly etiquette is expressed in letter writing by soldiers. Jackson, who always paid close attention to date and location of his letters, consistently started his prose with a variation of the same salutation: "My dear Wife with the greatest of pleasure I set myself to write you a few lines to inform you of my helth Which I am well at this present time and I hope when these few lines come to hand they may find you well as helth can ford."[40]

His formal tone sometimes drops into a more vernacular one, as when in March 1867 he writes, "My wife Lucey I have been a fishing. I have caught some fish as Big as a Baby."[41] The letters suggest a training in both phonetic spelling and formal letter writing style. When departing from rote salutation styles, we see Jackson sounding out and spelling words as he would pronounce them, with the end result being an approximation of his voice, a feature of the letters that must have been a comfort to those who heard his letters read aloud. Frederick Douglass biographer David Blight has observed that in letters to close loved ones from his childhood, Douglass adopted a vernacular style not seen in other correspondence.[42] As we read letters from soldiers, we must consider the creativity of expression allowed by writing and not presume that word choice, spelling, or sentence construction has anything to do with proficiency in reading or writing. The switch in his March 1867 letter from a formal salutation to the story about the giant fish provides a contrast in styles that is at the heart of great story and joke telling. For those listening to his letters, Jackson put himself firmly in the room with them.

The Post School

Most of the archaeological deposits associated with the barracks included artifacts related to reading and writing: parts of glass umbrella-shaped ink wells, broken pieces of school slates, slate pencil nibs, and pencil leads and tops (table 5.1). These are small but consistently found objects, sometimes occurring in deposits dating to periods when official schooling efforts were minimal, speaking to efforts arising from the initiative of the enlisted men. The archaeological materials show that despite the sporadic efforts of the post to meet its obligation to provide an education, soldiers were continuously engaged in practices related to reading, writing, and learning.

There were few school-aged children living at Fort Davis in the late 1860s to the early 1870s.[43] The lack of a post school, therefore, had an impact on soldiers who wanted to learn. For men who wanted to build a career within the military, the ability to engage in record keeping was essential for eventual promotion to the ranks of noncommissioned officers. The lack of formal opportunities for self-improvement meant that men who had come into the military literate were privileged over those who had not.

TABLE 5.1. *Writing-Related Artifacts from Enlisted Men's Barracks*

LOCATION	OBJECT FOUND	NUMBER
Enlisted men's dump	Light blue umbrella ink well	1
Hearth associated with 1872–1874 tent	Light blue 8-sided umbrella inkwell	1
Ashpit associated with 1874–1876 tent	Graphite slate pencil	1
	Fragment of writing slate	1
Mess hall of barracks HB-22	Knife-sharpened graphite pencil	1
	Light blue conical ink well	1
Yard of barracks	Knife sharpened graphite pencil points	2
Porch of barracks HB-22	School slate fragment with lines visible	1

The records at Fort Davis reveal at least four distinct efforts to provide a school for soldiers between 1867 and 1875. The earliest reference to the formation of a post school at Fort Davis is in 1869, two years after the post's reestablishment. Dr. Weisel's reports provide insight into this short-lived experiment: "A school for the purpose of instruction of soldiers has been for some months in successful function at the post. With a teacher employed and paid from post funds, but has been discontinued by reason of the teacher's salary being reduced and his leaving."[44]

A post school (or noted lack of one) is next mentioned in a January 21, 1871, letter from the post adjutant to Chaplain Manuel J. Gonzales of the Ninth Cavalry: "Sir, the commanding officer directs that a report of your duties as a school teacher and the name of each soldier or child of officers or soldiers whom you have taught on the post, the hours each day or evening for the school, whether or not divine service is held, if not, why not."[45]

The adjutant had to know that each of his questions would be answered in the negative. Gonzalez was first assigned to Fort Davis in November 1869 but not present at the post until November 1870. By the time he was asked about what he was actually doing about his duties, he had been on the post less than three months. On February 2, 1871, Gonzales decided to make an effort, and he requested of the assistant adjutant that "an order be given to

3 cm   0

FIGURE 5.1. Writing-related artifacts from Fort Davis: A. Front page of *Independent Fourth Reader* by J. Madison Watson, 1868/1876 copyright date. Book in author's private collection. B. Portion of letter from Anthony Jackson to Lucinda Jackson, dated April 22, 1868, enclosed in Lucinda Jackson Pension Application, Certificate 421209, RG-15, NARA. C. Partial base of blue-green glass umbrella inkstand from hearth feature. D. Fragment of school slate and graphite slate pencil from Fort Davis barracks. Photographs by the author.

the enlisted men who wish to attend the Post School, that they bring what school books they may have in their possession to the Chaplain's quarters, that he may report to the council."[46] The fragment of a post commissary lists Gonzales as purchasing twelve spelling books later that week and six more at the end of that month.[47]

Gonzalez's efforts did not last long. By May 1871, he was listed as on leave. He returned to post at the end of June, only to be transferred to Fort Stockton in November 1871. Dr. Weisel remarked on the school in his post reports: "During a portion of last year 1871, a post school was conducted by the Post Chaplain for the benefit of the officers' children and the troops—but was soon closed by the reason of the chaplain being ordered away."[48]

In early September 1872, attempts were made to locate the school books purchased by Chaplain Gonzales. Commanding Officer Andrews, trying to locate schoolbooks that the estate of Patrick Murphy, a local merchant (no relation to Daniel Murphy, the post trader), claimed had been purchased by the post but not paid for, sent a letter to Dr. Weisel, who had served as post treasurer (Weisel was now serving at Fort Richardson).[49] Andrews, finding no evidence of Weisel's having turned over school books to his successor, wanted the unpaid bill (the books had cost $8.70) reimbursed by the adjutant general, something that would not happen, he feared, without evidence of the actual goods.[50] This context is important, for it suggests that the search for school books was more about post accounting than working to ensure that soldiers had access to books. It seems likely that the student soldiers kept the books when the school shut, keeping on with their studies.

The cost of $8.70 is also instructive The front pages of the school books from the Independent Reader Series (discussed further shortly) show consistent prices for books in the series through the late 1860s and 1870s. A primary reader cost 18¢, the second 35¢, the third 50¢, the forth 70¢, the fifth 90¢, and the last in the series, the sixth, $1.00. Spelling books in the same series were priced 18¢, 35¢ and 20¢.[51] If the chaplain had been purchasing elementary books, those funds would have covered forty-three readers. The repeated purchases of books suggest that demand and progress were greater than the chaplain had anticipated.

In early 1873, efforts were made to start a third post school. On December 17, 1872, it was announced that in response to General Order No. 19, a post school would be established on or after January 1, 1873. The school would meet from seven to eight o'clock each weekday evening. The principle teacher would be Ordinance Sergeant John S. Holscher; Private James Johnson, Company A, Twenty-Fifth Infantry, would assist. Ordinance sergeants at this time were the only white NCOs found on the post. The men were to concentrate on reading, writing and the four simple rules of arithmetic. The school was to be located in "the stone building in rear of the south end of the line of officer quarters" (presumably a structure remaining from the first fort, perhaps the building that has been identified in some photos as first fort barracks).[52] Holscher and his assistant were to receive additional pay for their efforts; therefore, the assignment was not seen as a punishment. The ordinance sergeant never took over the school. Instead, on January 5, it was announced that because of demand and the small space of the school, multiple sections were to be offered at a variety of learning levels and that First Lieutenant Kendall would be detailed as superintendent of the school. Kendall would be relieved from one drill a day if other officers were available to cover the drill, but otherwise he was responsible for his duties.[53]

Whatever the reason for this assignment, Kendall took the position seriously. Kendall had graduated from Bowdoin College in Maine as part of the class of 1860.[54] A school publication describes him as interested in pursuing a career in journalism, and he was a member of the Athenaean Society, a student group dedicated to literary pursuits. He was quick to join the Union Army when fighting broke out, first joining the Eleventh Indiana Volunteers, then the Fourth New Hampshire Volunteers.[55] After his time with the Fort Davis post school, education became a theme in Kendall's career. He later served on detached duty from the Twenty-Fifth Infantry from 1876 to 1880 to serve as a professor of military science and tactics at Brooks Military Academy in Cleveland, Ohio. As a civilian, Kendall was noted for the work he did as a member of the Cleveland School Board.[56]

Kendall had a more expanded vision than Andrews had of what school studies might entail, and he did not limit the curriculum to reading, spelling, writing, and simple math. In January 1873, he requested a purchase to supplement the already existing supply of books. He asked for six fourth readers by Watson, eighteen arithmetic books, thirty-six primary arithmetic books (Robinson's), twelve advanced geographies, and seventy-two slate pencils. Kendall noted, "I would respectfully say that we have one dozen of the 4th readers now in use and the entire supply and the extra number is required to meeting increasing demand. It is in the best interest of the school that these books be furnished as soon as practicable to maintain a proper interest in the pupils who can be taught little else readings and spellings until the receipt."[57] Later, noted Black military chaplains like Colonel Allen Allensworth and Dr. T. G. Steward promoted a broad-based curriculum for Black soldiers, supporting coursework that provided opportunities for professional development and racial uplift.[58] Kendall's work with the school seems to have had the same goals.

In choosing to educate the men on the subjects of spelling, reading, geography, and math, we see a curriculum designed to make better soldiers, soldiers who could ultimately be effective NCOs. Scouting required reading maps, and when combined with basic mathematics, a soldier could estimate travel times and water and forage needs and do the accounting necessary for company records. The soldiers seem to have been offered not a remedial education but an education that would contribute to their professionalization.

When I first encountered Kendall's list of schoolbooks, although he provides incomplete references, I was excited to see that two authors were mentioned. This allowed me to track down existing copies and to examine directly what and how the soldiers were being taught. "Watson's 4th Reader" refers to one of the many reading texts published by A. S. Barnes and Company of New York. J. Madison Watson was involved in the authorship of two main reading series published by Barnes. He was sole author of the Independent Reader Series, which comprised six books: primary, second, third, fourth, fifth, and sixth. The series seems to have been established by 1860 and was in continual print through the 1890s. Accompanying the Independent Series was *Independent Child's Speech* and *Independent Complete Speller*. The other series published by Barnes was the National Series, for which Richard G. Parker was the primary author and Watson the secondary. This series also had six books and was more expensive. Barnes also published a *National Elementary Speller* and a *National Pronouncing Speller*.[59]

It seems likely, given that only one name was given and that Watson was second author on the other series, that the Independent Series was the one being used at Fort Davis in the Kendall-era school. Many examples of these texts still exist in digital or physical form. Because some of the books were purchased before Kendall took over the school, I worked under the assumption that the editions used would have been published no later than 1871, the year of Chaplain Gonzales's purchases. I found copies of the 1868 and 1876 editions. It appears that no different versions were published in the interim, and the 1876 edition appears virtually identical to the 1868 version. Therefore, the two volumes match what would have been used at the post.

Reading in the mid- to late nineteenth century, just as now, was taught using a variety of methods.[60] A review of the Independent Reading Series, authored by Watson, and the National Series, authored by Parker and Watson, shows that these authors favored a method that drew on phonetic approaches in the upper levels but used a combination of whole word, phonetic, and whole sentence methods to teach students. Students were encouraged to use a combination of rote memorization of whole words and phonetics. Standard cursive writing was taught in the elementary editions, with words shown in both typeset and script. The 1860 version of the *National First Reader and Word Builder* introduced single-lettered and two-lettered words in short sentences, slowly building up the number of letters in the words. The first lesson read as follows: "Ox. An ox. On an ox. Ah! He is on an ox. Ha, ha, ha! Ho, Ho, Ho! So he is. He is on it. Am I on an ox? Oh no; I am on no ox."[61] By lesson eleven, the vocabulary was up to three letters: "Do you see the boy? He has a gun. It is a new gun. His bag is on his hip. Did the boy rub, oil and fix the gun? Yes, and he put a wad in it too. It is our gun. We own it. Let the boy use it. May the boy aim the gun at a cow or kid? Oh, no; you may bid him hit an owl or the sly fox."

This passage, even in an early reader, demonstrates the role that school books had in promoting particular national agendas and ideologies. The vast majority of actors represented in the reader are boys and men. In a 128-page book, the word *girl* does not appear until page thirty-four, with the picture showing a little girl serving a boy tea.[62] It is not surprising to see that gun ownership, as part of an idealized pastoral life and constitutional right, would be featured even in an early reader. The readings also enforce politeness, kindness, and respecting one's parents. The ideological underpinnings of the reading series becomes more clear in the advanced readers, and by the fourth book, these are well-developed themes.

Men using the fourth reader were already proficient readers and writers. The emphasis on elocution ensured that readers could read and speak clearly with a standard form of pronunciation, and it complemented phonetic spelling techniques. The preface at the beginning of the book states that the work is intended for children between the ages of seven and twelve and that Webster's phonetic marks were used to facilitate proper pronunciation of words without being distracting to the reader. The readings are poems, short stories, and longer story extracts by authors including Charles Dickens, Elizabeth Barrett Browning, and William Wordsworth, clearly for more advanced readers. Reading aloud was a skill necessary for public speaking, an important genteel skill and a component of participatory democratic processes. Frederick Douglass, one of the greatest orators of the nineteenth century, would have been well known by reputation to soldiers who had followed political events, particularly given Douglass's strong advocacy for Black men's right to serve during the Civil War.[63]

The first part of the forth reader book, while focused on the practicalities of grammar and elocution, also drew on the works of well-known orators and writers through sentences used to illustrate principles. For instance, the "exercise on inflection" includes the following unattributed sentences: "The war must go on. We must fight it through. The cause will rise up armies; the cause will create navies. We shall make this a glorious, an immortal day. When we are in our graves, our children will honor it."[64] This unattributed quote is drawn from a speech delivered by Daniel Webster on August 20, 1826, "Eulogy on Adams and Jefferson."[65] While Webster was speaking of the Revolutionary War, the words, read in 1872, would no doubt conjure memories of the recently passed Civil War. Martial manhood, and the notion that full citizenship rights are earned by those who fought for them, is enforced throughout the schoolbook.

Other stories had the potential to speak to the experiences of the frontier military. The poem "The Washer-Girl" tells the story of a young girl who forgoes her own education to help care for her many siblings after her mother's death and her father's chronic illness. Army laundresses were frequently marriage partners for the soldiers. Many civilian Black women also turned to laundry work to support their families. Taking in laundry was laborious work, and the need for scalding water and chemicals made it dangerous as well. Because it could be done in the home, however, laundry work eliminated some of the kinds of interactions that left Black women prey to harassment and sexual abuse at the hands of white employers.[66] The poem extolling the virtues of the noble washer girl could resonate for many of the men.

"The Pasha's Son" tells of a British man who travels from Egypt to Central Africa recounting interactions with a central African ruler who keeps tamed wild beasts and the noble young son of a displaced Pasha who redeems his father's reputation in Egypt. It is not hard to imagine this selection drawing the interest of soldiers who would have had widely varying understandings of their relationship to Africa. Many men would have known about the recolonization rhetoric that circulated in the nineteenth century calling emancipated populations to be settled in Africa. Some northern-born soldiers may have personally known individuals engaged in such efforts or considered such possibilities for themselves. They may have also been aware of the justifiably anti-colonialist writings of Frederick Douglass, who saw recolonization as attempts to undermine claims of American-born Black men to citizenship rights.[67] Thus, while the reading series was intended to instill and enforce particular kinds of nationalistic and gendered ideologies in American students, it is also possible to see the ways these readings allowed Black soldiers to bring their histories and experiences to the materials.

The arithmetic book listed was surely *Robinson's Mathematical Series: First Lesson in Mental and Written Arithmetic*, published by Ivison, Blakeman, Taylor and Company of Chicago. This book was part of the American Educations Series of School and College Texts. I was able to examine an 1871 edition of the book. The editor of the 184-page book writes, "The aim has been not to load down the pupil with Arithmetic as a burden from without but to cause it to spring up within him by a natural and healthful process, that growing and unfolding, with his intellect, it may be organized, vital and indestructible part of himself." Lessons were organized to use mental calculations and board work to enforce teachings. The book presumes that pupils are familiar with counting but not with formal mathematics. Numbers are introduced as words and numbers in both Arabic and Latin forms. Mathematics is explained as the language of numbers, and a combination of pictures and word problems is used to teach students how to construct equations. Addition (and ability to read, add, and subtract numbers up to one hundred million), multiplication, division, fractions (including adding and subtracting them), currency (American and English units), and measures are covered.[68] .

While the information regarding the book *Advanced Geography* was too vague to track down a specific text, a quick review of period geography books shows that Lovell's Publishing of Ontario did an advanced geography book that focused on the study of world maps, whereas for English educators, *Advanced Geography* took students into the field of physical geography, with an emphasis on understanding landforms. World geography was a subject taught at West Point and several commissioned officers in the Black regiments were notorious for their poor exam results in the subject.[69]

Notes in the post returns observe beginning in February 1873 that the school was well attended and prosperous. On February 28, 1873, Kendall again approached Post Adjutant Cyrus Gray:

I have the honor to state that I consider the interests of the post school would be served by the appointment of Peter Hicks Principal musician of the regimental band as an assistant teacher thereof in place of Private Johnson now working in that capacity. The school should be, I think, self-sustaining as far as possible and the promotion of one of its members to the position of instructor should produce a good effect and serve as an encouragement to the others. There has been no neglects on the part of Johnson and he has performed his duty as faithfully as could be expected of him.[70]

The use of enlisted men in the school was an ongoing feature of Kendall's run as superintendent. While his stated goal was to encourage the other students, it is as likely that enlisted men had already been teaching one another to read and write, either before or in the service, and experienced teachers were among the troops. During the Civil War, soldiers developed schools and supported one another's efforts to learn and read.[71] Kendall's service with the Eighth US Colored Heavy Artillery in 1865 may have exposed him directly to these efforts. Any soldier who had participated in schools developed by the military chaplains (like Anthony Jackson) or the Freedman's Bureau Schools, would have been familiar with successful approaches to adult education and would have shared them with others. In drawing on soldiers to teach other soldiers, Kendall was not innovating but using practices established by Black troops in the Civil War.

In the March 1873 post return, Commanding Officer Bliss speaks to the success of Kendall's school: "The post school under the direction of Lt. Kendall is making excellent progress. There are two sessions daily attended by about 120 enlisted men who take an interest in their studies and make good progress." That same return lists a total garrison size of 182 men in residence. One hundred and twenty attendees represent an incredible rate of participation."[72] There are no orders demanding the presence of men at the school, as there would be in the late 1870s; therefore, these high numbers reflect the interest of the men and their motivation to learn.

In April, the school was moved to the church building north of the parade ground. Kendall asked that a private be detailed to keeping the chapel, where the school was held, open for night study: "I think it advisable to have the chapel open at all times of the day for the men so that they can spend leisure hours then in study."[73]

Although the bulk of teaching and study happened away from the barracks, parts of inkwells, pencils, school slates, and slate pencils found in and around that building show that studies also took place in the living quarters. While ink wells and pencils might speak to the letter writing and record keeping of a smaller number of soldiers, school slates and slate pencils were specific tools used by reading and spelling learners.

In May, other obligations started to distract Kendall from the school. Bliss reported that "Post school under direction of Lt. Kendell is doing very well but as Lt. Kendall is a member of a General Court Martial which meets almost daily, he is not able to give very great attention to the day school." [74] The school sessions were paused, and the school closed over the summer of 1873 because of heat and Kendall's absence on court-martial duty at Fort Stockton. There were plans to restart the school on September 15, 1873. Kendall wrote to the post commander on September 22, asking that the post school be reopened: "Sir, I respectfully state that I am ready to reopen the post school whenever the commanding officer sees fit to appoint the hours of session. I think that until the school gets into working order once session a day will be all that is necessary to wit from half an hour after retreat until tattoo." In addition to Musician Hicks as a teacher and Private Johnson as janitor, Kendall asked that Sergeant John Sample serve as an additional instructor.[75] The selection of Sample is surprising; recall that during his own court-martial, Kendall had smeared Sample, accusing him of being dishonest. Sample seems a strange choice for the school if Kendall believed his own assertions about the man's character. Yet as we will see, the nature of the major court-martial that occupied Kendall's time at Fort Stockton may have prompted this decision.

Assault on Free Expression at Fort Stockton, August 1873

Located roughly eighty miles east of Fort Davis, Fort Stockton seems like a different world. While the elevation of the Davis Mountains creates a visually stunning and relatively temperate climate, Fort Stockton is situated on a flat plain near a creek drainage. This drainage, Comanche Springs, regularly attracted bands of indigenous peoples watering their horses. Dusty and oppressive, Fort Stockton is the ugly sibling of Fort Davis, and it was often described in unflattering ways by officers and visitors alike.

Beginning in April 1873, Private John Taylor grew ill. He complained of a severe ongoing headache, and toward the end of his life, he suffered an inability to move, lapsed in and out of consciousness, and had seizures. The post surgeon, Peter J. A. Cleary, failed to treat the man. At one point, Cleary sent Taylor back to duty, accusing him of faking his illness. On another occasion, Cleary caused him to be confined to the guardhouse. Taylor died in mid-July, and the doctor, finding no conclusive autopsy results, diagnosed the cause of death as "nostalgia," a wasting disease. During court-martial testimony, a company captain suggested that Taylor died because he thought he was hoodooed, an opinion that Zenas Bliss, another member of the court-martial, shared.[76]

Men from three companies signed a petition detailing the horrors of Taylor's treatment and asking for an investigation of Dr. Cleary. The letter, signed initially by 126 men, emerged from a meeting in the company dining room of Company K, Twenty-Fifth Infantry, the deceased man's company. Because multiple companies were involved, the letter was delivered to the commanding officer rather than following the chain of command and submitting copies of the letter to each captain. There was no action on the letter for several days, then one of the officers realized that technically, the delivery of the letter was a violation of an articles of war. Each NCO was called into a meeting with their company officers to review the violation and give the men involved the opportunity to remove their names from the petition rather than suffer the consequences. Many men chose to remove their names, but others felt that to remove their names would be to admit that their statement was false and decided to move ahead with the consequences. These twenty-one men, mainly NCOs, were court-martialed as a group in one trial. They were charged with mutiny.[77]

The letter in question begins as follows:

> The undersigned enlisted men of the Command have the honor of most respectfully calling the attention of the proper authorities (through the Department and Post Commander) to certain facts relative to the death of Private John Taylor 2nd, Company K 25th US inf who expired on the 10th instant at the post, and from what we have witnessed, and from expressions uttered by the post Surgeon at different times. We believe the deceased came to his death from <u>intentional</u> neglect on the part of the post surgeon J.J.A. Cleary, USA who from malicious feeling of a personal nature refused to give or allow him proper treatment from the 30th day of April 1873 to the 7th day of July 1873 on which day he was conveyed to the Guard House . . . this strange and inhuman spectacle caused considerable excitement and sorrow among the men who witnessed it.[78]

The letter details Taylor's symptoms, his misery, and the surgeon's foul-language-filled responses. In hindsight, Taylor's head pain and subsequent deliriousness, bouts of unconsciousness, and weakness suggest that he may have suffered from a brain aneurism. While there was little that could have saved him, the account of his treatment shows that the man suffered needlessly, without comfort, and his suffering was intolerable to those who cared for him. The letter is a demand for accountability and recognition that no soldier could feel safe under Cleary's care.

During the trial, officers presented hearsay that the doctor feared for his life, and grumbling around the barracks suggested a possible violent uprising. An unnamed member of the court interrogated Captain Samuel Pelter, who was the most flagrant at repeating unsubstantiated gossip as part of his testimony. The member of the court forced Pelter to admit that he heard no mutinous talk himself. The court then asked, "When you informed the Noncommissioned officers of your company that the manner of their procedures was illegal and wrong, did you tell them the proper way to proceed to provide redress for their complaint, and if so, did they decide to follow such advice?" To which he admitted that he had not. The court then immediately asked, "Had you previous to the signing of the papers instructed the men in regard to the redress of wrongs and grievances?" Pelter responded that while at Fort Clark (two years earlier) the Articles of War were read once a month to the men. For one of the court members, whether the men had been properly educated about their rights and how to request them within the military structure was an issue in this case.

In their statement of defense, the defendants suggested education played a role in their actions:

> The paper we do not believe to contain anything of a mutinous or seditious character tho however the court will judge, if any improper language is made use of, it is caused by our want of education and proverbial inability to speak or write the English language properly . . . In conclusion we would ask the court if they find we have erred to take into consideration the fact that we have no advantages of education which would enable us to properly, at all times, to interpret the true meaning of regulations and articles of war.[79]

Twenty of the men were found guilty, with the specification wording changed from "mutinous" to "unauthorized" meetings and activities. The twenty-first man had expressed regret for his actions and attempted to remove his name after being charged, and all the members of the court sent a letter that successfully requested mitigation of his sentence. The convicted men were sent to Huntsville prison but were released under the order of C. J. Smory, then judge advocate of the Department of Texas, after six months of hard labor. Ellis Russell, the man credited with writing the petition for the men, settled in Galveston, Texas, after his release from prison, becoming the first Black postman in Galveston, and worked as police officer, customs inspector, and insurance agent before becoming an assistant to Norris Wright Cuney, a well-known Black political organizer and activist in central Texas during the late nineteenth century.[80]

Fort Stockton may have been eighty miles away from Fort Davis, but in the vast geography of west Texas, it was just next door. It was a place many infantrymen traveled to as part of their escort duty. The companies of the Twenty-Fifth Infantry serving there were men they had served with in previous postings. It is impossible to think that they were not aware of the case. In August 1873, as the court-martial of the men at Fort Stockton was scheduled to begin, Charles Southerner had gone on his shooting spree, aiming his gun at the commanding officer's house; Jonas Cox either willfully misheard or ignored an order to shoot the man and instead disarmed him peacefully. When Cox stated that he had not shot the man to avoid a mutiny, his words carried great weight given what officers believed was happening at Fort Stockton.

What, then, in light of this case, should be made of Kendall's asking that John Sample be added to the school? Sample, as recounted, had his history of demands for redress through writing. His situation was different; his demands for justice had been heard, not punished. He had followed the chain of command impeccably and had navigated the process unscathed. Kendall was serving with Sample at the time of the Goldsborough affair, and he would have known of Sample's protest.

Had Kendall been moved by the manly efforts of a community of men to protest a grave injustice that led to the death of their comrade? Had he been moved by the defense that without proper education, men could not be expected to know how to properly advocate for their rights? Someone on the court had clearly seen the relationship between the educational leadership of company captains and the ability of soldiers to understand and navigate processes. Was Kendall the officer who asked those questions, or was he influenced by the exchange? More important to consider, Was Kendall ensuring that the school would have a teacher who was not afraid to mount protest within the appropriate military structures and procedures? Was he recognizing that literacy for Black men was about more than simply having greater employment opportunities or the ability to read the Bible for oneself?

Whatever his motivations or inspirations, Kendall put aside his dispute with Sample to bring one of the most eloquent writers on the post into the school. By September 1873, the post was again under the command of Bliss, the man who had overseen the court-martial at Fort Stockton.

In 1873, after the first intensive post school had been running for six months, there is evidence in the archival record of people drawing upon literacy skills to demand citizenship rights. On July 30, 1873, laundress Christine Cooper wrote a letter directed to the post commander describing a confrontation between her and the chief musician of the Twenty-Fifth Infantry at her home. The conflict arose from her attempts to keep the man from bothering her husband, resulting in an injury to her arm and the arrest of her husband who had intervened to defend her. In her letter, Mrs. Cooper explained details of the case and the assurances she had received from the officer of the day that the musician was clearly in the wrong since he had been on sick leave that day and shouldn't have been away from quarters. She had not received any response nor did she see evidence that the offending party was going to be punished. She closes the letter, "I am trusting that you <u>will give this matter your early attention</u>" (emphasis in original).[81]

Another letter writer, in a July 27, 1873, letter addressed to General Augur and sent through four intermediaries—Captain David Schooley, Company E; H. B. Quimby, quartermasters department; Cyrus Gray, post adjutant; and Zenas Bliss, post commander—asked for lenience in the charges against a fellow soldier:

> Sir, I rekomends Private James Willson two you. I have known him two be faithful and trust worthy two. All of his duties that have been required he is a good mechanic and a useful man two the regiment and I think it is a Pity two see him go two Prison I think a disonerably discharge from the service is punishment enough for him he has been in the quartermaster department the biggest portion of his time also in the subsistant department and has proved himself two be trusty I have sent him off with detachment for nine and ten days acting in the capacity of a noncommissioned officer and therefore it look hard two see him go two prison.[82]

The careful reader may recognize James Wilson as the man whom Corporal Collins provoked by calling his mother a "bitch." The man writing in defense of Wilson, given the chain of command followed, appears to have been a noncommissioned officer in Company E, Twenty-Fifth Infantry. The writing does not match that of NCOs Anthony Jackson, Griffin Collins, or John Sample, men whose writing samples are available for comparison. The military had a policy of not responding to anonymous letters, so the effort put forward to help a comrade was in vain. Still, the letter represents a manly attempt to make a case for the qualities of a fellow soldier.

General Order No. 31 of April 10, 1874, relieved Kendall of his duty as superintendent of the post school.[83] Chaplain Mullins's arrival in 1875 coincides with the next iteration of a post school. A November 1877 bimonthly report written by George Andrews reports the school under Chaplain Mullins as being successful but inconsistently offered: "The post school which was reopened on Oct 1 is attended in large numbers and is producing most satisfactory results. I fear it will become necessary to reduce the number of sessions per week on account of the small accumulation of the post and the increased expense of lighting in consequence to the inferior candles on hand at the post."[84]

Again, expenses were seen as a justification to limit a soldier's educational opportunities. Despite obstacles placed in the way of soldiers, the archaeological and archival record demonstrates that education was part of their pursuit of self-improvement and that they used their education in their professional and personal lives as they worked toward fashioning themselves as citizens.

So what of Lemuel Johnson, whose letters to the secretary of war opened this chapter? Johnson and his fellow convicted deserters were sent to Baton Rouge Penitentiary to serve a ten-year sentence. Judge Adjutant J. Holt read Johnson's letters and forwarded them to the secretary of war on April 8, 1872, asking him to consider the irregularity of men being tried as a group, since, he argued, desertion was a crime undertaken by an individual, even if others deserted at the same time:

> No evidence was offered in the case and no facts in regard to the desertion appears even from the specifications except that the parties were gone only two days. The accused made a statement to the effect that he was forced to

desert by the arbitrary treatment of the first sergeant. . . . His ignorance of the rules of pleading ought not be allowed to prejudice his legal right and upon a review of his case by the Secretary of War, he should be entitled to the benefit of any legal defense in the proceedings against him.[85]

Holt recommended that Johnson be set free at once. The endorsement and notations on the letter suggest that Holt had already approached the secretary of war before and was asking him to reconsider. What happened is not recorded in the court-martial file, but Johnson's enlistment record notes his desertion but also states that he left the military at the end of his term of enlistment service. Johnson's letters found a receptive audience. In addition, a copy of Standard Order No. 84, signed April 8, 1878, remits the sentences of two of the other men involved in the same court-martial (Calvin Dudley and William Jones), freeing them two years early.[86]

6

※══○══※

SERGEANT SAMPLE'S
EYESIGHT

◆

In early 1865, stationed in Rock Isle, Illinois, the men of Company F, 108th United States Colored Infantry, were photographed at Gayford and Speidel's Photography Studio. First lieutenant T. F. Wright created an album from the carte de visites, carefully labelling each man's picture, and sent it to his mother.[1] Among the thirty-one men included in the album is seventeen-year-old drum major John Sample. Sample stands out in the album. While other men stand or sit stiffly, some with swords, some with rifles, some with one hand self-consciously stuck in their coats, Sample stands without props. His stone-faced expression contrasts with the baby fat sitting on his cheeks; his crossed arms project authority, while his stance, with one leg straight, one leg bent, expresses confidence. Looking at the image, the viewer can clearly see the twenty-one-year-old man who would later demand equal treatment for the men of his company.

The 108th was not Sample's first experiences with the service. From the fall of 1863 to the winter of 1864, he served as an "officer's man servant" for Captain Hogue of the Ninth Ohio Cavalry Volunteers. When Sample enlisted, he did so as a substitute for a Virginia farmer.[2] Prior to enlistment, Sample worked as a bartender.[3] When the Civil War ended, Sample picked up work as a waiter before enlisting in July 1867. When discharged at Ship Island, Mississippi, after his term of enlistment ended in 1870, he did not immediately reenlist. Schooley described Sample in his February 1, 1870, letter as one of the best soldiers in his company.[4] Sample reenlisted in Company E, Twenty-Fifth Infantry, in April 1870, earning an honorable discharge in April 1875. He took two weeks before reenlisting, this time in Company K of the Twenty-Fifth, and served

FIGURE 6.1. Photograph of John Sample, by Gayford
and Speidel, circa 1865. "A unique group of 31 individual portraits
of officers, non-commissioned officers, and enlisted men of
Company F, 108th United States Colored Infantry." Randolph
Linsly Simpson African American Collection, Beinecke Rare Book
and Manuscript Library, Yale University, New Haven, CT.

until May 1880. In July 1880, he enrolled in Company E, Twenty-Fifth Infantry, being discharged in 1885 in Indian Territory. Unknown to Sample, this would be the end of his military career. He presented himself in September 1885 for reenlistment in Washington, DC, but was refused because of his piles and rheumatism. He was thirty-seven years old. He stayed in Washington, DC, working for Harris House hotel on Pennsylvania Ave. Sample suffered ongoing eye troubles along with his rheumatism and piles, health problems arising from his military service.[5]

By 1887, his physical condition was deteriorating, and working was difficult. Sample applied for a soldier's pension in 1887. His file documents from 1887 to 1889 include his correspondence, in the same strong hand of his soldier days. His letters follow military format, expressing "his honor to be in communication" and signing "your obedient servant." He was a soldier by years of practice. Nonetheless, he was found to not have a ratable claim, and rejection was indicated as forthcoming. Then, during the review of his medical records, the pension commission investigator found a notation from 1885 stating that Sample was treated for "Tertiary Syphilis." Referring to his "vicious habits," his request was turned down for the first time in 1889.[6]

In 1891, Sample retained a lawyer to appeal and restate his claim. Sample was now living in the Old Soldier's Home in Washington, a charity hospital on five hundred acres of land north of DC's historic center. Veterans living there worked in exchange for food, housing, and medical services.[7] He asked for speedy review of the case, citing his dependence on charity. His tone is that of a man who still expects a resolution in his favor. From 1891 to 1901, Sample repeatedly returned to his claim. The application—a mix of documents stuffed together into a file, some documents clipped together, some hole punched and mounted to cardboard, their order an artifact of whoever reviewed the case most recently—includes almost a hundred pages. Included are depositions from two residents of the Old Soldier's home who had served with Sample at Fort Davis in 1877 and 1878: John Davis (Company A, Twenty-Fifth) and Aaron Robinson (Company C, Tenth). The men recalled Sample's medical problems, particularly with his eyesight. Davis remembered Sample's wearing dark glasses due to eye pain.[8]

Medical exams were ordered to search Sample's body for evidence of syphilitic scars. These were invasive exams, doctors examining him head to foot, poking sore gums, measuring pupil responses, examining his genitalia for malformations, squeezing glands in his throat, pulling his hair, probing his hemorrhoids inside and outside, and evaluating his fistula scar. I am reluctant to reproduce the accounts of the violence done to John Sample through these repeated exams, aware of the pornographic frame that recounting such violence creates and the ways that the archive has the power to reenact suffering.[9] Yet Sample submitted to these indignities, convinced that his body would provide a material counternarrative to the accusation of syphilis—a conviction whose corroboration, though ultimately ineffectual, took years:

The evaluation from the earliest exam in 1889: "Vicious habits: cervical, epitrochlear and inguinal glands, slight pharyngitis, no other evidence of. In view of record of syphilis the defect of the left pupil is possibly result of syphilitic iritis. No other evidence of vicious habits."[10] In other words, Sample suffered from none of the symptoms *exclusive* to tertiary syphilis, just ambiguous symptoms with any number of causes.

A doctor's evaluation from 1898: "We have examined carefully for syphilis but cannot find scars on penis, no eudurated glands, no evidence in bones, no evidence in throat or nose. No evidence of alcoholism."

A 1901 doctor's concurrence: "In short a thorough examination for the usual evidence of Old syphilitic infection reveals none whatsoever except the trouble in the left eye and that is not such as to be by any means certainly due to venereal disease. It might equally as well be attributed to rheumatism."[11]

Other reviews of his military medical records were made, and no others listed the 1885 tertiary syphilis diagnosis. Frostbite, diarrhea, dysentery, pneumonia, malaria, bronchitis, and iritis; these things he clearly suffered. R. C. Drum, the adjutant general of the Twenty-Fourth Infantry, provided records covering the same time Sample supposedly had syphilis and found no mention of it. Yet that first compilation of Sample's health records was treated as the authoritative document in this process—even when it became clear that the suspect entry was a misdiagnosis, a mis-transcription, or a mis-read by the investigator.[12] The first examiner said that Sample had been treated for syphilis and looked with bias for physical evidence, even his evaluation was ambivalent. The strongly worded dismissal of the diagnosis by later doctors could not override the convictions of the pension bureau.

Sample's continued iritis, his swollen and irritated eyes, drew suspicion. Syphilis is just one possible of cause of the condition. Parasites in undercooked food, fungal spores, shingles, viral infections, rheumatoid arthritis, and several genetic and autoimmune conditions can lead to iritis. Given that Sample spent his adult life in the cramped, unhealthy barracks of western forts and oversaw construction activities across the frontier, any number of causes could be responsible for his failing eyes. In a world without antibiotics, if Sample were suffering from tertiary syphilis, he would have presented with the symptoms and signs associated with the final stages of the disease; dementia, sores, and skeletal deterioration would have been present, recorded on his body.

Syphilis was more than a medical judgment; it was also a moral evaluation. In the 1880s, when Sample was supposedly diagnosed, syphilis was a label that included any range of venereal diseases and ailments. For decades, doctors thought that syphilis, gonorrhea, and bubo were three manifestations of the same illness that affected the blood. Just three years after Sample's death, wider use of microscopic evaluation improved diagnoses of syphilis and would have helped evaluate his case.[13]

Sample was aware of and outraged by the syphilis diagnosis. In a June 1897 letter to the pension commission, he wrote, "I never had any private disease. My record that says so is a mistake." In 1898, he submitted a notarized affidavit:

> I was treated in the Service at Fort Davis, Texas, 1878 and 1879 by Post Hospital. At Fort Sill for piles and I have had rheumatism. Eye trouble and fistula operated upon for that at Hospital and Old Soldiers House this city. I have treated myself for all these troubles having no money to employ doctors. I filed after Pension myself under Gen. Black for piles and eye trouble. I never had a venereal disease in my life and I make this statement under oath and on my own responsibility" [emphasis in original].[14]

By 1898, Sample's handwriting is declining, his script, though recognizable, is slanted, cramped, and halting. He writes quickly, likely in frustration. His efforts failed, and he ultimately abandoned his application after 1901. He died in 1905, in the Old Soldier's Home, and is buried in their cemetery. His stone, number 7109, reads, "Sergeant Major, Jno Sample, unknown to 1905." Sample considered his birth year to be 1848. He would have been fifty-seven years old.[15]

Black Soldiers' Relationships

Sample's experiences with the pension bureau reveals the lens through which Black men's intimate relationships were viewed. The pension commission evaluators were so consumed by the notion that Black men were sexually diseased that no other possibility could be considered. Their biases are symptomatic of the views held by a white supremacist patriarchy, which continued to construct Black men as less than human.[16]

This, like other racialized biases, was deep seated and often expressed by chaplains and officers serving with Black troops. They reported Black men as voracious in all appetites and prone to the vice of whoring and its medical aftermath. These stereotypes were essential flavors that seasoned the accounts of white men serving with Black troops, whether or not the men were conscious of their biases.[17] While testifying in a Freedman's Bureau case in 1864, Lieutenant Edwin Stivers (who would serve at Fort Davis beginning in 1872) opined that Black couples were never really married, that all of their marriages were "only pretend."[18] Colonel Andrews's obsession with the stereotype of Black rapists is seen in his excessive pursuit of Private Martin Pedee's case and was not expressed just at Fort Davis.

These attitudes meant that soldiers' loving and sexual relationships were understood through a biased gaze or were pointedly ignored. Soldiers technically needed an officer's permission to marry, but evidence suggests that many came into the service already married (like Anthony Jackson) and kept their relationships quiet, while others married after their enlistment. Records of desertion show that a passionate few left the military prematurely to pursue love.[19] How was military service entangled not only with the quest for citizenship rights, but also with understandings of manhood, womanhood, friendship, and kinship? The archival and archaeological records provide a small number of provocative insights into the range of intimate relationships soldiers engaged in—sexual intimacy, love affairs and marriage with women (and all the challenges those could entail), affectionate friendships and rivalries with other men, and those relations kept most quiet—loving relationships with other men.

Turning the Gaze toward the Fort's Women

Women were a crucial part of frontier life, both within and outside the post.[20] The military employed women as hospital matrons and military laundresses, while officer's wives hired women to work as cooks. Women could be found in the living quarters behind officers' kitchens, living in and around the hospital, or quartering in tents behind the barracks, with husbands or alone. In the northern post reservation, women lived in small clusters of adobes. Known by the military as "camp followers," they did laundry, baked, cooked, and dated the men as potential romantic partners or as part of economic transactions. Outside the post, more women lived and worked in proximity to the post, often in positions that provided services to the soldiers.[21]

Where women lived was one of the geographies that shaped men's movements through the post when they were off duty. The two-room kitchens behind the officers' quarters, where many Black men and women employed as cooks and servants lived, became social spaces. Since many of the people in these positions were former soldiers (and friends) or potential love interests, these spaces understandably drew soldiers. Officers saw this visiting as problematic. In February 1874, General Order No. 13 stated, "Hereafter no enlisted men will be permitted to sleep out of their barracks except those who are married and have their families living in garrison"; and Circular No. 8 in July 1874 stated, "Enlisted men are prohibited from visiting the kitchen or servants rooms in rear of the Officer's quarters."[22] Recall that earlier orders had informed soldiers that they could approach officer's quarters only from the back; Circular No. 8 now informed enlisted men that they could only approach officers' quarters from the back with an NCO escort. Wooing women living in these areas became more difficult. Officers recognized that married men could make better soldiers but apparently were not enthusiastic about the courtships that preceded wedded bliss.[23]

As per 1868 military regulations, each company or detachment of twelve or more enlisted men were entitled to hire one laundress for every nineteen or fraction of nineteen men, with no more than four laundresses to a company. Until 1878, "US Army laundress" was a position that came with rations, a mandated pay rate, housing, and travel expenses when moving with the company. Laundresses were housed in a variety of ways at Fort Davis, with some living in a rundown adobe near the commissary, some living in tents behind their respective companies, and others living with NCO husbands in tents in various locations. By the mid-1870s, a group of four laundresses and their families built adobe houses at the northeastern boundary of the post.[24] Military laundresses were women with economic security, making them interesting potential mates; soldier's wives regularly filled military laundress positions. Not all laundresses living near (or even on) Fort Davis were in the employ of the military. The rates charged by US laundresses could be undercut by civilians working as washerwomen.

A collection of houses lived in by laundresses, both official and otherwise, developed near the quartermaster's corral as early as 1868 and included civilian employees of the post, some of whom may have also sold their companionship to soldiers. These were spaces that could be sites of conflict. In 1868, Joseph Franklin of Company E, Forty-First Infantry, was court-martialed for attempting to rape Demetria Domingues, who lived with her husband in what was described as a "jacal" (a small adobe). Franklin had approached Domingues with another soldier and followed her into her home, asking in Spanish to have sexual intercourse with her. He threw five dollars onto her bed, began to undress, and attempted to embrace her. She rejected him but then took him to the home of another Mexican woman, who also turned him down. Domingues admitted that the soldier hadn't tried to force her. She was later heard fighting with her husband, who thought she was encouraging soldiers to come into the house. The details that emerged in the trial suggested that Franklin was brought to the house by a fellow soldier who told him that the woman was available for a price and who was confused by her unwillingness to engage with him specifically. The court decided that Franklin hadn't raped Domingues but that he had insulted her honor.[25]

The case shows the ambiguous spaces that existed in relations between soldiers and women living on the post. The development of formal brothels in the area, several run by former soldiers, clarified some of these boundaries. Social events like dances created circumstances where men's and women's expectations differed and conflicts arose, such as the disagreement between John Hewey and Annie Carter in 1872 (see chapter 4).

Relationships formalized by marriage existed on post. Several soldier-laundress couples have already been introduced in these pages. Mrs. Christine Cooper lived with her husband, Sergeant James Cooper, in what she described as "her house." The Coopers lived in the same part of the post as Domingues and her husband. Mrs. Cooper's letter described an 1873 assault on her by Musician Michael Truber, who swore at her, grabbed and bruised her arm, and waved a gun at her. A corporal of the guard intervened, and Truber and her husband were dragged off to the guardhouse.[26] As an employee of the US government, Mrs. Cooper wrote both as an autonomous person deserving of rights unto herself and as a wife in support of her husband. No response to Mrs. Cooper's letter has been found, but county court records show that Truber was arrested for assault five years later in 1878 and transferred to a civilian court for trial.[27] The archival record suggests that like other families at this time of change, men and women were negotiating what their respective rights were relative to the household, community, and nation-state.

Private Richard Henry Cuff was married to a laundress. His wife was also quartered near the quartermaster's corral and was probably a neighbor to the Coopers. Cuff's case demonstrates the challenges faced by dual military couples. Cuff was first court-martialed in December 1873 for fighting with a man who tried to stop him from taking wood from the quartermaster's corral; the wood was rationed for his wife. He was found guilty and sentenced to dishonorable discharge and hard labor. The sentence was mitigated and converted to a fine, but not before Cuff, apparently a hothead, attempted to intimidate witnesses from his first trial and found himself court-martialed again in January 1874. He was again found guilty.[28] This time, he was sentenced to hard labor and confinement in the guardhouse wherever his company was stationed, with a twenty-four-pound ball and leg iron attached to him for a period of three months. It is easy to see how quickly a couple's secure economic security could be upended by a partner's bad decision-making.

Annie Williams, accuser of Martin Pedee and wife of Corporal John Williams of Company E, Twenty-Fifth Infantry, was not a laundress. Perhaps this is why they found themselves living in a tent instead of a house near the quartermaster's corrals. Annie (maiden name Chinn) had been a domestic servant in the home of Frank Perry in 1870 at Fort Duncan. It is not known if she continued in domestic service at Fort Davis.[29]

Several other married couples appear in the 1870 census at Fort Davis. Henry Wiley, a hospital steward for the Ninth Cavalry, was married to Jane, a laundress. The couple had an eight-year-old daughter, Laura. Henry Wright of Company B, Ninth Cavalry, and his wife, Eliza, another laundress, lived at Fort Davis with their four-year-old son and two-year-old daughter. Corporal John Shanks (Company K, Ninth Cavalry) was married to Nancy Burch, who was "at home" with sixteen-year-old Eliza Shanks. Relationships to the head of household are not noted in the census of 1870, so it is unclear whether Eliza is a daughter, stepdaughter, or sister of Corporal Shanks. Corporal Ed McKenzie was married to Minerva, a woman of Mexican ancestry, who worked as a laundress and bought stolen boots from Solomon Moore in 1872. Mr. and Mrs. McKenzie were visiting in Archer Smith and his wife's kitchen on the January night in 1873 when the fight over a stolen overcoat broke out.[30]

For men and women who were enslaved before the Civil War, gendered relationships, marriages, and kinship did not conform to the heteronormative nuclear family glamorized in white middle-class proscriptive literature. Kinship during enslavement was expansive and inclusive in ways often incomprehensible to white people encountering them. Dylan Penningroth recounts records of refugees joining Union camps in families of two hundred or individuals who identified themselves as having as many as sixty parents.[31] Building family in the face of arbitrary separation by sale or inheritance, sexual violence, forced birth, and early death was a daunting task, and the results took many forms. These experiences shaped the expectations and hopes of Black men and women as they built intimate relations. Their ambitions were also, to differing degrees, affected by their conceptions of the relationships between citizenship, respectability, and belonging within the nation in their new status as freed people.

Differing expectations of emerging gendered roles could cause conflict within households. Who had the right to police behavior within the community could also be contentious. A memorable example of such a dispute took place in early November 1873, involving Laura Wiley and Solomon Powell of Company D, Twenty-Fifth Infantry.[32] Powell was witnessed chasing the twelve-year-old girl by the kitchen of Company E, Twenty-Fifth Infantry. He caught her, threw her on the ground, pulled up her clothing, and whipped her with a switch, exclaiming that he would "learn her how to talk about a man's mother." Four soldiers witnessed the assault. "All I saw was the prisoner whip her. He whipped her with a small switch; I don't think he hit her more than a dozen cracks with it," explained Private Benjamin Beasley. "The switch was no bigger than two foot long and wa'n't bigger than my finger. . . . He whipped her on her butt, he whipped her on her bare flesh." Beasley thought Laura was in pain because "she hollered, she cried, she did holler very bad."

Henry Wiley described himself as the servant of Dr. De Graw, the post surgeon. Laura was the daughter of his wife, hospital matron Mrs. Wiley. He described Laura's coming back crying. He examined her and found that the skin had been broken on her hip in several places and that her wrist was bruised and swollen. The court wanted clarification of whether she said she had been whipped or beaten, and he confirmed that she said she had been beaten.

In his defense, Powell described the girl as "noted for using all manner of low vulgar and obscene language to soldiers whenever she comes around the barracks, and the reason I whipped her was the she used such language to me about my mother and myself." A defense witness, Private William Pratt (Company D, Twenty-Fifth Infantry), stated that he knew the girl and "her character is not very good I should think from what she said to me, she called me a son of a bitch the other day. I have heard her say it to several soldiers and worse words than that, I heard her tell a soldier that his mother was a more of a bitch than she was herself."

Powell was found guilty and sentenced to lose $10.00 of pay for a period of one month. Assistant Adjutant General Augur found the sentence "totally inadequate" for the offense, but he confirmed it, opining, "As the prisoner brings witnesses to show the child had used certain language to him, he should have gone to her parents."[33] Augur thus sums up the social struggle at the heart of this conflict. Powell believed that his authority to administer corrective measures to the child was unquestioned. It is possible to see how martial citizenship would convey this inherently patriarchal authority to the soldier. The court-martial jury agreed with his assessment, giving him a slap on the wrist that drew no metaphorical or other blood. The hospital steward, the child's stepfather, represented her interests in the prosecution case, not her mother. The voices of the injured women are not heard, but judgment is clearly cast on them both. Mrs. Wiley's role as a mother is condemned in the court's approval of Powell's actions, and by extension, Henry Wiley's patriarchal control of his family is sanctioned as well.

Augur's response suggests his discomfort with this usurping of parental authority. The case also indirectly points to the ongoing violence of past enslavement in postbellum life. The soldiers who witnessed the beating seemed nonplussed by what they saw. The men serving in 1870s Fort Davis had been children during enslavement; a humiliating beating of a child does not seem to have struck them as anything but ordinary. The white officers hearing the case wanted specific details about the bareness of the girl's body, who disrobed her, and how she was disrobed, seemingly taking voyeuristic pleasure from the testimony.

The inability of Black men to claim a heteronormative patriarchal authority over the bodies of their mothers, sisters, wives, and daughters has been presumed by white men to have been an emasculating aspect of enslavement.[34] As freed people, Black men and women alike found themselves confronting white heteronormative assumptions about sex and gender roles. How they responded, and the ongoing historical implications for Black relationships today, is hotly debated in feminist circles, with feminist scholars like Tommy Curry arguing that intersectional analyses have failed to acknowledge the particular burdens of Black men, who have long been allies for Black women.[35] The conflict between Private Powell and Laura Wiley is a moment when conflict over what was proper behavior for men versus women bubbled into public.

Underlying the conflict was a notion about proper feminine behavior as well as the pejorative evocation of a maternal figure. Laura Wiley, on the cusp of womanhood, hung around the barracks and insulted men there with rough language. From a heteronormative notion of proper womanhood, if Laura was unwilling to act a lady, Powell was unwilling to treat her as one.

Many moments of disruption and differing expectations inserted themselves into mundane interactions between men and women. Abolition had been supported by suffragists who awaited their turn for citizenship rights, and women across the country had supported households while men fought the Civil War. Gender relations and norms were being challenged and re-scripted across the country during the postwar period. In this sense, Black families were no different from any other American families. The experiences of enslavement meant that Black couples brought different understandings, hopes, and expectations into their relationships as freed people. Normative feminine roles of mother and keeper of the hearth were attractive to some women who had been denied the ability to mother according to their own values during enslavement, which was quite independent of accepting a patriarchal power system.[36]

With this in mind, let us consider how these negotiations may have been materialized in the archaeology at the Fort Davis barracks and consider again the two yard features found: the archaeological hearth and ashpit and their associated materials. Both features suggest the presence of two distinct tent households. The hearth feature was located within a tent during its occupation, while the ashpit was located outside of a tent. The standard size for an officer's wall tent was twelve by ten feet, and the spatially discrete yet aligned nature of the two features suggests that two tents may have been simultaneously occupied at one point, with the tents in a row, occupying the area to the south and west of the unfinished dining hall of structure HB-22. There were no nails found in the area of the hearth, suggesting that the tent was not built on a nailed platform, but this would not preclude a set plank or log floors being laid in the tent or even a carpet flooring, as was found in the adobe houses excavated in the laundress quarters on post.[37] Window glass was found in fairly high densities compared to other parts of the yard, and this may indicate a canvas structure that had glass sewn into its window openings, not an unknown modification.

Colonel Andrews wrote in 1875 that in three years, the Twenty-Fifth Infantry's noncommissioned officers and members of the band had not been properly quartered since arriving at the camp.[38] Therefore, as stated in chapter

3, NCOs and band members were the most likely tent occupants. Court-martial testimony demonstrates that the only NCOs consistently described as occupying tents are those men who were married. Otherwise, NCOs like Anthony Jackson, Griffin Collins, John Hewey, John Chapman, and others were quartered in the barracks with the rest of their company. Given their status as NCOs, this would indeed be improper quartering. Musicians reportedly found housing in tents and abandoned buildings before the construction of their barracks. Band members would have occupied shelter tents, which would not have had a stove. Other possible tent occupants were women working as military laundresses. As of 1870, their tents were to be placed behind the barrack's sinks, and by 1873, many were living by the quartermaster's corral. Therefore, the most likely occupants for the tents in this area would have been married NCOs and their partners. The stove, as well as the ashpit, speak to the inhabitants' keeping a separate mess rather than using the shared dining hall and supports the interpretation that the tents were the homes of married couples. Given the dates of the deposits, only a few possible candidates for possible occupants emerge from the archival record.

Sergeant John Tonsell (Company F, Ninth Cavalry) lived with his wife, Laura, who was described as "keeping house," and their infant daughter, Catherine. The partial post-trader book shows Tonsell making purchases through 1871. Tonsell's date of service was to expire in August 1872, as much as maybe a year earlier than the tent site was abandoned.

The post-trader ledger also shows Sergeant Henry Washington (Company G, Twenty-Fifth Infantry) and his wife, Mary, making purchases in 1871. The Washingtons stayed awake after sunset, making multiple purchases of candles and writing paper. Given that Washington was discharged in 1875, he and his wife are strong candidates for occupation of one of the tents. A final couple whose occupation at the fort corresponds to one of the tent occupations are the aforementioned Corporal and Mrs. McKenzie, Company E. Stationed at the fort by May 1872 and married by 1873, the McKenzies are strong candidates to have occupied the tent associated with the later ashpit. While we cannot tie individual couples with any certainty to these households, it is important that the time frames of occupation do seem to correspond with known troop movements and with particular NCO families.

The archaeology of gender has been troubled by attempts to separate artifacts into girls things and boys things. Such an approach fails to recognize the multivalent nature of things and the failure of people to neatly fit into tidy, binary categories. When studying gender, it is more appropriate to think not about the gender association of things but about whether those things represent certain gendered practices.[39] For instance, a gendered-things approach to the barracks of Fort Davis would associate only two artifacts recovered from any of the deposits that might speak to the presence of women: a small cologne bottle that once held Hoyt's German Cologne and a busk from a corset. When one considers these two artifacts through the lens of gendered *practices*, however, the picture is more complicated. While one frontier resident associated the smell of Hoyt's German Cologne with the presence of prostitutes, perfuming is both a male and female practice. Hoyt's German Cologne also had a myriad of uses in Louisiana related to spiritual healing practices.[40] Corsets were more often than not worn by women, but cavalrymen were known to wear corsets for back support and health reasons. Domestic wares like ceramics are often seen to be the result of women's purchasing decisions, but at Fort Davis, the archival evidence suggests that the men of the companies and their officers were actively involved in the selection of ceramics. There was some sense among army officials that hot-beverage choices had a gendered dimension. In Billings's 1875 study of post health, the following observation about rations was made: "Tea is seldom drawn by the men, being mainly used by the laundresses."[41] Yet teacups and mugs alike are seen in the barracks trash deposit, the hearth assemblage, and the ashpit.

So if the hearth and ashpit were associated with married couples, is there anything about the contents of these assemblages that suggest different activities than seen in the larger trash deposit associated with the barracks? The three assemblages are difficult to compare to one another given the mixed use of the barracks' dump for the burned disposal of equipment and as trash deposits. However, a consideration of the materials suggests some interesting differences.

The ashpit is notable for the diversity of materials found within it, while also having a very small number of ceramics. A minimum of only four ceramic vessels were recovered, but two of the vessels represent types found nowhere else around the barracks: a bright yellow tin-enamel glazed teacup, probably of Mexican origin, and a yellowware whiskey flask. The other two ceramics, a plate and a platter, were of the plain white style that dominates all the barracks' assemblages. A pressed-glass bowl, of a style attempting to mimic hand-cut crystal, was also found. Other items of a personal nature from the ashpit included the previously discussed pocketknife, watch chain, and a black rubber dressing comb. Shoe aglets, boot eyelets (non-military), shell and Prosser-method buttons and suspender buckles also speak to non-military garments, some of the few found at the site.

The hearth ceramic assemblage is much more similar to the barracks' dump than the ashpit, perhaps not surprising given that the hearth (1872–1874) is roughly contemporaneous with the dump deposit (1869 to its end date of 1872/73). The ceramics from the hearth conform to the same styles seen in the overall dump deposit, just with a smaller diversity of vessel types than found in the dump. The only exception is a sherd from an embossed floral pattern that matches multiple examples found in the yard of the commanding officer's quarters. Two tumblers matching the ones used in company quarters were found bearing the mark of Company K at this same house, speaking to the movement of materials back and forth at different times. Materials could move between households through a variety of practices.

Plates move back and forth between domiciles as part of food sharing, a phenomenon that has been seen at other archaeological sites. The notion of the gift is of long-standing interest in anthropological studies, with the general recognition that any gift implies a reciprocal obligation.[42] For domestic servants, taking or receiving food from an employer's kitchen (a practice known as toting in the South), is a well-documented example of a gift that reinforced social and economic differences between employers and employees.[43] Noncommissioned officer's wives were not only employed as laundresses; they often held jobs before or after their marriages in the households of white officers. This lone ceramic may speak to an economic relationship between the occupants of the tents and officers' row.

Like the ashpit, which included Mexican ceramics and examples of decorative personal items, a pressed milk-glass bowl was one of the objects recovered from the hearth area. The barracks contained tableware and glassware not otherwise provided by the military, but decorative household wares are not part of that assemblage. Is decorating a practice that had gendered dimensions?

Katrina Eichner excavated two of four known households associated with the mid-1870s to 1880s laundress quarters located at the northwestern part of the post. These houses were lived in possibly as early as the mid-1870s and definitely in the first half of the 1880s, when the census describes them as residences of laundresses and the NCO husbands from the Tenth Cavalry. This is a distinct residential area separate from the cluster of married laundress and NCO houses described near the quartermaster's stables in 1873 and 1874.[44]

If the assemblages from those two houses are compared, using the analytical

Artifact Category	Laundress Quarter (HB-211)	Laundress Quarter (HB-212)	Hearth/ Tent (Near HB-22)	Ashpit (Near HB-22)
		PERCENT OF ASSEMBLAGE		
Clothing	10.0	8.2	14.6	48.1
Food service	5.0	14.2	21.9	5.5
Beverage service	3.8	4.0	17.0	5.5
Food storage	11.3	10.2	4.9	5.5
Alcoholic beverage storage	36.3	30.6	21.9	14.8
Nonalcoholic beverage storage	0	0	2.4	0
Cookware	3.75	2.0	0	1.9
Health care	16.3	16.3	4.9	5.5
Lighting	7.5	0	2.4	1.9
Literary	1.3	4.0	2.4	3.7
Tobacco	2.5	0	2.4	3.7
Weapons	2.5	8.2	4.9	7.4

categories used by Eichner, with the assemblages from the hearth (table 6.1), we see that the same range of activities is represented. However, there are more artifacts related to beverage and food service from the hearth than the laundress quarters, whereas more alcoholic beverage, food storage, and health-related items were recovered from Eichner's excavations at the laundress quarters. The smaller number of food storage–related artifacts from the hearth potentially speaks to the greater dependence of the tent occupants on the company mess. Cans and condiments accounted for food remains in addition to faunal remains.

Eichner has argued that the liminal space within the post, at the boundary of the property, made the laundresses' houses social spaces where soldiers could relax and socialize beyond the gaze of the officers and safely on the property of the post, beyond some of the troubles that could emerge once a soldier ventured into the civilian businesses. The adobe house sites studied by Eichner date largely to the period when companies of white enlisted men had joined the post, creating a very different racialized landscape for the Black soldiers to navigate. The founding of this neighborhood also seems to correspond with the greater regulation of socializing around the officers' kitchen quarters.[45]

A notable feature of the laundress quarters studied by Eichner, for our purposes, is the range of household materials that represent ornamentation: picture frames, figurines, ornaments, curtains, and carpets. Additionally, plain ceramics typical of family fare at the time are just one part of these assemblages, which include a wide range of colorful, decorated wares that contrast greatly with the barracks and tent materials. These items speak to efforts to render the space not just genteel but also beautiful, and they might be seen as the specifically gendered practices of homemaking.[46]

Archaeologist Diana diZerega Wall was the first to argue that the presence of gothic and plain-bodied ceramics so prevalent in mid-nineteenth-century middle-class households were material signifiers of women's participation in what became the "cult of true womanhood."[47] Yet the selection of these same kinds of kitchen furniture by men for demonstrating manly values of faith and gentility in the barracks, suggests that these plain table wares may be emblematic of notions of family shared by men and women alike, whether or not they were cohabitating. Therefore, for me, it is the colorful yellow teacup and glittering pressed glass from the ashpit and the milk glass decorative bowl and window glass from the hearth that quietly suggest that a woman trying to bring some beauty and light to a drab tent wall. If to be a homemaker came with expectations of bringing beauty to family life, imagine the frustrations of a woman married to an NCO at Fort Davis. Her husband had achieved the status of being a leader within his company, only to be housed in a tent. Her own ambitions to demonstrate her achievements as homemaker were thwarted.

Marriage after Service

The largest pool of people available for romantic pursuits was the civilian population. By 1870, Fort Davis was a town where half the civilian population claimed Mexican ancestry. The racial classification of this population was contested, with the census bureau telling enumerators to classify Mexicans as racially "white." Enumerators, hired locally and sometimes from the military post, expressed disagreement with this classification by noting in the margins which white people were Mexican.[48]

While intermarriage between races was prohibited by law in Texas, this hardly seems to have prevented unions between Black men and self-described Mexican women. Archer Smith (Twenty-Fourth Infantry), after his 1870 discharge, married a local woman named Lionicia. George Bentley, of Company K, Ninth Cavalry, married a woman named Conception after leaving the military in 1871.[49] After completing his enlistment terms in 1872, Randolph Wiggins, Company I, Ninth Cavalry, married a Mexican woman named Tula and became a Methodist minister in the town.[50] George McGuire of Company I, Ninth Cavalry, married Ewarda Rodriguez after his discharge in 1874 and continued to work on the post.[51] Robert Fair/Fayl, also of Company I, Ninth Cavalry, left the military in 1872 and settled in Fort Davis, becoming a Methodist preacher and in 1889 and marrying Pabla Casey.[52] Even in Jeff Davis County, a remote corner of west Texas named after the only president of the failed Confederacy, these marriages and military afterlives demonstrate the ways that Black soldiers merged into the local community. In each of these civilian households, the women are noted as "at home" or "keeping house," demonstrating that the families were able to economically sustain themselves without the women needing to engage in paid economic labors outside of the home—a hallmark of middle-class achievement and respectability. The work of fashioning manly gentility in the day-to-day habits of the military company may have served to shape soldier's expectations of home life.

Long-Distance Marriages

Not all married men at Fort Davis had their wives on post. Tracking who was married during their service at Fort Davis is significantly more challenging than tracing soldiers in civilian life. Unfortunately, the 1870 census did not collect marriage information as later censuses did, and the only way to identify married couples is based on whether they were cohabitating. In contrast, in 1880, individuals were asked whether they were married. In that census, twenty-eight men stationed at Fort Davis identified themselves as married even though only six men on base lived with spouses. Given that men were not permitted to be married when they entered the service and could marry only with permission, this speaks to the possibility that even more of the soldiers were involved in long-distance or secret marriages.

Sergeant Anthony Jackson was in one of these secret or unsanctioned marriages. Although letters from his time at Fort Davis no longer exist, letters dating to earlier in his military career give some sense of the challenges couples faced and provide insights into how Sergeant Jackson understood his role as husband and father. From the time that his unit left Virginia for North Carolina in 1867, there is only one documented visit between Lucrecia Jackson and her husband, in 1870. Without the later letters, it is impossible to know what the couple's plans for the future were. After his visit home, Jackson extended his term of service from three to five years in 1870. At the expiration of that original five-year term, February 2, 1872, he immediately reenlisted February 6 for another five-year period but died in May 1875.[53] Had he intended to remain in the service, or was he planning to return to his family with a nest egg?

Lucy Jackson, as indicated by Anthony's letters, lived in the midst of both of their families, surrounded by Anthony's uncle's family, her mother and siblings, and an extended network of friends and family to whom Jackson regularly sent his love and regard. There is no indication from anyone interviewed in the pension application that there was any discussion of Lucy Jackson's joining her husband on the frontier.[54] Of course, to do so would have stripped their two sons of the extended networks of support that surrounded them in Alexandria. The seemingly endless separation, which might seem strange to us, perhaps was not so foreign to a couple who had lived through enslavement and the disruption of war. Married in 1861, they lived together for six years before their separation. Between the Jackson's expiration of service at the end of 1869 and his reenlistment in February 1870, Jackson returned home to Alexandria, Virginia. Family and friends testified in the pension application that the two lived together during that several month period as loving man and wife. The visit resulted in another pregnancy. Only one letter submitted in the pension application dates to the period after his return to service, as he joined his company in Texas, but that last letter is equally loving. How the relationship faired over the next five years is unknown, and the family members interviewed for the pension would not have been inclined to mention if the couple experienced troubles.

The Jackson's long-distance marriage was complicated by Lucinda's inability to read or write. Jackson encouraged Lucinda to go to school. "You may goe to school if you want to I told you to go if you wants."[55] The letters take on a different cast when one understands that Lucinda Jackson could only hear her husband's words through a reader. Jackson in different moments attempts the floral love letters that the Victorian period was known for, but he had to write knowing that there would also be an additional audience. It must have also been frustrating to know that moments of marital tensions were open to others. Lucinda Jackson clearly feared early in their separation that her husband would become interested in another woman. Several of his letters attempt to reassure her that she didn't need to worry: "But the gals are far from us. No gals are aloud hear."[56] A letter written from Fort Macon on April 6, 1867, when their separation was still new, was filled with frustration and loneliness:

> I think you mite have riten me better letter then you did for I thought you would have treated me better than you did I have ritten 7 letters before now but I did not get any Answer from them tell today ... if you cant send me better ancars then you did doe not rite to me no more for I wont doe all for you that I can but you seame to think I have sum god dam wench with me if you cant find nothing to rite to me but a bout the gales."[57]

It is these moments of frustration sandwiched between expressions of love and longing and concern for his children and extended family that bring the Jacksons' relationship into aching clarity. Despite the pain of separation from his wife, children, and extended family, military service clearly provided Sergeant Anthony Jackson with something he valued beyond the monthly pay. The formerly enslaved man from Virginia had earned for himself a position of respect and authority, in a place that was as different from the Eastern Seaboard as one could imagine, a place that was increasingly seen in the national imagination as a frontier of great possibility. How many men serving at Fort Davis were in similar situations, juggling their duties as soldiers with their duties as fathers and husbands?

Manly Disputes, Manly Affections

Whatever their economic or romantic relationships with women, in day-to-day interactions, the soldier's world was filled with interactions with other men. The military caste shaped the kinds of relationships possible between commissioned officers and enlisted men. On January 17, 1885, Bigelow noted with disgust an interaction between a commissioned officer and an enlisted man: "Another scandal has lately occurred in the 10th Cavalry—Captain Keyes got drunk as Officer of the Day and hobnobbed in that condition with a colored soldier in the same condition, going over to the guard house with his arm around him."[58] While a primary focus of this work has been on the relationships between men based on rank, company, work obligations, and understandings of relationships between citizenship and service, I want to take a moment to consider more closely the affectionate bonds between men that developed as part of military service. Soldiers were more than coworkers; they lived, ate, ailed, traveled, and played together between their job duties. This close interaction, in close spaces, inevitably led to some of the rivalries and frustrations that been described in these pages. While documents like court-martial records focus on dispute, within their accounts are also stories of friendship and affection.

RITUALIZED DISPUTES

Several of the courts-martial discussed here involved an action referred to as "popping a cap." This expression exists in current-day parlance to mean shooting someone. The nineteenth-century meaning, however, is different in an important way. Prior to the development of bullet cartridges, which contain both black powder and an ignition source for that powder (primer), the primer for the gun was contained in a separate percussion cap that was handloaded on top of a nipple that had a channel leading to the powder chamber of the gun. The hammer hit the cap, exploding the powder and sending a flame into the powder chamber of the gun, causing it to explode (fire the gun). The cap represents a midpoint in the evolution from flintlock to metal integrated cartridges.[59]

The caps are found archaeologically as small, thin, almost daisy-shaped flat metal pieces (typically a copper alloy).[60] Importantly, one could make a bang noise by loading a cap but no other ammunition. This was popping a cap. The practice of shooting an unloaded gun at someone during a disagreement seems to be a frontier gloss on dueling. In court-martial testimony, the officers of the court typically tried to establish what the intent of shooting at someone was by asking whether there was ammunition in the weapon and how the weapon was pointed when discharged. Self-contained cartridges were developed earlier for rifles than for pistols and revolvers. When Fort Davis was reoccupied in 1867, soldiers were using .50-70 cartridges for the US Springfield model 1866, 1868, and 1870 rifles.[61] The .50-70 casings were used until 1873, with one being recovered from the bottom of the hearth feature. In contrast, it was the development of the single-action Colt revolver, tested by the military in 1872 and adopted in 1873, that heralded the introduction of integrated cartridges. The Colt Army model 1861, the revolver it replaced, was a widely held and popular gun.

TABLE 6.2. *Ammunition Recovered from* HB-22

CONTEXT	OBJECT	NUMBER
Barracks dump	Brass .50-70 rifle casing	1
	Brass .45-caliber casing	1
Hearth (1872–1874 tent)	Lead .45-caliber bullet, 250 grain weight	1
	Brass .50-70 rifle casing	1
Ashpit (1874–1876 tent)	Lead .45-caliber bullet, 250 grain weight	1
	brass 2 mm shot	1
	Brass 3 mm shot	1
Yard of HB-22 barracks	Brass Bennet primer pistol casing	1
Interior of HB-22	Fired lead bullet (indeterminate caliber)	1
	Brass 1 mm shot	1

Despite the post's being a military base, few gun-related artifacts were re-covered archaeologically (table 6.2). Post records show that men were carefully rationed ammunition as part of patrol duty. As part of their equipage, men had an ammunition cartridge box that was to keep ammunition dry and safe from accidental discharge. Early in the fort's reoccupation, enlisted men were responsible for their own arms. Thefts by the civilian population or sometimes by soldiers wanting to earn some extra funds led to greater control of weapons, with arms being locked up and access controlled by NCOs. Restrictions on per-sonal ownership of pistols and revolvers came later and were harder to enforce.

Both the hearth and the ashpit included a single example each of a .45 caliber bullet of the type introduced in 1873 for use in the Colt Single-Action Army 1873 revolver, but it may represent the presence of privately owned handguns. Neither bullet had been fired. There was some camp lore on the frontier about using gunpowder to cauterize wounds and snakebites, so the bullet's presence could speak to another use. For antebellum enslavers, the idea of a Black man with a gun was the source of night terrors and paranoia. For Black soldiers, handling, using, and developing proficiency in guns was part of a constitutionally protected citizenship right but also a way to participate in manly demonstrations of honor.[62]

An important relationship remembered by soldiers, Black and white, who served on the frontier, is that of the bunkie.[63] A bunkie was one's bunkmate, and when on patrol, the person one pitched a tent with, or when at post, shared a bunk. Today, Fort Davis's interpretive barracks is furnished with single bunks,

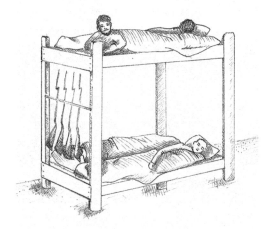

FIGURE 6.2. How double bunk beds were designed and occupied. Illustration by Merebeth Wilkie Antino.

but, at least in the early 1870s, there is evidence that the dormitories featured bunks designed for two men to share. Each man had his own "bed" (mattress), but the two mattresses were mounted on a single frame. The court-martial of James Wilson provides the clearest evidence of this arrangement at the post. Collins was asked if he and Private Gatewood shared a bunk. Collins stated, "No, they were in adjacent bunks." In his testimony, Gatewood described Private Wilson's placing money at the head of his bed and Collins then reaching over Gatewood's bunk to grab the money from Wilson's bed. Wilson and Gatewood were bunkies, and they were engaged in good-natured ribbing when Collins came into the barracks and inserted himself into their interaction.[64]

Roughhousing between male friends was a common nineteenth-century practice, which was formalized in some settings, such as fraternities or military academies.[65] In March 1870, at the post garden several miles from the fort, roughhousing had a tragic outcome. Private Jessie Quarren and Private David Boyd were described as "playing together" with carbines in the early evening. The men had picked up one another's guns and were play fighting in the adobe store house when Quarren ran outside. Boyd put down Quarren's gun, grabbed his sword, and followed his friend outside, where they continued to play fight. Quarren, unaware that his friend's gun was loaded, pulled the trigger, shooting Boyd in the stomach. Distressed by what had happened, Quarren exclaimed that he hadn't meant to do it, he didn't know the gun was loaded. Boyd died shortly after. When asked if there was any history of quarreling between the men, Private Henry Robinson provided a heartbreaking answer: "They were always playing like good friends while they were out at the garden." Private Ross Alsie agreed: "I have never seen them quarrel, there were always good friends."[66] Quarren, a veteran of the Civil War, was not charged in the shooting of his friend, which was ruled accidental. He left the military in 1874, at the end of his term of duty.

The nature of bunkie relationships suggests that men must have exerted some degree of choice over their sleeping companions, and it would be reasonable to expect that most men had some sort of friendly relationship, at least initially, with their bunkie. The use of double bunks, combined with crowded quarters, also provides some context to the degrees of irritation men developed with one another. Imagine any number of annoying habits one might confront in a sleeping partner: snoring, passing gas, talking, fidgeting. When one further considers that the soldiers at Fort Davis were overwhelmingly young men in their early twenties with the normal human urges and needs of men that age, the inconveniences of military barracks becomes manifestly clear, as is the usefulness of spaces like the unfinished HB-22 barracks. To illustrate this point bluntly, Dobak and Phillips found an 1892 record of Captain Sweet of the Twenty-Fifth Infantry reporting that a man in his company was ostracized by fellow soldiers because of his "vile habit of masturbation," which led the men to avoid him and not want to sleep near him.[67]

The sexual world of 1892, when this particular soldier was driven out of the military, was a very different one from that of the 1870s. The field of psychoanalysis and its reconceptualization of sexual desire as a psychological rather than a physical construct was still years away, as was the work of sexologists like Havelock Ellis.[68] The majority of the US populace understood reproductive health as related to the nervous system. Masturbation (onanism), same-sex desire, promiscuity, and lack of sexual desire were all considered to be manifestations of diseased nervous systems and failed morality. The male nervous system was seen as needing *some* release through sexual activity to avoid ill health, but not too much release, which could drain a man's vitality. A chronic masturbator could be easily recognized by his sickly pallor, poor posture, and weak constitution, but having no access to sexual relief could make a man agitated, nervous, and unhappy.[69] In the close quarters of the barracks, the acknowledgment of sexual need and companionship through formal or informal economic exchange systems is understandable. The empty barracks, located conveniently near the full ones, was an obvious place for rendezvous. The remains of liquor and tonic bottles deposited within the walls of the melting and abandoned barracks could easily be seen as having been consumed by romantic and/or sexual partners. Recall that Annie Carter, despite living at the Creek, was returning to the area of the barracks with her soldier friend. Perhaps they were looking for a private space like the empty barrack building. Yet the glass watch fob intaglio discovered along with these artifacts suggests that perhaps those romantic partners were not always a man and a woman.

MEN'S LOVING RELATIONSHIPS

The glass intaglio recovered from inside HB-22 was likely part of a watch fob. It was dropped there between 1869 and 1876, before construction was completed. Watch fobs, often used as wax seals, were common in the Victorian era. The intaglio depicts a classical figure, as indicated by the straight nose. Non-classical subjects on cameos and intaglios from the late nineteenth century feature small, upturned noses.[70] At first consideration, this figure appeared to be a Greek or Roman youth with a thick head of hair and a slightly downcast gaze.

Victorian-era cameos and intaglios represented particular persons from the Hellenic or the Roman world, with more generic representations becoming popular in the late nineteenth and early twentieth centuries. The popularity of Greek gods, goddesses, mythical beings, and warriors were part of the same nationalistic impulses that led to the collecting and reproduction of antiquities. While the elite sought antiquities, the upwardly mobile collected grand tour plasters, reproduction statuaries, lithographs, etched glassware, and transfer-printed plates featuring classical themes or ruins. Published catalogs of private and museum collections dictated decorative tastes. New archaeological art finds were quickly copied in consumer goods. The elite and upwardly hopeful alike decorated their homes with pieces influenced by the ancient world.[71]

During the period of 1850 through the 1880s, popular figures included Cupid and Psyche, Venus, Bacchus, Apollo, Hermes, and the Muses. Augustus and Julius Caesar and Mark Antony were portrayed less commonly but were also easily recognizable: Athena had her helmet or owl, Bacchus his grape headdress, Diane her bow, Mars his plumed helmet, and Apollo his lyre or cart. Each god or goddess had his or her identifying symbols associated with them to facilitate identification, signals as to their identity and symbolic meanings and associations.[72]

After a long and careful consideration of possible attributions, Antinous was found to be the best fit for the Fort Davis intaglio.[73] Antinous, the favorite lover of Emperor Hadrian, was often depicted with a downcast gaze and a lush

FIGURE 6.3. Antinous watch fob from Fort Davis and other nineteenth-century
Antinous items. A. Profile of the Ludovisi Altemps compared to profile of figure on Fort
Davis glass intaglio watch fob. Comparison created by Christopher Lowman using
Wikimedia Commons file: Antinous Ludovisi Altemps Inv8620n2.jpg. Note that the
visible ear, the lock in front of the ear the curls at the back of the neck, the toga over
the shoulder, and the mass of curls at the top of the head on the intaglio are very close
and suggest that one is a poor copy of the other. B. A nineteenth- century lava cameo, a
souvenir of the grand tour, showing the Antinous Mondragone. Author's private collection.
Photograph by the author. C. The full image of the watch fob recovered from
Fort Davis; D. A plaster cast of Antinous, a nineteenth-century souvenir of the
grand tour. Author's private collection. Photograph by the author.

head of hair. The Greek youth had been the emperor's love but had tragically
died in the Nile—a suicide in some versions of the tale, a willing human sacrifice in others. In his grief, Hadrian had Antinous deified, built a shrine at
his villa, and commissioned endless likenesses. Many examples of Antinous
were recovered during the excavation of Hadrian's villa, a popular stop on the
grand tours of the nineteenth century.[74]

Antinous appears in classical and nineteenth-century art as both himself
and other deities. In fact, Antinous took so many forms other than his own

that classical archaeologists, who work with a canon, have been frustrated by the quickness with which nineteenth-century archaeologists and art historians attributed to Antinous what are now thought of as classical-period generic Greek youths. A downcast gaze, pouty lips, and a head of J-shaped locks that cover the ear are now considered indicators of "authentic" classical-period Antinous by classicists. But in the nineteenth century, when this artifact was produced, the category was more expansive. One of the most popular images of Antinous in the Victorian period was the Antinous Mondragone. This bust was excavated from Hadrian's villa and is now in the Louvre. The lava cameo in figure 6.3 represents the Antinous Mondragone, showing that there is a precedent for his image circulating on jewelry.[75]

The Fort Davis Antinous seems to be based on the Antinous from Palazzo Altemps, formerly known as the Ludovisi Antinous. The Altemps has a visible ear and the random lock pattern. An overlay created of one image over the other left little doubt that one was emulating the other. There is good reason why the Ludovisi Antinous (and therefore the Fort Davis copy) fails to conform to clearly defined Roman patterns. Only the bust, nape of the neck, and back of the hairline date to the classical period. The face and remainder of the head were part of an eighteenth-century restoration based on antique portraits of Antinous. Thus, the Fort Davis Antinous is based primarily on an eighteenth-century restoration that was attempting to be authentically classical.[76]

Following the eighteenth-century excavations of statues and coins depicting Antinous, his image proliferated throughout nineteenth-century art and literature. It may have been his flexibility as a symbol of both masculinity and beauty, of youthfulness as well as classical knowledge, not to mention the veiled connotations of desire that accompanied the words "the emperor's favorite," that made him so popular a figure.

The homoerotic connotations of Antinous's image were sometimes explicit. The artist Simeon Solomon, who much like Oscar Wilde faced legal complications from being accused of sodomy, produced in the 1860s multiple paintings of Bacchus with the syncretized features of the youthful Antinous.[77] While images of Antinous with homoerotic content circulated widely, his literary debut in English is associated with poet John Addington Symonds's 1879 "Sketches in Italy" and his 1878 "The Lotus Garland of Antinous." Symonds's diary, published after his death, shows the incredible pain and confusion endured by a man who came of age in the mid-nineteenth-century aware that he longed for intense emotional connection with other men and admitting that he had a physical dimension. Symonds became increasingly convinced that his desires were part of his nature, not a moral failing, but he spent his life trying to resist that nature. Note that Symonds's publications postdate the occupation of the 1869–1876 deposit where the intaglio was found. By the 1870s, the term *Hellenism* was a euphemism for male-male desire, and within this discourse, the Greek youth came to represent male love and homoerotic desire.[78]

With entrenchment of the aesthetic movement in the mid-nineteenth century, the beauty of Antinous was seen as one of the finest examples of the male form. Oxford professor Walter Pater's studies of Renaissance art, first published in 1873, encouraged a sensibility that pushed for homoerotic understandings of the classical world and naturalized homoerotic desire, particularly in ways that emphasized pederasty. "Hellenic" relationships were based in teacher and learner binaries, asymmetries shaped by age, race, class, or some combination of the three. The elder man served as a mentor, expanding the horizons of his younger companion. Antinous, the Greek youth, and his older Roman lover fit this mold.[79] Karl Ullrich, a German who published (in German) the first widely circulated pamphlet advocating for the naturalness of manly love in 1865 celebrated Antinous.[80]

By the time he was sealed under the dirt floor of the enlisted men's barracks, Antinous was hopelessly tangled in a growing number of debates about manly friendship and love, same-sex desire, sexuality and identity, and pederastic relationships and morality. How on earth did Antinous find himself in remote west Texas? Here, the post and company libraries become essential to our considerations. Post or company libraries most likely included volumes on Greek and Roman mythology. Given the centrality of ideas about democracy drawn from the classical world, it would be strange if men seeking to establish themselves as citizens were not conversant in aspects of the ancient world. At least one NCO, Corporal Bowman, who would later serve at Fort Davis, was studying Greek mythology.

Ideas could enter the post through letters, newspapers, books, or visitors. San Antonio drew famous speakers on tour (including Oscar Wilde in 1882, speaking on art).[81] West Texas was not as isolated as perhaps it may seem. The Twenty-Fifth Infantry at Fort Davis had been previously stationed at Fort Clark, where a German watchmaker had been stationed—interesting given the connection of the artifact to watch furniture.[82] Large German immigrant populations settled in west Texas, providing a context where Ullrich's ideas could travel. Antinous could have served to note manly love or more specifically a relationship based in pederasty. There are any number of ways one can imagine an asymmetrical relationship emerging in the military: between white officers and Black enlisted men (like the situation described by Bigelow), between men born free versus men born enslaved, NCOs versus enlisted men, or men of different ages or education backgrounds.

For those unaware of Antinous's specific persona, the intaglio spoke to an engagement with classical literature and Greek culture. As a wax seal, the intaglio could have marked love letters. Given that this artifact was recovered in association with liquor bottles from an area that would have been private, we cannot dismiss that this Antinous signaled participation in debates about the naturalness of manly love, be it sexual, emotional, or both. Was this object accidentally left in an unfinished frontier barrack? Or was Antinous left as a token of heartbreak at the end of an affair? Or was he unceremoniously dumped when his owner became concerned his meaning was no longer secret?

Perhaps the careful reader will not be surprised that I will close this chapter the way I began, with attention to First Sergeant John Sample. When Martin Pedee was confronted with an accusation of rape, his defense was that he was asleep in his quarters—quarters that happened to be the private quarters of First Sergeant John Sample. A private asked by the court why Pedee was in Sample's quarters carefully answered, "No one else had any reason to be."[83]

Recall that Annie William's rape case was questioned by the assistant adjutant of Texas not because he doubted she had been attacked, but because he questioned her identification of Martin Pedee. You will recall that after screaming "Murder!" and drawing the attention of the guard, Annie Williams immediately named Pedee as her assailant and demanded that someone "go to John Sample's room and see if he was there." What if Mrs. Williams's intent was to punish Sample, not Pedee? After all, she was married to a corporal in Sample's unit. Sample received separate and private quarters as first sergeant; she and her husband lived in a tent. A promotion for her husband—or perhaps a demotion for Sample—could change that. We need to consider whether Mrs. Williams was being practical in naming Pedee as her attacker. Homosexual activity was punishable by court-martial. Naming Pedee and demanding that Sample's quarters be searched could have been intended to force the post to confront what must have been at least a source of gossip—that an NCO and private were engaged in an intimate relationship beyond that of normal bunkies. Perhaps Mrs. Williams dreamed of John Sample's quarters becoming her husband's, rescuing her from tent life.

Pedee and Sample had served together since 1867. Sample had been a drummer in the USCT; Pedee was a musician for the Twenty-Fifth Infantry. Both men served in the Civil War, both had been enslaved on the Eastern Seaboard in tobacco country. There is much in their history and shared experiences that could have drawn them to one another. In the post commander's own words, the members of the band were not properly housed, and given that context, Sample's sharing of quarters with Pedee could be seen as generosity toward a friend with no other housing options. The practice of putting men in double bunks and paired tents provided opportunities for contact and physical intimacy between men. Bunking with another man would not be reason to automatically support accusations of improper behavior, particularly if the other man in question had no assigned housing. In the same neglect of housing and overcrowding that caused so much grief to soldiers, it is possible to see how one pair of men may have used it to their advantage to claim a little joy.

The testimony to discredit Sample during Frederick Kendall's court-martial should in this context be reconsidered. As his fellow NCOs repeated opinions that Sample was "dishonest" or had a "mean reputation" in the company, we must contemplate whether these were coded expressions of homophobia. Kendall stated in his testimony that Sample was forced to testify against him, raising the possibility that Sample testified to prevent himself from being court-martialed.

What happened between Sample and Pedee following this court-martial? C. C. Augur wrote his letter mitigating Pedee's sentence on October 11, 1872. News had likely reached Fort Davis by October 19, when Colonel Andrews wrote to Schooley demanding to know why Sample had missed reveille and roll call. Schooley responded that "the Sergeant complained yesterday in the afternoon and the morning of being unwell. The Doctor gave him some medicine last evening, this morning his name was put in the sick book but he was not excused from duty," providing the sergeant with some cover.[84] Kendall was released on the October 20 from arrest, and combined with the (welcome?) news about Pedee's mitigated sentence, it isn't hard to imagine poor Sample wanting to delay facing his lieutenant.

Did their friendship survive what could be seen as Sample's betrayal? Notably, the two men were both subjects of garrison courts-martial in January 1874, shortly after Pedee's release from arrest. Pedee was charged with behavior prejudiced to good order and military discipline (Forty-Fourth Article of War), whereas Sample was charged with violation of the Twenty-First Article of War (an NCO being somewhere other than he was supposed to be). Unlike more serious general courts-martial, garrison court-martial records are often shoddily recorded, and for these cases, details of specifications were not recorded. Thus, it is impossible to know whether their cases were linked or if this is a very provocative coincidence.[85] After Pedee left the military, he and Sample went their separate ways.

Sample's remaining time at Fort Davis was no easier. He became the subject of vague accusations surrounding the theft of a trunk belonging to Captain Schooley in August 1873. A board of survey was convened in February 1874 to investigate whether he should be charged with theft of that trunk. He was cleared of wrongdoing, but one can only imagine what months of innuendo did to his ability to lead his company, as well as to disrupting his relationship with Schooley.[86] Sample finished his term of service in 1875, left Fort Davis, and joined a different company. His pension called on no one who had served with him in Company E, Twenty-Fifth. One might well wonder if the pension bureau's insistence that Sample was being denied a pension due to his "vicious habits" is another coded evaluation of his private life.

To return to the material record, my intention is not to place the Antinous in John Sample's hands. To do so would be to deny that there were probably many other men at Fort Davis who were sympathetic to Sample and Pedee's situation or were in similar arrangements themselves, living and loving in fear of retribution. Perhaps it is not necessary to point out that David Schooley, the steadfast defender of both men, was himself a life-long bachelor.

When Antinous was rescued from his muddy burial in the adobe melt of HB-22, he implored the archaeologists to consider what histories of Fort Davis had not been told. The Martin Pedee court-martial for rape is widely cited in the secondary literature, but no one has thought to revisit that crucial question: Why was Martin Pedee in John Sample's quarters? Instead, the attention of the historians is distracted by the tawdry details of a rape accusation, based on witness testimony that even the adjutant of Texas, sitting in San Antonio, could see was flawed. The stereotype of the Black rapist loomed large in the minds of some officers at Fort Davis, with potentially murderous consequences for at least one soldier.

7

DANIEL TALLIFERO'S CAP

On the morning of the November 21, 1872, a man screamed "Murder!" near the officers' quarters. Corporal Perry Davis was ordered by his sergeant to go arrest the man responsible. Davis found Hamilton Jones doing the yelling. It was learned, upon questioning Jones, that Charles Southerner had attacked him with his fists and a hatchet. Jones yelled to draw attention to his plight, only to find himself arrested.[1] When a few months earlier Annie Williams had screamed for help using the same call, "Murder!," the guard came to her aid. Why on that fall morning was a man who was doing the same thing, but near the officers' quarters, quickly quieted and arrested, as if *he* were committing an offense? What did the sergeant think was happening that morning when he heard the yell of "Murder"? Did he hear a call for help or an accusation?

Later that day, Colonel Andrews requested a coffin for Corporal Daniel Tallifero. Tallifero was shot through the head in the early morning on the back porch of Lieutenant Kendall's quarters. This chapter is about the last months of Tallifero's life and the remarkable and contradictory circumstances surrounding his highly publicized death.

The reader has hopefully come to realize that the events that took place at Fort Davis cannot be understood simply through a perusal of post records but that it must be understood as a locus where complex entangled personal histories, experiences, and relationships that predate and ultimately postdate the fort manifested in the everyday embodied lives of the soldiers and civilians living there. This is a work of history that considers the traces of the past collectively, as an assemblage larger than any single set of documents. Multiple temporalities are at play in any historical moment, be they an individual actor's understandings of past, present, and future or insights accessible to the researcher who seeks to understand a set of people in the longer contexts of their lives.

To understand the early hours of November 21, 1872, requires us to bring together a wide range of people, things, and entanglements that have been considered previously and to further examine connections not previously explored. Historians who have discussed this incident have looked at the small number of things—documents—directly related to the case. When the circumstances of Tallifero's death are seen through an archaeological gaze, a gaze that looks at all the assembled traces of post life from that time, a tear in the web of what was normal is rendered visible—procedures ignored, behaviors changed, evidence and narratives managed. Tallifero's death allows us to autopsy the racialized assemblage that came together to present him as a depraved monster, someone clearly less than human.

Assembling the Troops

May 1872 was a time of transition at Fort Davis. Commanding Officer William Shafter handed the post to George L. Andrews. The last of the Twenty-Fourth Infantry companies left the post. Fort Davis would host only one company of cavalry (Company I of the Ninth), which had arrived in July 1871, and four more companies of the Twenty-Fifth Infantry. Company G, Twenty-Fifth, which arrived in July 1870, would be joined by Company E in May. Company C would briefly stay at the post from May to August, and Company D, Twenty-Fifth arrived in mid-November.

For Colonel Andrews, service with the Twenty-Fifth in west Texas was still new. Andrews had served in the Civil War, attaining the rank of lieutenant colonel in 1864. He served as the superintendent of regimental recruiting service in 1865–1866 and commanded Camp Cook and Fort Shaw, Montana. The reorganization of the military in 1869 left him unassigned. He served as the superintendent of Indian affairs for Arizona territory. He was assigned to the Twenty-Fifth Infantry in January 1870 and promoted to the colonelcy on January 21, 1871, at which point he joined his regiment, commanding Fort Clark.[2] Here he would have first come to know Cyrus Gray, Edwin Stivers, and H. B. Quimby, men he would work closely with at Fort Davis. Andrews arrived at Fort Davis with men from the Twenty-Fifth Infantry he knew and trusted. As he settled into the post, he worked to develop patronage relationships with men already stationed there.

Once at Fort Davis, Andrews became consumed with creating an orderly transfer of command. With Stivers and Quimby, he began to inventory and analyze post materials Quantities of medicinal alcohol (identical in every way to non-medicinal alcohol) were missing from the post hospital, ultimately contributing to Andrews's fixation on misplaced spelling and reading books purchased by Chaplain Gonzales. While the books were found safely in Adjutant Cyrus Gray's possession, the missing alcohol, after several accusations against Dr. Weisel, was found to have been stolen by a hospital steward.[3]

Separately, weapons were missing from Company I, Ninth Cavalry. Missing guns were a feature of post life, with carbines and other weapons stolen from barracks by civilians, former soldiers, or soldiers.[4] The guns in question disappeared under Shafter's command. In tracing Company I's problems with weapon theft, I came upon across a familiar name: Sergeant John Hewey. Hewey was named in a December 1871 letter from Shafter to the commanding officer at Fort Bliss explaining that sergeant Hewey would be escorting a prisoner to that post. The man in question was a citizen named Harris who was believed to have stolen carbines from Fort Davis. Hewey was the principle witness against the accused who was to be tried in a district court.[5] Shafter acknowledged that the theft of arms had been carried out "to a considerable extent and with complete impunity so far."[6] On April 4, Harris escaped from custody, and Shafter wrote to explain the situation to the assistant attorney general of Texas:

> On the 9th of November 1871 a Carbine was stolen from the Quarters
> of Company I Ninth Cavalry. On the 11th of the same month Sergt John
> Hewey of Company I of the Cav reported to me that John H. Harris had
> been seen with the Carbine and that he was then in a House a short distance
> from the post. I had him arrested and brought in with the Carbine which
> was fully identified by the number which was recorded in the Ordnance
> Book of the Company I Ninth Cavalry. Harris when questioned as to how
> he came in possession of the carbine stated that it had been sent him by a
> Soldier to sell and that he knew it was stolen at the time he received it.[7]

Hewey's presence as both informant and travel companion to the prisoner draws attention to him, particularly since Company I, Ninth Cavalry, seems to have had ongoing problems with arms disappearing while he was sergeant. General Order No. 58, issued May 2, 1872, called for a board of survey "to examine and to fix responsibility for the loss of 2 spencer carbines and 3 Remington Pistols, the property of the US and for which Captain Frank Bennett Ninth Cavalry is responsible."[8] The ordinance survey for Company I, Ninth Cavalry, was forwarded to the chief ordinance officer of the Department Texas that same day.[9]

Shafter soon left Fort Davis and Company I, Ninth Cavalry, behind, but questions surrounding the ordinance inventory of Company I remained for Andrews to answer. In June, the captain of ordinance of the Department returned Company I's inventory, noting that "attention is accorded to the discrepancy between the dates named in the affidavit marked I and D which refer to the loss of one Remington pistol in the possession of Private Tallifero."[10] Andrews sent a tart reply, condemning the actions of two privates who failed to store the carbines in the place designated by the company command, claiming that they were following the orders of an unnamed sergeant.[11] I can find no explanation of the fate of Tallifero's missing revolver.

A survey of company ordnance inventories is revealing. Company I, Ninth Cavalry, did not complete their March 1872 inventory until May 18. They reported eighty-nine Spencer carbines (.50 caliber), eighty-six percussion cap Remington revolvers (.44 caliber), and eighty-four light cavalry swords. The June 30 inventory listed significantly fewer weapons: sixty-nine Spencer carbines, eighty Remington revolvers, and the same number of cavalry swords, a loss of twenty-six guns total. In the September inventory, the Spencer carbines had been replaced with eighty sharp rifles (.50 caliber).[12] Whatever was happening in Company I, a number of weapons were no longer in the company, and at least some of those were lost to theft.

By the time Andrews was installed as commanding officer at Fort Davis, Hewey was fresh off a ten-day leave to visit his parents in New Orleans after escorting prisoners to the Baton Rouge penitentiary.[13] Hewey somehow ingratiated himself to Andrews, who not only took his side when confronted with conflicting testimony between an NCO and two privates, but also cosigned a letter asking for a mitigated sentence after Hewey's August court-martial. Likewise, Tallifero's lost revolver did not affect him; he was promoted to corporal in late May 1872 under Colonel Andrews's command.

Tallifero was twenty-five years old in 1872, one of the older men in his company. He was born in Fairfax, Virginia. He had enlisted in Washington,

DC, where he was a laborer, for a five-year term of enlistment in October 1869. At five feet six, Tallifero was hardly a tall man, but he was tall enough to join the cavalry and taller than many soldiers. Before coming to Fort Davis in June 1871, he had served at Fort Quitman. Sitting directly on the Mexican border, the post offered many temptations for soldiers serving there, and the courts-martial from 1869 to 1871 include murder, brawls, whoring, jumping the border regularly, and lots of intoxication.

Hewey and Tallifero are notable as two men who avoided general court-martial while at Quitman. While Hewey shows up with great frequency in the records of Fort Davis, Tallifero, like most soldiers quietly doing their jobs, spent his first year at post with no mention. In the months before his death, he becomes archivally visible, with the loss of his revolver, his promotion, being named in late July for escort duty, and finally, for serving as a witness for the defense in Sergeant Hewey's court-martial.

Based on his choices of Cyrus Gray and H. B. Quimby, men he has previously served with, as adjutant and post quartermaster, Andrews was a man who liked to keep a loyal staff near him. We have evidence that Andrews used officers to report on other officers. Kendall expressed outrage during his August 1872 court-martial that Gray reported a private conversation between them to Colonel Andrews, a conversation the prosecution attempted to weaponize against Kendall. Andrews's actions suggest that he was grooming Hewey and Tallifero for patronage relationships. Since they lived in quarters with the enlisted men, NCOs had greater access than commissioned officers to the goings-on in the barracks. Men who had been personally promoted by the colonel, like Tallifero, or who protected by him, possibly like Hewey and Tallifero both, would potentially feel indebted to their benefactor.

THE SUMMER OF 1872

Andrews would need his allies. The summer of 1872 would prove a chaotic one (see tables 7.1; 7.2). Dysentery would reemerge as a health threat on the post, killing seven men between the end of May and October. The resurgence of dysentery, an ailment that killed so many men at Fort Davis in 1867 and 1868, corresponded to the departure of Dr. Weisel in May 1872. The doctor was apparently not making idle boasts when he argued that his interventions in the police of the fort had eliminated the disease.[14] Deaths from sickness were interspersed with violent ones. On July 14, William Donaldson, after being insultingly compared to a horse, started a day-long confrontation in the neighborhoods surrounding the fort, culminating in the death of Old Man Cotton (chapter 1).

Shortly after Cotton's death, Andrews learned of civil unrest near Chihuahua, Mexico. Refugees were flocking to Presidio Del Norte. The colonel kept troops from Company C, Twenty-Fifth Infantry, stationed in Del Norte.[15] On July 25, Andrews commanded troops at Del Norte to disarm any one attempting to enter US territory from Mexico.[16] Five days later, Andrews called for "Quartermaster Sergeant Albert Fowler, Corporal Daniel Tallifero and 9 privates CO I report to Post Adjutant for Special Instructions. The detachment will be mounted, armed, and provided 10 days rations."[17] Tallifero and men from Company I, Ninth Cavalry traveled with Colonel Andrews and officers Gray and Sanborn as their escort. Since no Ninth Cavalry officers were involved in the patrol, Tallifero would have reported directly to Andrews as his commanding officer. Andrews knew and decided to trust this freshly minted corporal. The five hundred or so Mexican refugees in Del Norte were found to offer no threat of danger, and Andrews recalled troops to Fort Davis.[18]

Upon Andrews's return to post, Chaplain Barr's alcoholism could no longer be tolerated, and he was arrested on August 8. The following night, August 9, Annie Williams screamed "Murder!" from her tent and accused Martin Pedee of attempted rape. The visit of Captain Albert Morrow to post on the August 15 and the resulting party led to the arrest of Frederick Kendall for being "crazy drunk." On August 17, Kendall was put into arrest, a sentence to be served in his quarters. Kendell's arrest put his company in a difficult situation. Captain David Schooley's ongoing leave left Kendall commanding Company E. Schooley returned on August 18 and returned to command of his company on the August 19.[19]

Whatever rest and relaxation poor David Schooley may have enjoyed during his three months away must have been greatly diminished by what he faced on his return. A soldier he had worked with and admired since 1867 was accused of attempted rape by the wife of another of his NCOs, and his former housemate, a lieutenant he had served with since they were in the Fortieth Infantry together, was under house arrest and awaiting court-martial. And what of First Sergeant John Sample? Kendall openly accused Sample of being forced to testify against him during his court-martial, and Sample's fellow NCOs were equally angry with him. Certainly, some of their hostility could be attributed to disapproval of whatever relationship Sample had with Martin Pedee. But

TABLE 7.1. *Officers on Post, May 31–November 1872*

NAME, RANK, COMPANY, AND REGIMENT	MAY 1872	JUNE 1872	JULY 1872	AUGUST 1872	SEPTEMBER 1872	OCTOBER 1872	NOVEMBER 1872
George Andrews, lieutenant colonel, Twenty-Fifth Infantry, commanding post	X	X	Detached service	Commanding, returned August 8	X	X	
C. L. De Graw, USA, captain and assistant surgeon							X
Cyrus Gray, first lieutenant, Twenty-Fifth Infantry, post adjutant	X	X	Escort to commanding officer	Returned August 8	X	X	X
H. B. Quimby, first lieutenant, regimental quartermaster sergeant	X	X	X	X	Since September 6, thirty-seven days leave	On leave	X
D.E. Barr, chaplain, Twenty-Fifth Infantry	X	X	X	In arrest since August 8	resigned	-	-
D. D. Vanvabzah, captain, Company D, Twenty-Fifth Infantry							Arrived November*
James H. Patterson captain, Company G, Twenty-Fifth Infantry	X	X	Escort to CO	Returned August 8	X	X	X
Frank T. Bennett, captain, Company I, Ninth Cavalry	X	X	Commanding post	Relieved of temporary command August 8	X	X	X

Officer							
Jacob Paulus, first lieutenant, Company C, Twenty-Fifth Infantry	x	x	Company transferred	–	–	–	–
David Schooley, captain, Company E, Twenty-Fifth Infantry	On leave	On leave	On leave	Returned August 19	x	x	x
Frederick Kendall, first lieutenant, Company E, Twenty-Fifth Infantry	x	x	x	Relieved of company command August 19	In arrest since September 13	Released from arrest October 20	Sent on road construction November 11, called back November 21
Washington Sanborn, first lieutenant, Company G, Twenty-Fifth Infantry	x	x	Escort to commanding officer	Returned August 8	x	x	x
W. W. Tyler, first lieutenant, Company I, Ninth Cavalry	x	x	x	sick	Sick leave since September 8	Sick leave	Sick leave
Henry D. Landon, second lieutenant, Company E, Twenty-Fifth Infantry					Assigned to unit, on three months graduation leave	Absent without leave, October 1–10	x
Wallace Tear, second lieutenant, Company G, Twenty-Fifth Infantry	x	x	x	Commanding recruits	x	x	x
J. M. McDonald, second lieutenant, Company I, Ninth Cavalry	x	x	x	x	x	x	x
Thomas Landers, acting assistant surgeon	x	x	x	x	x	x	x

TABLE 7.2. *Calendar of Events, May–November 1872*

DATE	NOTABLE HAPPENING(S)
May 26	Companies C and E, Twenty-Fifth Infantry, arrive, Colonel George Andrews takes command.
July 14	William Davidson shoot and kills Old Man Cotton.
July 31	Corporal Daniel Tallifero escorts Colonel Andrews, Captain Patterson, and Lieutenants Sanborn and Gray to Del Norte to observe refugees at Mexican border.
August 8	Colonel Andrews and escort return to Fort Davis. Chaplin Barr put in arrest.
August 9	Martin Pedee accused of attempted rape by Annie Williams.
August 11	Corporal Griffin Collins sent to stage duty at El Muerto Station with Privates William Smith, William Johnson, and Moses Stewart.
August 15	Chaplin Barr's resignation accepted by Colonel Andrews. Captain Albert Morrow visits post, officers convene in sutler's for drinks, Frederick Kendall spends the night there after celebrating too much. Lieutenant Cyrus Grey assigns Kendall to be officer of the day for the August 16.
August 16	Virginia Kendall reports her husband sick. Lieutenant Kendall shows up for roll call, heads back to quarters to sleep.
August 17	Lieutenant Kendall placed in arrest.
August 18	Captain David Schooley returns from leave.
August 19	Lieutenant Kendall removed from command of Company E, Twenty-Fifth Infantry.
August 20	Lieutenant Kendall leaves arrest to attend court-martial.
August 21	Privates William Johnson and William Smith decide to chase a herd of deer at El Muerto and get hopelessly lost. Sergeant John Hewey shoots at Felix Johnson and Annie Carter.
August 26	Chaplain Barr leaves Fort Davis for San Antonio.
August 27	Sergeant Hewey's court-martial takes place
August 30	Privates William Johnson and William Smith are returned by stage to Fort Davis in a "wretched condition."
September 3	Lieutenant W. W. Tyler goes on sick leave.
September 13	Lieutenant Kendall taken off of court martial duty and back into arrest.

September 16	Lieutenant Kendall's court-martial convenes. Sergeant Anthony Jackson and First Sergeant John Sample get in an argument over what orders were given to one Private Solomon Moore, who is arrested for being absent from duty.
September 19	Solomon Moore is court-martialed, Jackson and Sample dispute one another's testimony.
October 1	Martin Pedee court-martial for attempted rape begins.
October 11	Assistant adjutant Department of Texas approves finding of Pedee trial but mitigates sentence, sends letter to Fort Davis.
October 19	Sergeant John Sample misses roll call. Schooley reports him sick on the nineteenth, puts him on sick book for twentieth.
October 20	Lieutenant Kendall released from arrest and returned to duty.
November 11	Lieutenant Kendall, Sergeants Anthony Jackson, Edward McKenzie, John Williams, Griffin Collins, and twenty-four privates of Company E, Twenty-Fifth Infantry, including James Wilson, sent to do road work in Limpia Canyon until November 30.
November 20	Corporal Daniel Tallifero is recorded in burial register under this date.
November 21	Corporal Daniel Tallifero shot dead. Second Lieutenant Harry Reade sent to retrieve Kendall from Limpia Canyon. Colonel Andrews writes letter explaining Tallifero shooting and contesting Pedee sentence mitigation to the assistant adjutant general, Department of Texas. Lieutenant Edwin Stivers writes a letter to New York with this date. Hamilton Jones is arrested for yelling "Murder!" at officers' row.

there could be another, more timely explanation—they could have known that he was lying under oath about Kendall.

Left without the support of his absent captain and pitted between a desire to salvage his own accomplished career and his concern for his company-mate and friend, Sample must have felt that his world was collapsing. While we cannot know Sample's thoughts and feelings, there is some evidence regarding how he may have found himself with no choice but to testify against his company lieutenant. Within the post, close to Colonel Andrews, was an officer who had known John Sample longer than anyone else: First Lieutenant H. B. Quimby, post quartermaster. Quimby had served during the Civil War as second lieutenant for the Company I, 108th USCI, the same regiment and company as Sample.[20] If there was anyone outside of his company who would be in a position to provide a long-term perspective on John Sample's character strengths and vulnerabilities to the colonel, it was Quimby. It is not hard to imagine Sample's being pressured to testify against Kendall once Kendall made the mistake of drinking too heavily and Mrs. Williams made her fateful accusation.

Soon, two NCOs with whom Andrews had nurtured alliances would also become entangled in a court-martial case. Just two days after David Schooley's return, John Hewey was arrested for shooting at Felix Johnson and Annie Carter by the blacksmith's shop, and two soldiers were reported to have deserted their posts at the El Muerto stage station.

Schooley's return may have solved Company E's command problems caused by Kendall's arrest but not the problem of his court-martial service. Kendall was named as a member of a general court-martial called at Fort Davis. On August 20, Andrews wrote to the assistant adjutant of Texas stating that to enable the court-martial, Kendall must be released from arrest. On September 3, Standard Orders arrived removing Kendall from court-martial duty and replacing him with Schooley. The timing of the orders meant that Kendall served on the Hewey trial, which was held on August 27, less than a week after the alleged shooting incident, but not Martin Pedee's, which did not begin until September 19, five weeks after the first accusations.

Sergeant Hewey's court-martial has already been considered at length, but it is worth briefly returning to several aspects of the case. First, Kendall's agreement to sign the letter requesting clemency was undertaken while Kendall himself was awaiting court-martial and probably hoping for whatever good graces he could muster with his commanding officer. Second, Tallifero's willingness to steadfastly testify that Hewey held a stick, not a revolver, may have been an act of self-preservation as much as protection of a senior NCO. Recall that Hewey innocently asserted that he no longer had a gun, having relinquished it "some time ago." Was the stick Hewey wielded that night Tallifero's unaccounted for and missing revolver?[21] No wonder Tallifero clearly remembered seeing a stick in his sergeant's hand. The decision of the officers on the court-martial to ask for a mitigation of the sentence demonstrates that they had no problems with the testimony of the defense witnesses, or at least that they tacitly approved the evidence of their demonstrated manly support for their NCO.

Kendall's court-martial took place on September 16, three days before Pedee's began. Sample testified against his first lieutenant and endured the testimony of his fellow NCOs calling him a liar and a man of poor reputation. But when Pedee's court-martial ended, he had not been called as a witness, nor had the uncomfortable question "Why did you know it was Martin Pedee in John Sample's quarters?" been answered, a silence clearly heard today.

As October turned to November, the post prepared for the arrival of Company D, Twenty-Fifth Infantry, and Lieutenant Kendall, acquitted and returned to duty, was ordered with twenty-eight men to undertake road repairs away from the post:

> Lt. Kendall, Serg Anthony Jackson, Corporals Edward Mc Kenzie, John Williams and Griffin Collins and twenty-four privates Company E 25th, including James Wilson on extra duty in the Quarter Master's will proceed to a point on the road running through the Limpia Canyon and make such repairs and changes in the road as may be necessary. Lt. Kendall will report to Post Command for instructions with date of return Nov. 30, 1872.[22]

They were told to pack one wall and eight common tents, tools, fuses and blasting powder.[23]

Perhaps some of the names listed sound familiar. Corporal Edward McKenzie, despite being called by the prosecution, provided testimony in Pedee's trial that suggested he did not believe Annie Williams's accusation. John Williams was married to Annie, Pedee's accuser. James Wilson was named by Henry Sappho as the person who heard him yell that Pedee was asleep in Sample's room and could not have committed the attack. Griffin Collins was also one of the men who asserted that Sample was dishonest, as did Anthony Jackson. Perhaps as the men made the northward march to Limpia Canyon, they grumbled among themselves, debating whether this work detail was retribution against them for recent events. Three of the men left wives back at the garrison—McKenzie, Williams, and Kendall—at a time when Colonel Andrews suggested to the assistant adjutant of Texas that it was cruel to send married men on details away from their fearful wives (chapter 2).

Company D arrived the day after the detail from Company E left the post. Their arrival placed more strain on the officers' quarters than on the barracks, where being overcrowded and under-provisioned was a fact of life. Once again, the post was filled with new people, things to be unpacked, and the general chaos accompanying new troops' arrival. For Andrews, the incoming officers included more people he served with at Fort Clark. For officers' wives and families, the arrival of Company D meant the addition of another family with young children, another mother to be a potential friend and source of support. Mrs. Gray and Mrs. Stivers would have already known one another from Fort Clark, but there is no evidence that Mrs. Kendall and Mrs. Stivers had ever met before. That would soon change.

Excavating Tallifero's Death

And now we have arrived at a moment I have dreaded. It is time for Daniel Tallifero to die. There is no way to tell it gently—he died from a bullet to the head. Even so long after he died, I find his death unsettling, not only for the violence of the act but for the violence of the *remembering* of his death, as recorded in the archive and in historians' retellings. No one has ever defended Tallifero or questioned the circumstances of his demise.[24] The representation of historical violence against Black bodies is often a voyeuristic reanimation of that violence in the present, and Tallifero's death is an example of such an archival violence. He is killed again and again in history books, a sacrifice to the stereotype of the Black rapist.[25] As a white woman writing in the twenty-first century about nineteenth-century Black men, I am very concerned about how I represent these men's lives, and want to proceed in a manner that respects and preserves their dignity. Just as it was necessary to share some indignities endured by John Sample, in Tallifero's case, certain descriptions cannot be avoided. I include them only to build my counternarrative surrounding his death.

Archaeology is foremost the study of actions. People do things and leave traces. They set up campfires, they clean stoves, they buy dishes (and break them), they sweep their yards, they cook dinner, they throw out their trash. These are things people do that we can study from the traces of those actions. Documents are merely products of things people do—filing taxes, buying houses, enlisting in the army, testifying in a court-martial, reporting purchases, writing letters to loved ones. As an archaeologist, I find myself thinking as much about why words were committed to paper as about the words put on that paper. This version of Fort Davis's past has been told by someone who studies traces of actions, and it explains how I have come to understand Daniel Tallifero's death very differently from other historians, holistically drawing on the assemblage of the material traces—artifacts, documents, bodies, technologies, landscapes—that allow us to understand a past actor's movements.

Tallifero's case drew my attention for three reasons. Two are historical, one is modern, but all three are painfully relevant to our contemporary world. The first two are related explicitly to the necropolitical power of the state invested in the military. This case underscores the general lack of attention paid to investigating soldiers' violent deaths when white civilians were potentially involved. Post records include the deaths of several men "at the hands of persons unknown."[26] This failure to pursue the killers of Black soldiers is another space through which necropolitical power was enacted. Secondly, as I will discuss, the accounting of the case is odd, for lack of a better term. The corporal's actions as described simply do not make sense. The response of officers to the incident also does not match responses of these same officers in other similar circumstances. This raises for me, when combined with further complications raised by the broader material and archival record, the possibility that the corporal died under circumstances other than those reported.

The third reason the case drew my attention had to do with the racial and cultural upheaval in which we in twenty-first-century America are now so enmeshed. The seemingly endless incidents of Black men and women dying at the hands of law enforcement and vigilantes and the media accounts of those horrific injustices colored the entire period of my work on this research project, and I could not help but wonder if our understanding of the processes and structures that denied an accounting of Daniel Tallifero's death in the past could somehow be used to dissemble these structures in the present.

As I will explain, when the assemblage of actions, or the things people did, involving the case are considered as a whole, incongruities emerge. In particular, the actions undertaken by Colonel Andrews and Lieutenant Stivers suggest a cover up; yet their descriptions of the event are primary sources used by historians reporting the event. Instead, evidence suggests that Tallifero was killed by another soldier, most likely a commissioned officer. This represents the ultimate in the state's necropolitical power.

Finally, there is a rhetorical question for us to consider: How does the failure of historians to pursue answers about the deaths of Black men in the past naturalize the ongoing and appalling rates of state-authorized murder by unpunished police officers, through unsolved homicides, and by the unequal application of the death penalty? In these pages, I have attempted to do what no other historian has done: to gather those scant details about Daniel Tallifero's life. His life mattered. One hundred and fifty years later, I sincerely believe that the circumstances of Daniel Tallifero's death still matter, too.

In the early morning hours of November 21, Corporal Daniel Tallifero was shot dead on the back porch of Lieutenant Kendall's quarters. Kendall was away from his quarters on a road-construction detail. Virginia Kendall was at home with their three children. Shortly following this event, Colonel Andrews sat down to write a letter to the assistant adjutant general of Texas. The letter had three parts: the first part described Tallifero's death; the second (discussed in chapter 2) described unsubstantiated accounts of multiple attempts at assault by Black soldiers across Texas and the fear of leaving their wives alone experienced by soldiers detailed away from post; and the third demanded that the mitigated sentence for Pedee be rethought and his original sentence reinstated.

Let us look now at the first part of the letter, Andrews's description of Tallifero's death:

> Between one and two o'clock this morning Corporal Daniel Talliferro Company I 9th cavalry while attempting to force an entrance into the sleeping apartment of the wife of 1st Lieutenant F. A Kendall 25th infantry was shot by Mrs. Kendall and instantly killed. Lieut. Kendall is absent from the post on detached service and during his absence, a young lady, the daughter of one of my officers, has been the companion of Mrs. Kendall at night.
>
> It appears the ladies retired at the usual hour and were awakened by the sound of breaking glass. Mrs. Kendall arose and reaching over her sleeping children raised the window curtain and discovered a man at the window. She ordered him away and threatened to shoot him if he did not go. To this order he gave no heed but continued leisurely to remove the pieces of broken glass from the sash and when he got ready he thrust his head through the opening (the sash was nailed down) when Mrs. Kendall fired the ball taking effect on the top of the man's head the blood shooting into the room, his cap also falling in the room while the man fell back from the window on the porch dead, this in brief are the circumstances.[27]

But Colonel Andrews was not the only person writing that day (or at least dating his correspondence that day). The recently arrived Lieutenant Edwin Stivers of Company D, Twenty-Fifth Infantry, also wrote a letter. His letter seems to have addressed some of the strange or problematic descriptions in Andrews's account. His was sent to the *New York Herald*, one of the best-selling newspapers of the day. It was a paper that the post subscribed to by 1881 and was likely one of the many newspapers subscribed to by the post library in 1872. Stivers's letter would appear in the post on December 8, 1872. It would be republished in its entirety in the *Chicago Tribune* and abstracted and retold in dozens of national newspapers between December 1872 and January 1873:

A Plucky Woman.
To the Editor of the Herald:
Four times within as many months effort have been made by some Black-hearted rascals at this post to effect an entrance into the sleeping apartments of the families of the officers of the garrison during the absence of the officers on their several duties.

A diabolical attempt was but a few nights ago made upon the family of one of the civilian employees of the government at the post. A feeling of dread apprehension and insecurity has for some time prevailed among the officers and their families, except a few who pooh-poohed and said that it was all imagination, but by the heroism of Mrs. Kendall, wife of First Lieutenant F. A. Kendall, Twenty-fifth infantry, one of the devils at last has learned that there is a God in Israel, and the doubters are silenced.

About two o'clock this morning Mrs. Kendall, whose husband is temporarily absent on duty, was awakened by a noise as of someone breaking in the sash of a window opening from her sleeping apartment upon the porch in the rear. She promptly awoke her companion, a young lady, and daughter of one of the officers of the garrison, and asked in a loud voice, "Who's there?" Receiving no reply, the plucky little lady took her revolver and listened. Bits of broken glass continued falling on the floor, convincing her that the fiend was persisting in his efforts to enter the room, and then, with the consciousness that on her depended the safety of herself and companion from a fate worse than death, and doubtless, their lives and those of her three little children, she called several times, "Who's there?" and receiving no reply, she stepped to the window, and aiming over the bed occupied by her little ones, at the head just being thrust through the broken sash, fired. She heard instantly after the fall of a heavy body on the porch and a stifled groan.

Being awakened by the shot, I, in company with others, hurried to the spot and soon a squad of the guard were on hand with preparations for removing the carcass. An examination proved him to be Corporal Talliferro, a hideous negro belonging to Company I, Ninth United States cavalry, one of the companies composing this garrison.

The bullet had penetrated the skull and must have killed him instantly. With assured esteem, yours,

E. J. S. First lieutenant Twenty-Fifth United States Infantry.[28]

The reader must see the similarities in the outlines of the two stories. Stivers's version has made several improvements on Andrews's and could be read as a second draft of the original. First, Andrews's description of the man slowly removing pieces of glass from the window because the sash was nailed shut is ungainly. Why would a man being threatened with being shot calmly remove sherds of glass methodically so he could insert his head through the window? It struck me as implausible when I first read it, and now, after many readings, that sense has only grown stronger. Stivers's version smooths the narrative by having the sash broken. Stivers avoids mention of the blood, and importantly, he loses Tallifero's cap from the narrative. Stivers's account makes it clear that the purity of the young women and children is at stake and uses appropriately melodramatic language.

That Stivers would write to newspapers about the event is odd; he is not an officer in the company where Tallifero served, nor is he in the same company as Kendall. He did not hold a post-wide position of authority that would obligate him to report this incident. He is also not the husband of the menaced woman. Yet he may have had a personal connection to the case. Both letters note the presence of a young lady, the daughter of an officer who was also at the Kendall's, but neither names her. Stivers had a fourteen-year old daughter, the only officer's child on base old enough to be referred to as a "young lady" and be a companion to Mrs. Kendall during her husband's absence. Stivers's involvement makes more sense from this perspective. Still, his decision to write to a major newspaper and report this event, naming Mrs. Kendall and Lieutenant Kendall while protecting the identity of his daughter and providing just enough of his own identity to be legible to officers familiar with the Twenty-Fifth Infantry, is interesting. If his account proves embarrassing, none of the embarrassment is his family's. And recall: there is no evidence that Kendall and Stivers had any personal connection; they had not yet even overlapped physically at Fort Davis.

How does Andrews's letter compare with others he wrote? Writing on July 20, 1872, Andrews informed Augur about the Cotton case:

> Enclosed do find proceedings of a board of Officers convened by orders of these headquarters to investigate a shooting affair in the vicinity of the post on the 14th last resulting in the death of one Cotton. William Donaldson, who appears to have been the principle actor is now confined in the guard house of this post and George Fitzsimons is to be obtained at any time. The affidavits attached to the proceedings are all original documents as is also the "ante-mortem" statement signed by W. S. Cotton. The pistols with which the shooting was done are in my possession. I respectfully request you will take such action as may be necessary on the case and have the state police take the parties into custody."[29]

Note that it was Andrews, freshly arrived on post, who decided to make an investigation of the case, calling for an inquest, for which a detailed transcript of multiple interviews was preserved, interviews that included the accused. Likewise, he seized the weapons involved. The contrast between the Cotton case and the Tallifero affair is quite striking. No one was interviewed, there was no inquest or formal investigation, and there was neither an autopsy nor an examination of the weapon involved.

One could argue that it would be unseemly to submit Mrs. Kendall and her unnamed companion to the terrible strain of reliving the events of the previous night. This would, of course, be keeping with the ideas of femininity that circulated at the time. Yet we see the victims testifying in the two previously described courts-martial involving rape accusations at Fort Davis. Demetria Dominguez testified about Joseph Franklin's alleged assault in 1868, and Annie Williams testified about her attack during Andrews's command. Could race have been a factor? The other two women were described in census records as people of color. Yet recall that in his letter to Augur, Andrews described Mrs. Williams as a white woman (chapter 2). Why is there recorded testimony of Williams's complaint but none for Mrs. Kendall? Still, even if one wanted to sincerely protect Mrs. Kendall's and Miss Stivers' delicate sensitivities, that would not preclude questioning other people—the men who found the body, his superior officers, the men who bunked with him. If Andrews was truly concerned about a rapist or rapists running loose on the base, why not do a thorough investigation to root them out? Would it not have been appropriate to determine whether the corporal was responsible for the alleged string of attacks, including possibly the one against Mrs. Williams? Why was there no inquest? Why the continued obsession with Pedee?

For me, these departures from normal practice—the failure to call for an investigation and the decision of an officer to write to the press detailing this event—combined with the oddness of the account led me to have serious doubts about what was said in these two letters. Historians have generally cited only Colonel Andrews's letter to Augur when referencing the case, and they have generally avoided citing the most outlandish parts. As far as I have seen, no one else has found the Stivers letter, and nor has anyone questioned the veracity of Andrews's account, although Adams, in his study, at least raises the possibility that Tallifero's motive was burglary.[30]

The case has troubled me since I first read Andrews's letter, and the more I pursued additional information, the more disturbed I became. I have questions I would have liked addressed in an inquest:

Given that Tallifero was on duty as corporal of the guard just a few weeks earlier during the midnight hour, a fact we know from the Hewey court-martial testimony, was he on guard duty at the time of the incident?

If Mrs. Kendall was loudly asking her potential assailant to go away, why did no one else hear her? Mrs. Williams was able to make herself heard across the parade ground.

Who was officer of the day? Who lived in the officers' quarters next door? With the changing residences typical of new troop influx, had the Kendalls recently moved quarters? The quarters were designed with two rooms separated by a central hallway with an entrance door in the front and back. Why did the companion, who was apparently also awakened, not run out the front door and get help? Or at least run out the front door and scream like Mrs. Williams?

Unfortunately, we have no witnesses to answer these questions, but we can further interrogate the rest of the record—again, from an archaeological perspective, looking at what people did and did not do. But most importantly, we can interrogate the record by considering the material traces available to us. My efforts are not intended to push a particular alternate theory, but rather to do what was not done at the time: investigate the death. After all, the man has been accused for 150 years of being a failed rapist, but that claim has never been submitted to any kind of inquiry.

Given the potentially questionable motives behind the words spoken about this case, we need to turn to the world of material things to evaluate the accounts provided. Things have their own nature, their own physicality that subjects the world around them (including humans) to their particular agency.[31] In Kendall's court-martial testimony, the ability of the thick tufts of grass on the parade ground to make soldiers trip and render their gait unsteady was discussed. The structure of percussion cap guns, which required them to have two distinct loading procedures, allowed men to engage in harmless displays of aggression. The variety of ceramic designs marketed to consumers allowed the men to choose wares that communicated particular stories about themselves and their ambitions. How might things implicated in the telling of this incident shed further light on what did or did not happen?

TALLIFERO'S BODY

Daniel's body was taken from the back porch of the Kendall's quarters, presumably to the hospital; C. S. De Graw, assistant post surgeon, who arrived days earlier from Fort Clark with Company D, examined the body. The surgeon's notes for November 1872 echo the narrative presented by Andrews and Stivers.

> No events transpired to make note of save one—on the night of the 20th about 2 o'clock am Corporal Talifera [*sic*] I Co 9 attempted a forcible entrance into the sleeping apartment of Mrs. Lt. Kendall, whose husband was absent at the time on duty. Mrs. Kendall warned the man from the window but he persisted in his efforts. Driven to desperation Mrs. Kendall seized a revolver and fired as the scoundrel had succeeded in getting his head through the break he had made in the window. She fired sending a bullet through his brain killing him instantly.[32]

When Tallifero's mother applied for a pension in 1873, the doctor's account of the body was extracted from hospital records. The summary suggests that the weapon involved was specifically a Colt revolver.

> The ball entered from about the vertex of the skull, passing downwards almost perpendicularly smacking the vasilar process of the occipital bone and lodging as nearly as could be determined, about opposite the last dorsal vertebra. The body, evidently from the course of the ball had been in a bending position. Owing to the want of proper facilities no "postmortem" was made. The course of the ball was determined by a probe improvised from heavy wire.[33]

It would be worth asking what facilities De Graw expected to conduct an autopsy. A bone saw would be used to open the top of the skull, thus allowing the removal of the brain to assert the actual trajectory of the ball and to recover it. Since gunshot wounds in the living too often required amputation, the surgical bone saws needed to undertake an amputation would have been available and would have been the same tools used in an autopsy. Granted, in 1872, the post hospital was a thrown-together jumble of rotting adobes from the first fort that held twelve patients. While sporting a surgery room, it was not a structure to inspire confidence.

Still, Dr. Weisel, who had left the post a mere six months previous, had performed autopsies in the same facilities. In the March 1871 accidental death of Private David Boyd, Weisel's autopsy was part of the inquest record. Likewise, when Private Anderson died, victim of an off-base shooting by parties unknown in October 1870, Weisel did an autopsy of the man, tracing the pathway of the bullet across his body cavity and into his ilium. In Merryweather's case, Weisel identified the deadly shot as having been made by an army pistol, based on recovery of the ball. By July 1873, when the hospital was still in desperate condition, De Graw decided he could perform autopsies at the post, investigating the fatal self-inflicted shooting of Private Frazier, Company E, Twenty-Fifth Infantry.[34]

Of course, in the case of Private David Boyd, the autopsy results were presented as part of an inquest; as noted, no similar investigation was called for in the Tallifero case. Perhaps De Graw, a recent addition to the post in 1872, did not understand that his work conditions would not improve, or perhaps the description of events provided by Colonel Andrews (De Graw's short account clearly echoes the accounts of Andrews and Stivers) made De Graw feel the hassle of an autopsy was not required.

I consulted a bioarchaeologist about the description of the bullet's trajectory through the corporal's skull. Based on the details of where the bullet lodged, it had to enter the skull not from the forehead, as one might imagine for a man with his head raised to look while entering through a window, but from the top of the head, with the face lowered.[35]

THE WEAPON

De Graw's account is the only one that identifies the gun as a Colt. Stivers described the weapon as a "revolver." Andrews merely mentioned Mrs. Kendall's threatening to shoot and then shooting, but he makes no reference to the

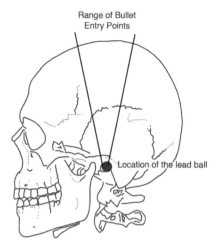

Range of Bullet
Entry Points

Location of the lead ball

FIGURE 7.1. Reconstruction of bullet trajectory through the skull, based on post surgeon's description of Daniel Tallifero's fatal wound. Illustration by the author.

weapon. Given that the shot was taken in November 1872, the gun in question was most likely a Colt Army 1860. The Colt Army model 1860 was the most widely produced and used handgun during the Civil War, with 200,500 produced between 1860 and 1873, at least 127,156 of which were purchased by the military. The gun weighed 2.74 pounds and had a barrel of either 7.5 or 8 inches in length.

The revolver was a percussion cap; therefore, in addition to loading each chamber with powder and ball, a copper percussion cap with mercury fulminate needed to be placed on each of the chamber nipples (figure 7.4). Soldiers typically used paper to wrap the ball and powder together in a cartridge for easy loading. Otherwise, loading required thirty grains of black powder, followed by wadding or grease (to prevent chain firing, when multiple chambers discharged at once, a common cause of soldiers shooting their fingers off) and the ball. The lead ball or bullet, .454 inches in diameter, was loaded into the chamber via the loading lever. To ensure a tight fit and proper firing, it was not unusual for a small ring of lead to be shaved off the ball or bullet during loading. Unloading was only possible by discharging the weapon. The Colt's second site was only visible when the gun hammer was cocked, a feature that had implications for taking aim.[36]

My knowledge of guns is limited, and I wondered about the circumstances under which Mrs. Kendall took her single shot. Civil War reenactments being popular, YouTube is an excellent source of information on how to load,

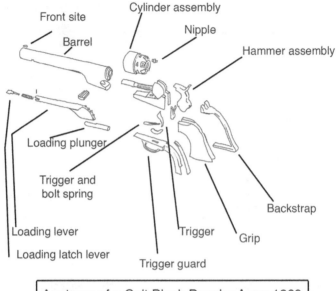

Front site
Cylinder assembly
Nipple
Barrel
Hammer assembly
Loading plunger
Trigger and
bolt spring
Backstrap
Loading lever
Trigger
Grip
Loading latch lever
Trigger guard

Anatomy of a Colt Black Powder Army 1860

FIGURE 7.2. The anatomy of a percussion-cap weapon (a Colt Army 1860 black powder revolver), after gunpartscorp.com/gun-manufacturer/colt/ black-po-revolvers/1860-army. Illustration by the author.

shoot, and care for black-powder weapons. These resources helped to refine my thinking.[37] I first considered the loading of the weapon. The full moon had occurred on November 15, so by the early morning of the twenty-first, it was waning but would still provide some light through the window, and was presumably how Mrs. Kendall would see the intruder—backlit by moonlight.[38]

None of the accounts refer to Mrs. Kendall's lighting a lamp or going to get a gun; it is just there, presumably close to hand in the bedroom—on a high shelf? In a drawer? She is not mentioned as loading the gun. Although it is not inconceivable that a loaded gun was left in the house ready to use, and leaving safety concerns aside, there were practical reasons for not leaving a weapon of this type loaded with black powder lying around. Black powder is hydrophilic and draws moisture, leaving the gun prone to rusting or misfire. Failure to care properly for one's firearm could lead to permanent damage of the weapon, making it significantly less likely to perform as expected. In one video on black powder, the owner of a replica Colt Army 1860 advised that the gun be given a preliminary clean in the field after firing, and once back home, that the gun be given a more thorough going over. Since this revolver would have been a personal weapon (the revolvers issued to the cavalry at this time were "Remingtons using percussion caps," with the infantry being issued rifles, not pistols), one might assume that the sidearm was cared for with greater attention than similar weapons used by troops.[39] So if the weapon was left loaded for Mrs. Kendall, there was some risk that if she needed to use it, it would not perform as needed under duress, and the only way to unload the weapon would be to later discharge it.

The Kendalls' three children were young, five years old and younger. Today, many people would balk at the idea of leaving a loaded gun accessible to small children, particularly in a time before safety locks. For the officers of the Twenty-Fifth Infantry and their families, the dangers of leaving loaded weapons around the house were too well known. The account of the Grays' having lost a child to a gun accident in the home had traveled through the Twenty-Fifth at the time of the child's death, and the officers would most likely have known of the tragic tale.

One way that this kind of gun could be left loaded with some modicum of safety would be to leave the first chamber of the revolver empty. If that were the status of the Kendall's weapon, Mrs. Kendall would have had to have shot twice, once with an empty click, the next with the deadly load. Given what we have learned of the common practice of snapping a cap, perhaps the best safety measure would be to leave a percussion cap alone on the first chamber. If a child got hold of the gun and discharged it, the noise would alert the adults before the next shot could be fired; or, in the case where one had to threaten an intruder with deadly force—the scenario that Stivers and Andrews described Mrs. Kendall facing—a warning cap could have been snapped as a way of scaring an intruder or attacker before using deadly force. These are questions that could have been addressed in an inquest. Instead, we are left wondering if Mrs. Kendall fumbled to load the gun in the dark, if the gun was left loaded, and what previous experience she had handling weapons. Despite the "stand and deliver" mythology popular among some Americans today, the reality of one lucky shot across a bed exacting such a perfect delivery on the head of Daniel Tallifero seems unlikely if one pauses to consider the realities of the technologies and circumstances involved.

Both accounts describe Mrs. Kendall as simultaneously going to the window and firing over the sleeping children just as the head enters the window. Is the bed propped against the window? Next to the window? This is unclear. But if she held the gun directly, or nearly directly, against the man's head, then the need to aim from distance was moot. Instead, we must imagine a most unlikely scenario: a distraught Mrs. Kendall placing a gun, with great determination, near the corporal's head for a kill at close range, while the corporal, ignoring her, went about moving glass from the window frame.

Does the damage sustained by the corporal from his mortal wound clarify the circumstances of his shooting? Abraham Lincoln was shot at close range with a .44 caliber bullet to the head by the same size ammunition that killed Tallifero, so it is useful to compare the resulting damage. The following excerpt is from Dr. J. J. Woodward's report on the autopsy of the president, on April 15, 1865:

> The ball entered through the occipital bone about one inch to the left of the median line and just above the left lateral sinus, which it opened. It then penetrated the dura matter, passed through the left posterior lobe of the cerebrum, entered the left lateral ventricle and lodged in the white matter of the cerebrum just above the anterior portion of the left corpus striatum, where it was found.
>
> The wound in the occipital bone was quite smooth, circular in shape, with beveled edges. The opening through the internal table being larger than that through the external table. The track of the ball was full of clotted blood and contained several little fragments of bone with small pieces of the ball near its external orifice.[40]

Like Lincoln, the ball that killed Tallifero stayed lodged in his head, with no exit wound. Also like Lincoln, Tallifero seems to have been killed at close range. Unlike Lincoln, whether Tallifero was assassinated is harder to determine.

THE QUARTERS

To understand the movements of people on the early morning of November 21, it would be useful to know where they resided on the post. We have considered before which troops lived where. Based on the best available information, in November 1872, Company I, Ninth Cavalry, occupied the southern dormitory of HB-20, while Company G, Twenty-Fifth Infantry, bunked in the northern dormitory. HB-21 was shared by Company E and D of the Twenty-Fifth, with Company E most likely in the northern dormitory, the side where the first sergeant quarters were, and Company D in the northern half of that building.[41]

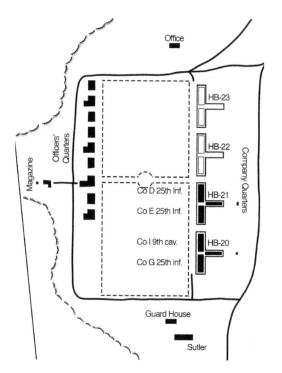

Office

HB-23

HB-22

Officers' Quarters

Magazine

Company Quarters

Co D 25th Inf.

Co E 25th Inf.

HB-21

Co I 9th cav.

HB-20

Co G 25th inf.

Guard House

Sutler

FIGURE 7.4. Officers' quarters as they appear today. Photograph by Katrina Eichner.

Today, if visiting the national historic site, one sees a tidy row of officer's houses situated on the western edge of the parade ground, but not all of these buildings existed in 1872. While the construction of officer's quarters was prioritized over the construction of enlisted men's in the 1860s and 70s, the same funding and labor issues that plagued the construction of enlisted men's housing effected commissioned officers as well.

By November 1872, ten buildings were completed on officer's row: the commanding officer's quarters (HB-7), located across from the flag pole; three captain's quarters (HB-5, HB-9, and HB-12); and six lieutenants' quarters (HB-4, HB-6, HB-8, HB-10 and HB-13).[42] Captains' houses featured three rooms, lieutenants' quarters two. At times when the post was crowded, officers' families reportedly had to double up. When men were single, this was much of a hardship, but for lieutenants with wives and children, this could mean very cramped quarters.

The May 1872 post returns lists eleven officers plus the chaplain and an assistant surgeon (table 7.1). The chapel contained living quarters, and presumably the assistant surgeon could occupy quarters in the hospital, but based on documents, he could occupy officer quarters. This means that there was at least one more officer, if not two more, than available houses. Captain David Schooley was on leave when his company arrived, and he is not included in these counts, but based on rank, he was eligible to demand a captain's house. In November, with the arrival of Company D, Twenty-Fifth Infantry, and H. H. Landon, the freshly graduated second lieutenant in Company E, fifteen men (the new post surgeon held the rank of captain) were eligible for nine quarters (excluding the commanding officer's quarters).

By November 1872, three commissioned officers, all lieutenants, lived with wives and children: Kendall, Gray, and Stivers. Kendall and his wife, Virginia, had three children. Cyrus Gray and his wife, Ellen, had a three-year-old daughter. The biggest family among the officers was that of Edwin J. Stivers and his wife, Kasia. Their eldest daughter, Lissette, was the oldest officer's child on post at fourteen, but her three siblings were seven or younger. Unfortunately, we have no sense of how any of the quartering played out, except in one case: the Kendalls. Conveniently, Kendall's walk between the Company E barracks and his home was the subject of considerable interest, and it appeared in his court-martial transcript. It was estimated by viewers that when Kendall trudged across the uneven surface of the parade ground from Sergeant Sample's quarters, it required him to walk a distance of between 250 and 275 yards. This

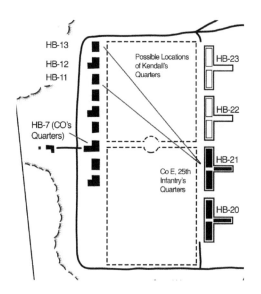

FIGURE 7.5. Location of Kendall's quarters in August 1872, based on court-martial testimony. Illustration by the author.

means that if Company E was bunked in HB-21, as archival evidence suggests, the only possible lieutenant's quarters that the Kendalls could have occupied was HB-13, the building farthest north on officer's row. If I have miscalculated, and the company was in HB-20, then it is possible that that HB-11 was their quarters, but for either location, HB-13 is the best fit.

If they occupied HB-13, the Kendall family had no neighbors to the north, and a captain (or captains) immediately to the south. If in HB-11, there was a captain to the north and another lieutenant's family to the south (possibly the Stivers?). The unfinished barracks would have been immediately across the parade ground. The 1872 plan shows an office just north of the parade ground and centrally located (probably the adjutant's office, where court-martials were heard), and further north, along the canyon wall, the first chapel (and second school location), approximately 240 yards due north of the HB-23 barracks. Behind the officers' quarters was sentry station number five, just west of the commanding officer's quarters. This was a quiet part of the post relatively speaking.

Of course, this description of the Kendall's housing is as of the September court-martial; the assignment of quarters could have changed with the arrival of Company G in the second week of November. But this is the best information available to work with. Both HB-11 and HB-13 were adobe structures with shingle roofs, measuring twenty-one by forty-eight feet. Each room measured eighteen by five feet, with the center hallway measuring twelve by eighteen

FIGURE 7.6. Layout and plans for lieutenants' quarters at Fort Davis. Illustration by the author, based on Greene, *Historic Resource Study*, descriptions and Fort Davis, Captains' Quarters, Fort Davis, Jeff Davis Country, TX HABS TEX, 122-FODA, 3-(sheet 2 of 3), Library of Congress Prints and Photographs Division, Washington, DC. Illustration by the author.

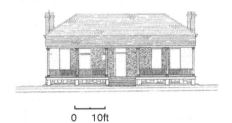

0   10ft

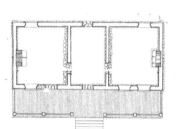

Layout of Lieutenant's
Quarters

feet. Windows and doors were located on the eastern and western sides of the quarters so that residents in quarters on either side could not peer into each other's bedroom windows. The front and back entrances opened into a central hallway with another room opening on either side, and each had a front and back porch or veranda. A two-roomed adobe kitchen measuring seventeen by twenty-eight feet was to the rear of the building. Each room had two windows in the front and two in the back.

In Andrews's account, because the sash was nailed shut, sherds of broken glass had to be carefully removed from the pane before Tallifero could stick his head through; Stivers altered that story, making the sash broken. What agency of the windows were the authors attempting to thwart? When an architectural Historical American Buildings survey was done for the officers' quarters and men's barracks in 1980, the windows were noted to be of a standard factory manufacture, measuring ninety inches high and forty inches wide and having twelve glass panes. The pane size was not recorded, but based on these measurements, each pane would be no larger than 13 1/3 inches wide and 23 inches high.[43] Here, perhaps, is part of the problem. I am not a particularly large or a particularly small person—my shoulders measure 15.5 inches across (I stand two inches shorter than Corporal Tallifero). I could stick my head through Mrs. Kendall's window pane, but I most certainly could not fit any more of my body through. To do that would require me to attempt to put a hand through the window to balance myself on one hand and twist sideways to take advantage of the height of the pane to put my shoulders through sideways, an uncomfortable proposition that leaves one quite vulnerable.

If the assailant was actually truly trying to break into the house (instead of merely conveniently sticking their head through a window pane too small to enter the house so they could be shot in the head), it is necessary to break the sash. And in Stivers's version of the story, that is what happened. If one has just broken a sash to enter a sleeping chamber, the easiest course of action would not be to go head first, but to kick it out with one's army boots to avoid glass cuts and to bend as one stepped through the window.

Andrews's belabored description of the head through the window, the cap falling into the room, and the blood splashing into the room, seem to have been included to place Tallifero definitively in the sleeping chamber. His dead body, located on the back porch, would necessarily suggest other possibilities to those who saw it.

DANIEL TALLIFERO'S CAP

To someone unfamiliar with Fort Davis, the presence of a man on the back porch of an officer's quarters (or anywhere near) in the early morning hours could be seen as suspicious; yet when approaching an officer's quarters, there was no other place a Black man was allowed to go. Soldiers were prohibited by their commanding officer from going to the front door. The shooting happened at a time when we know from Hewey's court-martial that in mid-August, the corporal had been serving as corporal of the guard. At that point, he was stationed at the cavalry corral (station number 6). As discussed in chapter 4, station 5 was located behind the officers' quarters at the magazine. One can imagine any number of reasons why a man on patrol might end up behind the officers' quarters, especially if there were honest concerns that several rapists were loose on the post. Perhaps a concerned Andrews had even asked Corporal Tallifero to check in on the Kendall household in the lieutenant's absence, given how worried he was about marauding rapists.

This brings us to Corporal Tallifero's cap. Soldiers wore their uniforms both on duty and off. They communicated their status in particular ways, be it tucking in their smocks, unbuttoning jackets, or not wearing their caps. The caps were emblazoned with a man's regiment and his company and either a bugle for the infantry or crossed sabers for the cavalry. Wearing a cap in the middle of the night while in the commission of a crime might not have been the smartest thing to do unless one were a civilian impersonating a soldier while undertaking a crime. But wearing a cap while at work on guard duty? Yes, that was appropriate. Mrs. Kendall was no stranger to military life, and she would have been able to quickly read a uniform. Would she have made a different decision about the man's intents in seeing his uniform? So presenting Tallifero's cap as falling into the room either after he thrust his head through the window or as he was shot through his head presents a problem. The cap was too potentially troublesome to stay in the narrative; it begged for certain questions to be asked and answered. It had to be removed—not from Tallifero's head, but from the story. Stivers's version mentions no cap.

Summary of the Evidence: What the Word Choices Do; What the Materials Say

All the accounts of the evening's events rely upon Daniel Tallifero breaking a hole in a window through which he could not fit more than his head. The accounts ask us to believe that when intent on committing a crime, a man entered a window head first and continued in his attempts even when a gun was waved in his face and put to his head. To account for the incontrovertible reality of the location of the gunshot wound on the top of Tallifero's head, and to establish the possibility—if not the likelihood—that the fatal wound was an execution shot and not a shot taken in self-defense, we must place Tallifero on his knees at the time of the fatal shot. The accounts also make it clear the fatal shot had to be fired by one Mrs. Kendall.

Despite noting the presence of an unnamed companion, the accounts also require us to believe that no one screamed in fear or decided to run out the front of the house while the would-be intruder was on his knees in the back. Mrs. Kendall may have been committed to protecting her children; the young lady was not. Even from the most isolated of the barracks, she would have needed to run only a dozen or so feet to reach the front door of the next house; after all, the only officer off post at the time was Lieutenant Kendall. Any other officer was likely to be in their quarters. It is possible that the girl was frozen in fear, and I don't want to minimize whatever terror might have been felt if this indeed, improbable and as strangely handled as it was, was what the women experienced.

Mrs. Kendall was the woman who anticipated the trouble her husband would be in if found drunk on duty, so she was quick thinking. Both accounts suggest that the women were awake, so it is hard to imagine Kendall's not giving some sort direction to the younger woman, even if it were just to "run and get help." If she worried that they faced a "fate worse than death," wouldn't it be natural to send the younger woman from the house while Mrs. Kendall confronted the intruder with the gun? The narrative relies on feminine passivity. There is no mention of Tallifero's being armed, and again, it is hard to imagine what kind of threat he would have been while stooped on his knees.

Ignoring the problems of the narrative, what work does this particular story of Tallifero's death accomplish? First, it diverts attention from the mute testimony of the material contradictions by mobilizing the specter of the Black rapist, a profoundly powerful stereotype broadly used to justify deadly violence against Black men. Second, by putting the gun in the hands of a woman, the weaker sex, the easily traumatized sex, it renders the shooting a clear case of self-defense. This is an easier narrative to relay than the alternate suggested by the scant evidence—that a Black man was shot through the top of his head while on his hands and knees at close range.

Can you imagine an alternate narrative that fits the available evidence? I have. I first tried to imagine a scenario in which Mrs. Kendall actually did shoot the young corporal. Some unpublished speculations have suggested that the young woman had invited the man to see her while she was away from her family. In this scenario, Mrs. Kendall shoots him to protect the girl, not knowing why he is there. There are multiple problems with this narrative. First, this interpretation still draws on stereotypes of Black men as constant pursuers of white women. If invited, why the broken window? Why the necessity of putting his cap in the house if he potentially had already been there? And why would the newspaper article draw attention to the presence of the young lady if she had solicited the man's attention? Why not leave her out of the account?

There is another possible scenario. What if Colonel Andrews had asked the corporal to put a scare in Mrs. Kendall while her husband was away? If he were one of the pooh-poohers of the idea that there were rapists at large on the post, sending Kendall away and arranging for the terrorizing of his wife would make sense. Perhaps Andrews underestimated Mrs. Kendall, who shot the intruder. Not having an inquest could protect the commander, but why would Stivers be involved in writing a newspaper report? Why would the story change from Andrews's letter to the report? I set about imagining a series of events that would most coherently fit within the assembled evidence from different people, places, things, and temporalities.

Imagine this scenario. A corporal on duty in the small hours of the morning is spotted moving around in the dark by an officer who is checking on the house in which his teenaged daughter is staying (possibly just next door from his own quarters). The sinks were behind the officers' houses, and a man going to relieve himself in the small hours of the morning would have every reason to be outside (whether or not he walked as far as the sink). This officer has only recently arrived on post, but he has heard about the recent case of attempted rape. This officer is not a particular fan of the Black troops and has expressed negative attitudes regarding the morals of Black men and women. Convinced he is catching a rapist lurking near where his daughter is sleeping, the confrontation escalates. Perhaps the Black man attempts to defend himself, or perhaps, not understanding the racialized assemblages at play, he tries to calm the man. The white man thinks he sees a weapon being drawn. He pushes the Black man down and shoots him through the head, awakening the garrison. Confusion ensues, and the man is identified, perhaps as someone who was on guard duty. A story is needed. The commanding officer has served with this man, so they devise a story, but it requires someone to have shot the man, someone who will not be prosecuted.

As someone whose husband was just court-martialed, Mrs. Kendall understands the incredible dependence of army wives and children on their husbands. This officer would not merely be kicked out from the army, he would face a possible murder charge and possibly time in a penitentiary. His wife and four children would be ruined, left to starve. She agrees to be party to the cover-up, not to save the officer, but to save his family. To ensure that she doesn't change her mind, the story is quickly communicated to headquarters, and for extra insurance, after consideration, it is refined, improved, and sent to the *New York Herald*. There is one audience in mind for that letter to the editor: not the nation, but the post itself. The story in official form, with the authority of the newspaper behind it, will come back to Fort Davis in print for everyone to read, quelling any whispered concerns that something *else* happened. Otherwise, why would a letter to the editor need to be written? No one did such a thing in any previous case.

An inquest is not ordered. Because an inquest would require that the woman testify under oath, it would require other people to provide accounts of the events before, during, and after the shooting; it would require the seizure and examination of the gun; and it would necessitate an autopsy. An inquest could expose the identity of the young woman and threaten her reputation. Perhaps during an inquest, Kendall's belief that the post commander was out to get him would be repeated. Perhaps the clearly punitive nature of the road-building detail would be discussed during testimony. Perhaps the coincidence that the "attack" happened against the wife of an officer disliked by the commanding officer by a man who had been personally trusted by the commanding officer might also be mentioned. An autopsy is not needed in the absence of an inquest, and an autopsy would only threaten to reveal more information than necessary. We can only speculate, but the actions we can see, the assembled traces of this event, underscore that the words do not add up.

Colonel Andrews and Lieutenant Stivers correctly understood the story of a white woman killing a Black man who was threatening her virtue and the lives of her children and companion would cause such a visceral response in the white men who heard it that they would fail to dissect the story further. No one would need know that the dead man had been promoted to the rank of corporal by the commanding officer, and no one would need know that the commanding officer had trusted this man to lead his own escort to the southern border.

I am not saying this is what happened in the early morning hours of November 21, 1872. I am saying that given the evidence available, it could have happened. In fact, this narrative provides a better explanation that includes a wider assemblage of evidence than previously considered. All that was necessary was to ask the question, What if the commanding officer was lying? In the American justice system, we rely on the notion of reasonable doubt as a standard of proof to validate a criminal conviction. My intent is not to prosecute Colonel Andrews, Lieutenant Stivers, or Mrs. Kendall and her companion. I am presenting a defense of Corporal Daniel Tallifero, whose mother was told that he died an attempted rapist, whose service record in the National Archive has more documents related to his death than to his life, a man who has continued to be represented as a failed rapist in the secondary literature of the Black regulars. I have presented as full an accounting of the evidence as still available from the fort during that time and from that night and the way it was handled.

Have I convinced you? Do you agree that something is not right in the existing accounts of that night? Do the silences trouble you? Can you imagine Daniel Tallifero dying, shot not during the commission of a crime but for being Black in the wrong place at the wrong time, being shot for being a Black man simply trying to do his job? Have you considered the evidence I presented fully? If so, perhaps we have given Tallifero the least that a soldier is due: a fair hearing.

Aftermath

As Corporal Tallifero's body lay in the hospital, a private was arrested for screaming "Murder!" by the officer's quarters. If Private Jones had run directly from his fight with Southerner behind the barracks to the closest officer's quarters, he would have been near Colonel Andrews's quarters when he yelled—a scream for help that a sergeant heard as an accusation.

Colonel Andrews's writing wasn't limited to his letter that day. He also wrote Standard Order No. 167, ordering Second Lieutenant Harry Reade of Company G, Twenty-Fifth Infantry, to proceed to Wild Rose Pass to relieve Kendall and send him back to post. What happened when he returned? We cannot be sure. Kendall was eventually named as head of the post school, a position that would limit his time away from his wife. Was this a quid pro quo with the commander? The colonel saw the position of school superintendent as a privileged one when he first assigned it to the ordinance sergeant. Given that he had no affection for Kendall, Kendall's assignment to the school seemed strange. Kendall took advantage of this role to create a curriculum that gave soldiers access to the knowledge necessary for career advancement in the military, education that would prepare them for work as noncommissioned officers. He ensured that their teachers included a man who understood how to protest ill treatment within the proper chain of command.

Stivers's letter to the *Herald* had its own extraordinary life. While not published until December 8, 1872, the *Herald* letter propelled the story of the plucky lady killing the Black would-be rapist to a national audience, reaching all four corners of the continental US and most places in between. Not surprisingly, Republican-leaning newspapers took a less fantastical take on the story, while southern papers described Tallifero as "hideous," "giant," or "huge." Andrews and Stivers deployed the stereotype of the brutish Black rapist and set him free to run up the administrative ladder of the military and the national media, a media that was increasingly hungry for lascivious and sensational content. The country was more than happy to consume a story that represented a Black soldier as less than human.[44]

The news of the event as told by Stivers was spreading across the country when Judge Adjutant Gender J. Holt sent the following response to Andrews regarding both Pedee and Tallifero, dated December 18, 1872:

> Respectfully returned with full concurrency in the opinion expressed by General [William T.] Sherman that the wife of Lieut. Kendall was perfectly justified in shooting Corporal Tallifero while forcing an entrance to her sleeping chamber. The record in the case of musician Pedee has been carefully examined and the conclusion reached that the mitigation of the sentence ordered by General Augur was called for by the strong doubt raised by the testimony as to the guilt of the prisoner. After a comparison of the statement of the woman immediately after the alleged assault upon her with those made by her as a witness in the trial added to the evidence given for the defense it is felt that on the question of identity the preponderance of the proof was against the prosecution.[45]

Daniel Tallifero is buried in San Antonio's National Cemetery, in plot I o 1548; in cemetery notes, his death date is listed as November 20, 1872. His stone is bright white and shows his rank as corporal and names him as a member of the Company I, Ninth Cavalry. It is a quiet and respectful stone that belies the turmoil surrounding his death. He is buried not far from Sergeant Anthony Jackson and other men who died at Fort Davis.

Martin Pedee, Fort Davis's other accused rapist of 1872, finished his term of imprisonment in October 1873 and left the military soon after. He moved north, to Vermillion County, Illinois, working as a farmer, and later, as a barber in the town of Caitlin. He married twice. The first marriage ended in divorce due to complaints of alcoholism. His second marriage came shortly before his death, to a much younger woman, perhaps to gain her a widow's pension after his death. He had no children. In 1887, Pedee became the subject of national news when he became the first Black man to be elected as a police magistrate in the state of Illinois. Upon his death, he was buried in the Oak Grove Cemetery in Caitlin. His place of burial and marker long since had disappeared. In April 2019, thanks to local historian Larry Weatherford, the community dedicated a new marble military memorial to Private Martin Pedee, Civil War and Frontier Veteran. Far from Fort Davis, he was remembered as a "brave man who fought for his own freedom, the freedom of others and for his country, overcoming great prejudice and obstacles along the way."[46]

EPILOGUE

⋯⇒◉⇐⋯

Archaeology provides a different lens through which to look at the history of African American service. Patricia Limerick has poetically argued that western history is embedded in the soil, layered and concretized, sometimes buried and sometimes visible at the surface.[1] As an archaeologist, this stratigraphic imagery appeals to me but is too simplistic. A different part of western history emerges when we look at the soil—not a better or more truthful part of history as some archaeologists might argue, but a different one, a more holistic one.

What I have argued for here is not just a historical archaeology but an archaeological approach to history, one that sees all potential traces of the past—be they objects, words, soil stains, environmental evidence, buildings, images—as part of a complex and entangled assemblage through which we can study the ecologies that shaped and were shaped by humans. To be an archaeologist is by its nature a commitment to reassembling sets of things that were inter- and intra-related.[2] We have often chastised ourselves as a discipline for destroying the very thing that we study, the so-called archaeological record.[3] We may disassemble earthly depositions to recover traces they contain, but ultimately, we are builders. We create insights into the human condition.

Some have recently argued that archaeology is best understood by its original Greek roots—as the study of "old things," but this definition restricts those of us who have fought to ensure that archaeology remains a practice rooted in anthropological thought and those of us who see archaeology as having the potential to affect change in the future, not just imagine the past.[4] The enduring nature of things—indeed, the ontologies of things—should not and cannot be ignored, as I hope I have demonstrated in this in retelling of a Fort Davis past. However, I am attentive to Karen Barad's recognition that all observable phenomena emerge through the apparatus that renders them visible and are inherently political, not neutral. Therefore, an attentive scientific practice must be clear about defining and recognizing its ethical stakes.[5] For me, the ethical grounding of this project is aiding in the dismantling of anti-Black racism, through an attention to how racializing assemblages creating systemic inequality emerged through the intra-actions of people places and things. While archaeology is attentive to temporal relationships, is it not contained to a single time period. The world created at Fort Davis is intrinsically tied to our past and future, and by considering it, we have only made it more so something that exists in our present.

To be an archaeologist is not merely to think about old things. It is also to think about how we understand people from the traces left behind, to think about the relationships between time, space, people, places, and all the *thingy* things of the world and the mattering of those things. And if we think about that in its purest terms, then all we experience as humans through our limited powers of observation is part of the archaeological record. Our craft as archaeologists is in identifying and recovering traces and assembling together meaningful sets of them—things that share appropriate contexts, associations, and proveniences. We assemble things not randomly but through an understanding of what and how things articulate with one another, how things have journeyed to the places where we have found them, so that we can consider what those articulations have meant, what they could mean, and how they can matter.[6] The "assemblage" is at the core of archaeological thinking, but the rest of the social sciences have taken the word as their own, popularizing it as something not quite the same as archaeologists conceptualize it.[7]

The men and experiences discussed in these pages are just a sample of the totality of traces these men left behind, but it is a collection of traces that have been holistically assembled with attention to particular temporalities that were meaningful within a soldier's world, within enlistments, company stations, a career, life before and after soldiering. I think what has emerged is an essence of the complexities of the worlds Black men navigated as individual and groups of soldiers in a postwar world that was debating what role and future they were to play in the nation, while they themselves attempted to answer those same questions.

Alexander Weheliye has proposed that we seek to recognize particular kinds of assemblages: racializing assemblages, those sets of processes and practices that seek to naturalize the ways in a given society that some people are valued and others are not. I see necropolitics (Mbembe's construction) as the most obscene of racializing assemblages—the ultimate in the state's biopolitical power. But the state's political power is not limited to killing those who are less than human.[8] As Jasbir Puar has observed, the state also wields the power to debilitate, and that right to maim effects racialized, queer, and disabled populations disproportionately, particularly those who inhabit intersectional spaces.[9] At Fort Davis, a number of interlocking racialized assemblages are rendered visible through an archaeological approach to history. Though myriad discomforts were endured by all frontier soldiers, regardless of race— cramped housing, unreasonable labor demands, food insecurity, arbitrary judicial sentencing, misuses of power by some NCOs and commissioned officers—Black bodies were regularly subjugated in ways that made those discomforts more frequent, more intense, and more debilitating, not just in the military but beyond, with indignities that were theirs alone to bear, including long periods of being stationed in undesirable posts in the West because of notions of the heat tolerance of Black bodies.

It has been argued by some that the military was not a racist institution, despite the undeniable presence of many racist men in its ranks.[10] I hope I have demonstrated that the situation was much more complicated. We can see in the ways that orders were constructed and enforced (or not enforced) the ways that racist notions beget racist practices, practices that become institutionalized and ultimately become so naturalized that they are rendered invisible. Sergeant Anthony Jackson died at Fort Davis, in pain from an undiagnosed abdominal condition. As a Black man in the military, he had endured years of what Puar has called "biopolitical risk."[11] His body had endured a seven-week stint of yellow fever and years of being under-rationed for his expected workload. Sergeant John Sample also endured the cumulative impacts of military services' debilitating impact. Both men also lived with the need to disguise their personal lives—one married in secret, the other drew suspicion that he did not conform to heteronormative expectations. Nor were they alone. Starving soldiers became part of the landscape, unexamined murders normal, barracks filthy from overcrowding standard issue, epidemics of dysentery commonplace. Yet these risks were read not as indications of the institutional failure of military negligence but as the fault of soldiers, not as health misdiagnoses, or the failure to provide an education, or as a way to avoid punishing the malpractice of a surgeon or to justify denial of a pension but as a mark of the soldiers' personal moral failures. It is in this way that the army supported the necropolitical and debilitating agendas of the United States, a government that at state and federal levels balked at fulfilling the promises of liberty and equality that emerged following the Civil War, a government that turned a blind eye as white supremacist violence eroded the life, liberty, and citizenship rights of Black people in and outside the military. The soldiers may have been supporting the settler colonial agenda of the United States, but the United States, as embodied by the actions and practices of its representatives (from officers to the secretary of war), too often saw these men as less than human.

Yet to focus just on the racializing assemblages is to ignore the other stories that emerge out of the material traces of Fort Davis and to ignore the incredible creative agentive and community-building power of the soldiers. These were men collectively engaged in denouncing anti-Black racism through the examples of their lives and fighting for access to their constitutionally assured citizenship rights. Black men and women emerge from the soil and the archive as persons demanding to be recognized as fellow humans. They supplemented their diet through the acquisition of additional food sources, built homes out of canvas, found private spaces to assure intimacy, remembered their collective history through kitchen furniture, and worked to continue their educations themselves even when the post failed to do so. Their voices resonate from court-martial transcripts, demanding their manly contributions be recognized, arguing for just treatment and their human right to justice. What to call these parallel assemblages, these assemblages that speak to their own assertions of their humanity? For Wehiliye, the answer is clear: once we strip away the veneer of racializing assemblages, we are left with the base of all life: flesh—flesh that lived, loved, endured.[12]

By taking a micro-historical approach, considering a smaller number of people as they interacted over a smaller span of time, by pausing and looking closely at the spaces in which they lived and the things they used, we can see the diversity and complexity of frontier experiences. While a Sergeant Hewey may have used his position to engage in questionable practices, a Sergeant Sample used his position to assert for citizenship rights and better treatment. Sergeant Major William Henderson, Sergeant John Chapman, and Private Lemuel Johnson all argued for their rights and dignity through the written word. While Corporal Griffin Collins might have used his power to taunt the men serving with him, Private James Wilson stood up to defend his bunkie. Collectively, the men sought and worked toward social uplift, working at their studies in the crowded barracks and tents even when the post offered no schooling. Through their collective efforts, the men built a living space that allowed them to create a material world that documented their dignity, shared experiences, and commitment to martial manhood and citizenship. Through the spaces they made and the things they acquired and used, the men of Fort Davis materialized their ambitions and desires.

White officers were entrenched parts of the military structure, a structure that may have misrepresented the murder of Corporal Daniel Tallifero as a justified killing. Still, individual choices could make a difference in soldier's lives. A Colonel Andrews may have hounded a man falsely accused of rape, while a General Augur intervened and mitigated or overturned unfair sentences. A Lieutenant Cyrus Gray may have devalued soldier's lives and lashed out in anger with racialized insults, but a Lieutenant Kendall envisioned a school curriculum that encouraged upward mobility in the military for dedicated soldiers. In short, we can see that what individuals chose to do mattered, both for the negative and the positive. It is a scale of history that forces us to acknowledge today that actions can have ongoing consequences at different scales of social experience.

And despite archival practices that sought to render the lives of these men invisible, we see in the material record of Fort Davis the great pains that soldiers took to counter the racialized stereotypes that hounded them beyond the boundaries of enslavement. We see their efforts to create homes within the mess halls of the barracks and to demand they be treated with dignity and respect, and we see their efforts at uplift through education. We also see the ways they navigated interpersonal relationships with one another— loving, hateful, affectionate, competitive, resentful—relationships in all their humanity. While these are dynamics that played out in many western posts, through historical archaeology we can see the beautiful messiness of clearly human lives in all their complicated glory.

NOTES

✦━◦◗◖◦━✦

Prologue

1. Andrews to AAG, November 21, 1872, NMRA 66-783(7675)-1, FODA.
2. Dobak and Phillips, *The Black Regulars*, 197; Leiker, *Racial Borders*, 85–86; Thompson, "The Negro Soldiers on the Frontier," 231–32; Wooster, *Frontier Crossroads*.
3. Adams, *Class and Race in the Frontier Army*.

Chapter One

1. Douglas, "Why a Colored Man Should Enlist."
2. Standard Order No. 96, Inquest into shooting of Cotton, July 16, 1872, NMRA 66-783(7675)-6, FODA.
3. US Population Census 1870 Presidio County.
4. FTD_SoldierDatabase.xlsx, database of soldiers who served at Fort Davis, Fort Davis National Historic Site Reading Room, Fort Davis, Texas.
5. Wooster, *History of Fort Davis, Texas*.
6. Standard Order No. 96, NMRA 66-783(7675)-6, FODA.
7. Wilkie, *The Archaeology of Mothering*.
8. Frederick Kendall, GCM KK-260; James Wilson GCM PP-3257; Griffin Collins GCM PP-3254, RG 153, NARA.
9. Wilkie, *The Archaeology of Mothering*.
10. "Battle Unit Details," The Civil War, National Park Service, accessed June 1, 2020, nps.gov/civilwar/search-battle-units-detail.htm?battleUnitCode =UUS0064RIOOC.
11. For example, Du Bois, *Black Reconstruction in America 1860–1880*; Fanon, *The Wretched of the Earth*; Curry, *The Man-Not*; McKittrick, *Sylvia Wynter*; Weheliye, *Habeas Viscus*; and Wynter, "Unsettling the Coloniality of Being/ Power/Truth/Freedom."
12. Dobak and Phillips, *Black Regulars 1866–1898*; Schubert, *On the Trail of the Buffalo Soldier*; Schubert, *Voices of the Buffalo Soldier*.

13. GCM William L. Henderson, PP-142, RG 153, NARA; FTD_SoldierData base.xlsx, FODA.

14. Emberton, *Beyond Redemption*; Kinder, *Paying with Their Bodies*.

15. Henderson GCM PP-142, NARA.

16. Curry, *Man-Not*; Weheliye, *Habeas Viscus*; Wynter, "Unsettling the Coloniality."

17. Fowler, *The Black Infantry in the West*; Leckie, *The Buffalo Soldiers*; Nankivell, *Buffalo Soldier Regiment*; Shellum, *Black Officer in a Buffalo Soldier Regiment*; Steward, *Buffalo Soldiers*.

18. Leonard, *Men of Color to Arms!*.

19. Donaldson, *Duty beyond the Battlefield*; Hayes, *Slavery before Race*; Jackson, *Creole Indigeneity*; Weik, *The Archaeology of Antislavery Resistance*.

20. Mbembe, *Necropolitics*.

21. Adams, *Class and Race*; Leiker, *Racial Borders*.

22. Dobak and Phillips, *Black Regulars*; Schubert, *On the Trail*; Schubert, *Voices of the Buffalo Soldier*.

23. For example, Tsing, *The Mushroom at the End of the World*; Latour, *Reassembling the Social*.

24. In my thinking on racialization and its processes and materialities, I am particularly influenced by Battle-Baptiste, *Black Feminist Archaeology*; Bonilla-Silva, *Racism without Racists*; Chen, *Animacies*; Collins, *Black Feminist Thought*; Hartman, *Scenes of Subjection*; Snorton, *Black on Both Sides;* Omi and Winant, *Racial Formation in the United States*; and Weheliye, *Habeas Viscus*.

25. Omi and Winant, *Racial Formation*.

26. Snorton, *Black on Both Sides*.

27. Chen, *Animacies*; Ingold, "Materials against Materiality"; Latour, *Reassembling the Social*.

28. Donaldson, *Duty beyond the Battlefield*; hooks, *We Real Cool*; Leiker, *Racial Borders*; Leonard, *Men of Color*.

29. Blight, *Frederick Douglass*; Douglas, "Why a Colored Man Should Enlist"; Johnson, *Negroes and the Gun*.

30. Higginson, *Army Life in a Black Regiment*.

31. Lucinda Jackson, Widow Pension, Certificate 421209, RG 15, NARA.

32. Dobak and Phillips, *Black Regulars 1866–1898*; Foner, *The United States Soldier between the Two Wars*.

33. Brooks, *Captives & Cousins*; Donaldson, *Duty beyond the Battlefield*; Gwynne, *Empire of the Summer Moon*.

34. Cimprich, *Fort Pillow*.

35. Dobak and Phillips, *Black Regulars 1866–1898*; Emberton, "'Only Murder Makes Men'"; Leiker, *Racial Borders*.

36. Alexander, *The New Jim Crow*; Curry, *Man-Not*; Mbembe, *Necropolitics*; González-Tennant, *The Rosewood Massacre*; Muhammad, *The Condemnation of Blackness*; Roberts, *Killing the Black Body*.

37. Gannon, "Unearthing the True Toll"; González-Tennant, *The Rosewood Massacre*.

38. Billings, *A Report on the Hygiene of the United States Army*.

39. Adams, *Class and Race*; Foner, *United States Soldier*; Leiker, *Racial Borders*; McChristian, *Regular Army O!*; Rickey, *Forty Miles a Day on Beans and Hay*.

40. Donaldson, *Duty beyond the Battlefield*; Harris, *Negro Frontiersman*.

41. Donaldson, *Duty beyond the Battlefield*, 38–39, 113–14.

42. Leckie, *The Colonel's Lady on the Western Frontier*, 132.

43. Donaldson, *Duty beyond the Battlefield*; Shellum, *Black Officer*.

44. Gellar, "Building Nation"; Novak and Warner-Smith, "Assembling Heads and Circulating Tales," 71–91; Stocking, *Victorian Anthropology*.

45. For example, Donaldson, *Duty beyond the Battlefield*; Horne, *Black and Brown*; Leiker, *Racial Borders*; Leonard, *Men of Color*. For a discussion of military settings creating conducive environments for supporting multiracial communities, see McKibben, *Racial Beachhead*.

46. Carrera, *Imagining Identities in New Spain*; Loren, "Corporeal Concerns."

47. US Populations Census Presidio County, 1880; 1900; 1910; Casey, *Alpine, Texas*.

48. Donaldson, *Duty beyond the Battlefield*; Leiker, *Racial Borders*.

49. Utley, *Fort Davis National Historic Site*; Wooster, *History of Fort Davis*.

50. Greene, *Historic Resource Study*; Utley, *Fort Davis National Historic Site*; Wooster, *History of Fort Davis*.

51. Dobak and Phillips, *Black Regulars 1866–1898*; Fowler, *Black Infantry*; Leckie, *Buffalo Soldiers*.

52. Raht, *The Romance of the Davis Mountains*; Scobee, *Old Fort Davis*.

53. US Census Presidio Country, 1860; 1870; Greene, *Historic Resource Study*; Raht, *Romance*; Wooster, *History of Fort Davis*.

54. Shafter to AAG, February 12, 1871, NMRA 66-783(7675)-1, FODA.

55. Ibid.

56. McIntrye and Studd, *Terrestrial Vegetation*.

57. Eichner, "Frontier Intermediaries"; Wilkie et al., *Report of the University of California Berkeley's 2013 Archaeological Research*; Wilkie, Eichner, and Rodriquez, *Report of the University of California Berkeley 2015 Archaeological Research*.

58. Eichner, "Frontier Intermediaries"; Wilkie et al., *Report of the University of California Berkeley's 2013 Archaeological Research*; Wilkie, Eichner, and

Rodriquez, *Report of the University of California Berkeley 2015 Archaeological Research*;

59. For difficulties of working in military contexts associated with Black regulars, see Brown, Zapata, and Moses, *Camp Elizabeth*; Cheek, *The Fort Concho Trash Dump*; and King and Dunnavant, "Buffalo Soldiers and Apaches."

60. Schiffer, *Formation Processes of the Archaeological Record*.

61. For historical archaeology, a great example of this is the important archaeologist Stanley South, who hoped to create a set of methodologies that would wean archaeologists off their use of documents. See South, *Method and Theory in Historical Archaeology*.

62. The National Historic Preservation Act of 1966 and supporting state legislation provides structure for evaluating historic architecture, landscapes, and archaeological sites. Like any environmental legislation, it is vulnerable to political whims; see https://www.achp.gov/sites/default/files/2018-06/nhpa .pdf.

63. Bennett, *Vibrant Matter*; Chen, *Animacies*.

64. Weheliye, *Habeas Viscus*.

65. Willis and Krauthamer, *Envisioning Emancipation*. For discussions of epidermalization and biological counters, see Fanon, *Black Skin, White Masks*; Frankenberg, *White Women, Race Matters*; Omi and Winant, *Racial Formation*; and Smedley and Smedley, "Race as Biology Is Fiction."

66. Martin Pegee Pension, Certificate 792614, RG 15, NARA.

Chapter Two

1. This account is reconstructed from witness testimony, Martin Pedee GCM PP-2809 RG 153, NARA.

2. Greene, *Historic Resource Study*.

3. Account of board of survey, January 4, 1868, NMRA 66-783(7676) 6, FODA.

4. GCM John Hewey PP-3257; James Wilson PP-3254; Griffin Collins PP-3257, RG 153, NARA.

5. Eichner, "Queering Frontier Identities."

6. In February 1871, Standard Order No. 34 specified that the "laundress tents are to be pitched behind the respective companies and are to face the east." This would have placed the laundress' quarters near the sinks, presumably a less than desirable location. NMRA 66-783(7675)-3, FODA.

7. Photograph on file, FODA.

8. Greene, *Historic Resource Study*.

9. Billings, *Outline Description of U.S. Military Posts*.

10. Greene, *Historic Resource Study*, 94.

11. End of year fiscal report, 1869, SR-FODA-10, FODA.

12. Inspection report of the post of Fort Davis Texas, by Lt. Col. James H. Carleton, Acting Assistant Inspector General March 6, 1871, SR-FODA-5, FODA.

13. August 30 letter, William Shafter to Adjutant General Department of Texas regarding post repairs, SR-FODA-6, FODA.

14. January 12, 1871, letter from Thomas Hunt, requesting wells in back of officers' quarters, NMRA 66-783(7675)-1, FODA.

15. Dickson, "Museum Spotlight."

16. Billings, *Report on the Hygiene.*

17. May 1872 post description provided by Assistant Surgeon D. Weisel, NMRA 63-15(1946), FODA.

18. March 31, 1873, Monthly Inspection Fort Davis, prepared by Major Zenas Bliss, NMRA-66-77(7675)-7, FODA.

19. Andrews to AAG, November 1873 letter in NMRA-66-783(7675)-1, FODA.

20. Bell, *Mosquito Soldiers*; Brock, *Justus von Liebig*; Ellis, *Yellow Fever & Public Health in the New South*; Sokolow, *Eros and Modernization*; Magner, *A History of Infectious Disease*; Tesh, "Miasma and 'Social Factors' in Disease Causality."

21. Brock, *Justus von Liebig*. Recipes included in Weisel to company captains, April 12, 1869, SR-FODA-4, FODA.

22. Clary, "The Role of the Army Surgeon in the West."

23. Billings, *A Report on the Hygiene of the United States Army.*

24. Weisel in Billings, *A Report on the Hygiene of the United States Army.*

25. Twenty-Fifth Infantry Band quote.

26. Billings, *Report on the Hygiene.*

27. King, "Buffalo Soldiers and Apaches."

28. Quartermaster General of the Army, US *Army Uniforms and Equipment, 1889*; Geier, Orr, and Reeves, *Huts and History.*

29. Barnes, *Cartridges of the World*; NMRA 816(8091), FODA.

30. Barnes, *Cartridges of the World.*

31. Guerin, *Mountain Charley.*

32. Greene, *Historic Resource Study*; McChristian, *The U.S. Army in the West*; Newman, "A Dating Key for Post-Eighteenth Century Bottles."

33. Martin Pedee GCM PP-2809, RG 153, NARA.

34. Martin Pedee enlistment papers, November 27, 1866; November 27, 1869, Enlistment Papers United States Army 1798–July 14, 1894, Pearceson, Henry to Pedrick, William E., Box No. 612. RG 94, NARA.

35. National Park Service, "Battle Unit Details."

36. Martin Pedee Pension Certificate 792614, RG 15, NARA.

37. David Schooley to adjutant Twenty-Fifth Infantry, Cyrus Gray, February 1, 1870, enclosed in Edward Hinks's reports relative to the condition of Twenty-Fifth Infantry and failure to secure re-enlistments, Records of the Adjutant General's Office 1780–1917, Records of Divisions, Recruiting Division, 1814–1914, LR 1862–1882, 1870 (C-H) vol. 45 of 120 PI 17 entry 471, RG 94 AGO, NARA.

38. Frederick A. Kendall GCM PP-2749, RG 153, NARA.

39. Elijah Fillmore GCM PP-2876, RG 153, NARA.

40. Frederick Kendall GCM PP-2749; KK-260 RG 153, NARA.

41. Blight, *Frederick Douglass*; Bowdoin College, "Obituary Record"; Orth, *A History of Cleveland, Ohio*.

42. Dobak and Phillips, *Black Regulars 1866–1898*, 27; Fowler, *Black Infantry*; Frederick Kendall GCM KK-260, PP-2749, RG 153, NARA; Orth, *History of Cleveland, Ohio*.

43. Frederick Kendall GCM PP-2749, RG 153, NARA.

44. John Sample pension application 600330, RG 15, NARA.

45. John Sample to David Schooley, April 1868, RG 98 US Army Commands Second Military District 1867–1868, letters received 1868(Book II) S-79-S-301, Jan–May 1868, NARA.

46. Wooster, *History of Fort Davis*.

47. January 10, 1870, letter from Shafter to H. Clay Wood. NMRA 66-783(7675) 1, FODA.

48. Medical Record for month of January 1869, NMRA 63-15(1946), FODA.

49. Billings, *Report on the Hygiene*, 15.

50. Register of burials relocated from Fort Davis, 1886, SR-FODA-1, FODA.

51. Girard to AAG, undated 1879, NMRA 63-15(1946), FODA.

52. Receipts, April 12, 1869, Weisel to CO, SR-FODA-4, FODA.

53. Brock, *Justus von Liebig*.

54. William Smith GCM PP-2809, RG 153, NARA.

55. Martin Pedee GCM PP-2809, RG 153, NARA.

56. Ibid.

57. Mbembe, *Necropolitics*, 38.

58. Billings, *Report on the Hygiene*, 10.

Chapter Three

1. Pedee GCM PP-2809, RG 153, NARA.

2. Adams, *Class and Race*; Cheek, *Fort Concho Trash Dump*; Custer, *Boots and Saddles*; Herskovits, *Fort Bowie Material Culture*; Kinevan, *Frontier Cavalryman*; Leckie, *Buffalo Soldiers*; Rickey, *Forty Miles a Day*.

3. For example, John Crutchfield (GMC PP-142) was charged with theft after picking up an officer's dropped change, James West (GCM PP-1712) stole rations, William Cuff (GCM-PP-3657) allegedly stole lumber, John Hewey (GCM PP-4581) took a basket of food and ceramics, George Brown (GCM PP-2839) took uniform items, and Solomon Moore (GCM PP-2875) sold stolen army boots (RG 153, NARA).

4. See especially Leach, *Land of Desire*; Logan, *The Victorian Parlour*; McDannell, *The Christian Home in Victorian America*; Mullins, "Racializing the Parlor," 158–76; Schlereth, *Victorian America*.

5. Although modern hindsight allows us to see clearly that the seeds of Jim Crow were being planted shortly after the war, it is important to acknowledge the ways that Black men could imagine a different future based on the world they had inhabited and the changes they had seen in their lifetimes. For discussions of how freedom was understood and celebrated, see Blight, *Frederick Douglass*; and Clark, *Defining Moments*. For considerations of the development of veteran's organizations, see Kinder, *Paying with Their Bodies*. Essential readings on Reconstruction include Du Bois, *Black Reconstruction*; and Litwack, *Been in the Storm So Long* and *How Free Is Free*.

6. Examples of archaeological works that speak to African American awareness of broader discourses on citizenship and the politics of gentility include Battle-Baptiste, *Black Feminist Archaeology*; Delle, *The Archaeology of Northern Slavery and Freedom*; Mullins, "Racializing the Parlor"; and Wilkie, *Archaeology of Mothering* and *Creating Freedom*.

7. Du Bois, *The Souls of Black Folk*.

8. Dobak and Phillips, *Black Regulars 1866–1898*; Leckie, *Buffalo Soldiers*.

9. Pedee Certificate 792614; S. Jackson Certificate 779638, RG 15, NARA.

10. US Census 1870 Presidio County, Texas

11. Mahon and Danysh, "A Diverse Half Century, 1866–1915"; Stubbs and Connor, "Indian Wars Period."

12. Rickey, *Forty Miles a Day on Beans and Hay*.

13. Billings, *Report on the Hygiene*, 10.

14. I am intentionally not disclosing the locations of deposits at Fort Davis. The property is open to the general public and vulnerable to what is known in some circles as "relic hunting," which persists despite the liming and burning discard practices of the military, which often leaves artifacts in poorly preserved and often unrecognizable condition.

15. See, for example, Godden, *Encyclopedia of British Pottery and Porcelain Marks*; Kovel and Kovel, *Kovels' New Dictionary of Marks*; Lehner, *Lehner's Encyclopedia of U.S. Marks*.

16. South, *Method and Theory*.

17. See Wesler, "Assessing Precision in Formula Dating." For prehistoric applications, see Christenson, "A Test of Mean Ceramic Dating."

18. Quartermaster General of the Army, "US *Army Uniforms and Equipment*"; McChristian, *Headgear, Clothing, and Footwear; The U.S. Army in the West*; and *Weapons and Accoutrements*.

19. McChristian, *The U.S. Army in the West*.

20. Herskovits, *Fort Bowie Material Culture*; McChristian, *The U.S. Army in the West*; Quartermaster General of the Army, "US Army Uniforms and Equipment."

21. Ibid.

22. Quartermaster General of the Army, "US Army Uniforms and Equipment."

23. McChristian, *Weapons and Accoutrements*, 10.

24. Field, US *Infantry in the Indian Wars*, 21.

25. William Harris GCM PP-2356 shows that men would carry their money in their caps. James Wilson GCM PP-3257 includes descriptions of boxes and stashing goods at the head of bed. Henry Lovett GCM PP-3603 describes different places men tried to stow belongings RG 153, NARA.

26. RG 393-BRIEDS, NARA.

27. Lucinda Jackson Widow's Pension Certificate 421209, RG 15, NARA.

28. Keefer, *Slavery*, 20.

29. L. Jackson Certificate 421209.

30. George Thompson, member of the Thirty-Ninth Infantry and discharged before the unit moved to Texas, married his wife while still in the USCT and stationed in Donaldsonville, Louisiana, where she lived until his discharge. In her pension application, she had to gather witnesses to attest to when they were married, and she admitted that they married without his commander's knowing. Ellen N. Thompson, Widow Pension Certificate 566032, RG 15, NARA.

31. Quoted in Schubert, *Voices of the Buffalo Soldier*, 85.

32. Alcohol is mentioned in a number of cases; for example, Private Frank Cates (GCM PP-1712, NARA) stole and sold shoes to buy a bottle of whiskey, while Henry Lovett (GCM PP-3603, NARA) was arrested for hollering loudly as he walked back to the barracks in a drunken state after taps.

33. Udolpho Wolfe advertisement, *New Orleans Daily Crescent* (November 30, 1859), 4, CA-LOC; "Udolpho Wolfe Dead," *Daily Dallas Herald*, advertisements 1869–1876 (March 11, 1901), CA-LOC.

34. Lockhart, "The Origins and Life of the Export Beer Bottle."

35. Eichner, "Frontier Intermediaries" and "Queering Frontier Identities."

36. Jenks and Luna, *Early American Pattern Glass 1850–1910*; Jones and Sullivan,

The Parks Canada Glass Glossary; McAllister, *Collector's Guide to Yellow Ware Book III*; Wilson, *Bottles on the Western Frontier*.

37. Rickey, *Forty Miles a Day*.
38. Fox, *The Archaeology of Smoking and Tobacco*; *Veuve Hasslauer Successor of Gambier*.
39. Fike, *The Bottle Book*; Lyons, *Montgomery Ward & Co*.
40. Israel, *1897 Sears, Roebuck & Co. Catalogue*; Lyons, *Montgomery Ward & Co*.
41. Billings, *Report on the Hygiene*, 40.
42. FODA Trader, FODA; Leckie, *Colonel's Lady*.
43. Shafter to Wood, August 15, 1871, NMRA 66-783(7675)-1, FODA.
44. Bederman, *Manliness and Civilization*; Blight, *Frederick Douglass*; Emberton, *Beyond Redemption*.
45. Jones, *Labor of Love, Labor of Sorrow*; Penningroth, *The Claims of Kinfolk*; Stevenson, *Life in Black and White*.
46. Jones, *Labor of Love*; Somerville, *Queering the Color Line*; Wilkie, *Archaeology of Mothering*.
47. Crenshaw, "Demarginalizing the Intersection of Race and Sex"; Flewellen, "Locating Marginalized Historical Narratives"; Lee and Scott, "Introduction: New Directions in African Diaspora Archaeology"; Snorton, *Black on Both Sides*.
48. See Black, *Dismantling Black Manhood*; Curry, *Man-Not*; Johnson, *Black Masculinity and the Frontier Myth*; Lemelle, *Black Masculinity and Sexual Politics*; Richardson, *Black Masculinity and the U.S. South*.
49. Higginson, *Army Life*.
50. Andrews to Augur, November 21, 1872, NMRA 66-783(7675)-1, FODA.
51. Blaszczyk, "The Aesthetic Moment."
52. Wetherbee, *A Second Look at White Ironstone*; *White Ironstone Notes*.
53. Caldwell, "'Flower of the Lily.'"
54. Clark, *Defining Moments*; Emberton, "Only Murder Makes Men"; Glatthaar, *Forged in Battle*; McPherson, *The Negro's Civil War*.
55. Cunningham, *The Collector's Encyclopedia of American Dinnerware*; Dieringer and Dieringer, *White Ironstone China*.
56. Miles and Miller, *Price Guide to Pattern Glass*.
57. Greene, *Historic Resource Study*, 145.
58. Barber, *Marks of American Potters*; Blaszczyk, "Aesthetic Moment"; Cheek, *Fort Concho Trash Dump*.

Chapter Four

1. John Hewey GCM PP-4581, RG 153, NARA.
2. National Park Service, "Battle Unit Details"; John Hewey, 1866, 1871, EN-LIST, NARA.
3. "William Branch, San Antonio, Texas."
4. The men were Privates Walken Gillmore and James Kelley, Company I, Ninth Cavalry. Both men were acquitted. John Hewey GCM PP-4581, RG 153, NARA.
5. Hewey 1875, ENLIST, NARA.
6. See Adams, *Class and Race*; Dobak and Phillips, *Black Regulars 1866–1898*; Donaldson, *Duty beyond the Battlefield*; Leiker, *Racial Borders*.
7. Dobak and Phillips, *Black Regulars 1866–1898*; Donaldson, *Duty beyond the Battlefield*.
8. Post Commander to AAG, March 20 1868, NMRA 66-783(7675)-1, FODA.
9. Donaldson, *Duty beyond the Battlefield*.
10. Schubert, *Voices of the Buffalo Soldier*, 85–86.
11. Griffin Collins, GCM PP-3257, RG 153, NARA.
12. "William Watkins, Texas."
13. Dobak and Phillips, *Black Regulars 1866–1898*; Donaldson, *Duty beyond the Battlefield*; Kenner, *Buffalo Soldiers*.
14. Sea, "James G. Birney."
15. Birney to Parrington, March, 1868, SR-FODA-9, FODA.
16. Dobak and Phillips, *Black Regulars 1866–1898*, 18.
17. Foner, *United States Soldier*.
18. John Chapman, GCM PP-3657, RG 153, NARA.
19. Ibid.
20. Courtney Pension Certificate 117424, RG 15, NARA.
21. Jonas Cox GCM PP-3607, RG 53, NARA.
22. Smith et al., *The Reminiscences of Major General Zenas R. Bliss*, 413.
23. Ibid., 414.
24. Wooster, *History of Fort Davis*.
25. Donaldson, *Duty beyond the Battlefield*; Wooster, *History of Fort Davis*.
26. Utley, *Fort Davis*.
27. Standard Order No. 27, March 25, 1870, NMRA 66-783(7675)-3, FODA.
28. Dobak and Phillips, *Black Regulars 1866–1898*, 200.
29. Henry Jenkins GCM PP-3052, RG 153, NARA.
30. Donaldson, *Duty beyond the Battlefield*.
31. Post returns, May–November 1872, NMRA-172, FODA.
32. Andrews to Barr, August 4, 1872, NMRA 66-783(7576)-1, FODA.

33. Dobak and Phillips, *Black Regulars 1866–1898*; Donaldson, *Duty beyond the Battlefield*; Wooster, *History of Fort Davis*.

34. Chaplain Report, May 30, 1875, NMRA 65-855(10427)-2, FODA.

35. Post Returns, May–November, 1872, NMRA-172, FODA.

36. General Order No. 11, March 24, 1872, NMRA 66-783 (7675)-4, FODA.

37. Foner, *United States Soldier*.

38. General Order No. 22, October 24, 1870, NMRA 66-783(7576)-2, FODA.

39. Greene, *Historic Resource Study*; Levi Scott GCM PP-2418, RG 153, NARA.

40. John Hewey GCM PP-2839, RG-153, NARA.

41. Greene, *Historic Resource Study*; Alfred Taylor GCM PP-2809, RG 153, NARA.

42. Greene, *Historic Resource Study*; Nicholas Johnson GCM PP-142, Henry Cuff GCM PP-3657, RG 153, NARA.

43. Jordan Hudson GCM PP-3257, RG 153, NARA.

44. Dobak and Phillips, *Black Regulars 1866–1898*, xvi.

45. Greene, *Historic Resource Study*; Wooster, *History of Fort Davis*.

46. Taylor, *Texas, My Texas*.

47. Samuel McKinney GCM P-2356, GCM Richard Thompson PP-2356, RG 153, NARA.

48. McChristian, *Garrison Tangles in the Friendless Tenth*.

49. Allen to Andrews, January 25, 1875; Tyler to Andrews, undated, SR-FODA-5, FODA.

50. Richard Roper GCM PP-2812, RG 153, NARA.

51. Tyler to Andrews, undated, SR-FODA-5, FODA.

52. George C. Mullins to post adjutant, December 7, 1878, SR-FODA-5, FODA.

53. Hewey GCM PP-3935, RG 153, NARA.

54. Griffin Collins, GCM PP-3257, RG 153, NARA.

55. Standard Order No. 36, May 6, 1869, NMRA 66-783(7675)-3, FODA.

56. Brune, *Springs of Texas*.

57. Standard Order No. 90 November 4, 1869, NMRA 66-783(7675)-1, FODA.

58. Ely, *The Texas Frontier and the Butterfield Overland Mail*; Scobee, *Fort Davis Texas*; Utley, *Fort Davis*; Wooster, *History of Fort Davis*.

59. Sullivan Pension Certificate 1174241, RG 15, NARA.

60. Shafter to Wood, February 1, 1871, NMRA 66-783(7675)-1, FODA.

61. Utley, *Fort Davis*.

62. Utley, *Fort Davis*; Scobee, *Fort Davis Texas*.

63. "William Branch, San Antonio, Texas."

64. "William Watkins, Texas."

65. Porter, "The Seminole Negro-Indian Scouts."

66. Smith et al., *The Reminiscences of Major General Zenas R. Bliss*, 430.

67. Ibid., 431.
68. Brown et al., *Camp Elizabeth*; Herskovits, *Fort Bowie Material Culture*.
69. Scobee, *Fort Davis Texas*.
70. Hester, "The Prehistory of South Texas."
71. Wilkie, "Glass-Knapping at a Louisiana Plantation."
72. Weik, *The Archaeology of Antislavery Resistance*; "The Role of Ethnogenesis."
73. Shafter to Taylor, January 1871, NMRA 66-783(7675)-1, FODA.
74. Moore to Fort Davis, November 10, 1873, SR-FODA-5, FODA.
75. Keesey to CO, October 13, 1875, SR-FODA-5, FODA.
76. Henry Browler GCM-PP 1645, RG 153, NARA.
77. John Hewey, GCM PP-2839, RG 153, NARA.

Chapter Five

1. Enclosures in file, Lemuel Johnson GCM PP-2356, RG 153, NARA.
2. Greene, *Historic Resource Study*, 170.
3. Adams, *Class and Race*; Dobak and Phillips, *Black Regulars 1866–1898*; Kenner, *Buffalo Soldiers and Officers*.
4. See, for example, Douglass and Jacobs, *Narrative of the Life of Frederick Douglass*; Northup, *Twelve Years a Slave*; Truth, "Ain't I a Woman?"
5. Chen, *Animacies*.
6. Letters of Anthony Jackson enclosed in pension application of Lucinda Jackson, cert 421209, RG 15, NARA.
7. Battle-Baptiste, *Black Feminist Archaeology*; Deetz, *In Small Things Forgotten*; South, *Method and Theory*; Wilkie, *Strung Out on Archaeology*.
8. Hume, *Historical Archaeology*.
9. Wilkie, *Strung Out on Archaeology*.
10. Tsing, *The Mushroom at the End of the World*.
11. Adams, *Class and Race*; Dobak and Phillips, *Black Regulars 1866–1898*; Fowler, *Black Infantry*; Kenner, *Buffalo Soldiers and Officers*; Leckie, *Buffalo Soldiers*; Rickey, *Forty Miles a Day*; and Wooster, *History of Fort Davis*, all make some sort of allusion to the lack of Black soldier's representation in the archival record. A rare alternate take is Schubert, *Voices of the Buffalo Soldier*.
12. Don Rickey Papers, WH986, Western History Collection, Denver Public Library.
13. Multiple letters from Corporal James F. Ukkerd, Corporal Joseph Merryweather, and Corporal A. Franklin, Twenty-Fourth Infantry, while leading the detachment at Barilla Springs in 1880, NMRA 66-783(7675)-8, FODA.
14. Ukkerd to James, August 10, 1880, NMRA 66-783(7675)-8, FODA.
15. Dobak and Phillips, *Black Regulars 1866–1898*.

16. Billings to AAG, February 10, 1876, SR-FODA-3, FODA.

17. Billings 1872, Enlist, Ancestry.com.

18. Dobak and Phillips, *Black Regulars 1866–1898*, 272–78.

19. Ibid.

20. Courtney Pension, certificate 1174241, RG 15, NARA.

21. Lucinda Jackson, widow's pension, cert 421209, RG 15, NARA.

22. Williams, *Self-Taught*.

23. Sample to Schooley, March 16, 1868, US Army Commands 2D Military District 1867-1868, LR 1868 (Book II) S-79-S-301, January–May 1868, RG 98, NARA.

24. Ibid.

25. March 17 endorsement, Ibid.

26. April 1 endorsement, Ibid.

27. Sanford to Van Horn, April 28, 1868, RG 98 US Army Commands 2D Military District 1867-1868, LR 1868(Book II) S-79-S-301, January–May 1868, RG 98, NARA.

28. Rickey, *Forty Miles a Day*.

29. Hull to Van Horn, April 18, 1868, RG 98 US Army Commands 2D Military District 1867-1868, LR 1868(Book II) S-79-S-301, January–May 1868, RG 98, NARA.

30. Ibid.

31. Kendall GCM, PP-2749, NARA.

32. Glatthaar, *Forged in Battle*, 169–173.

33. Smith et al., *The Reminiscences of Major General Zenas R. Bliss*.

34. Reports to Lieutenant Colonel Hinks relative to the conditions of recruitment for Twenty-Fifth Infantry (twelve enclosures), February 1, 1870, Records of Divisions Recruiting Division 1814–1913, Letters Received, 1862-82, 1870, vol. 045 of 120 PI 17 entry 471, RG 94, NARA.

35. Chosey to Gray, February 24, 1870, Reports to Lieutenant Colonel Hinks relative to the conditions of recruitment for Twenty-Fifth Infantry (twelve enclosures), February 1, 1870, Records of Divisions Recruiting Division 1814–1913, Letters Received, 1862-82, 1870, vol. 045 of 120 PI 17 entry 471, RG 94, NARA.

36. Post Description, May 1872, NMRA-63-15(1946), FODA.

37. Papers Received at Post Library, November 1, 1881, NMRA 66-783(7675)-2, FODA.

38. Kinevan, *Frontier Cavalryman*, 44.

39. McChristian, *Garrison Tangles*.

40. August 19, 1869, letter, Lucinda Jackson widow's pension, cert 421209, RG 15, NARA.

41. Ibid., March 27, 1867 letter, Anthony to Lucinda Jackson.
42. Blight, *Frederick Douglass*, 164.
43. US Population Census 1870 Presidio County, Texas.
44. D. Weisel, March 1869 Monthly report, NMRA 63-15(1946), FODA.
45. Gerhard to Gonzales, January 21, 1871, NMRA 66-783(7675)8, FODA.
46. Gonzales to Gerhard, February 1, 1871, NMRA 66-783(7675)8, FODA.
47. Transcript of commissary fragment, Fort Davis, Texas NHS.
48. D. Weisel, May 1872 Monthly report, NMRA 63-15 (1946), FODA.
49. The books, purchased between February 20 and April 26, 1871, were likely the books listed in the ledger. In his forensic accounting, Andrews also found a July 11, 1871, receipt for additional books that had been signed by Gonzalez.
50. Andrews to Weisel, September 2, 1872, NMRA 66-783(7675)-1, FODA.
51. Watson, *The Independent Fourth Reader*.
52. Standard Order No. 51, December 17, 1872, NMRA 66-783(7675)-3, FODA; Greene, *Historic Resource Study*.
53. General Order No. 1, January 5, 1873, NMRA 66-783(7675)-3, FODA.
54. Orth, *History of Cleveland, Ohio*.
55. Bowdoin College, "Obituary Record," 142.
56. Ibid.
57. Kendall to Gray, January 13, 1873, SR-FODA-1, FODA.
58. Donaldson, *Duty beyond the Battlefield*.
59. Watson, *Independent Fourth Reader*.
60. Williams, *Self-Taught*.
61. Parker and Watson, *The National First Reader and Word Builder*.
62. Ibid.
63. Blight, *Frederick Douglass*.
64. Watson, *Independent Fourth Reader*.
65. Webster, *The Great Orations*.
66. Eichner, "Queering Frontier Identitiesm," "Frontier Intermediaries"; Wilkie, *Archaeology of Mothering*;
67. Blight, *Frederick Douglass*; Lapsansky-Werner and Bacon, *Back to Africa*; Wilson Jeremiah Moses, *Liberation Dreams*.
68. Barr, *Robinson's First Lessons*.
69. Dobak and Phillips, *Black Regulars 1866–1898*.
70. Kendall to Gray, February 28, 1873, NMRA 66-783(7675)-1, FODA.
71. Williams, *Self-Taught*.
72. March 31, 1873, post return, NMRA-172, FODA.
73. General Order No. 21, April 5, 1873, NMRA 66-783(7675)-3, FODA.
74. Bliss to AAG, May 1873; NMRA 66-783(7675)-6, FODA.
75. Kendall to Gray, September 22,1873, NMRA 66-783(7675)-1, FODA.

76. Smith et al. *The Reminiscences of Major General Zenas R. Bliss*, 469–70.

77. The other men were George Roberts, John R. Jones, Thomas Lee, Isaac Lewis, Absalom Ely, Daniel Landron, John Johnson, Edward Gaston, Houston Shelton, John Thomas, Jefferson Santifer, Ellis M. Russell, Jacob Lione, Jacob Richardson, Payton Cook, Barney Hiter, John Lee, George Ringold, Henry J. Johnson, and John H. Wheeler: GCM PP-3542, RG 153, NARA.

78. GCM PP-3542, RG 153, NARA.

79. Ibid.

80. Eskow, "Sympathy for the Loss of a Comrade."

81. Cooper to Bliss, July 30, 1873, NMRA 66-783(7675)-1, FODA.

82. Anon to Bliss, July 27, 1873, NMRA 66-783(7675)-1, FODA.

83. General Order No. 31, April 10, 1874, NMRA 66-783(7675)-3, FODA.

84. November 3, 1877 post report, NMRA 66-783(7675)-6, FODA.

85. Lemuel Johnson, GCM PP-2356, RG 153, NARA.

86. Ibid.

Chapter Six

1. Randolph Linsly Simpson African American collection, Beinecke Rare Book and Manuscript Library, Yale University, New Haven, CT.

2. Bradley, *Bluecoats and Tar Heels*, 195.

3. John Sample Pension Application, 6003300, RG 15, NARA; Sample enlistment papers, Enlist, NARA.

4. Schooley to Gray, February 1, 1870, RG 94 Recruit, NARA.

5. John Sample Pension Application, 6003300, RG 15, NARA.

6. Ibid.

7. Austermuhle, "What's the Story behind D.C.'s Old Soldiers' Home"; Dobak and Phillips, *Black Regulars 1866–1898*;

8. Sample Pension Application, 6003300, RG 15, NARA.

9. See Browne, *Dark Matters*; Fanon, *Wretched of the Earth*; Hartman, *Scenes of Subjection*; Weheliye, *Habeas Viscus*.

10. Sample Pension Application, 6003300, RG 15, NARA.

11. Ibid.

12. Post hospital records were kept in ledgers with scores of entries per page and many, many columns. It would be easy for a post surgeon to write the wrong diagnosis next to a soldier's name, or more likely, a hurried investigator to attribute someone else's syphilis to Sample.

13. D'Arcy, "On Recent Advances in the Surgical Treatment of Syphilis"; Fleck, *Genesis and Development of a Scientific Fact*.

14. Sample Pension Application, 6003300, RG 15, NARA.

15. "Sgt Major John Sample," Find A Grave, findagrave.com/memorial/21922912 /john-sample.
16. See, for example, Curry, *Man-Not*; McKittrick, *Sylvia Wynter*; Richardson, *Black Masculinity*.
17. Adams, *Class and Race*; Donaldson, *Duty beyond the Battlefield*; Leiker, *Racial Borders*.
18. Penningroth, "Freedpeople's Families in the Age of Emancipation."
19. Ibid.; Edward Mark QQ-2972, RG 153, NARA.
20. Adams, *Class and Race*, 175–76.
21. Charles Smith GCM PP 4206, RG 15, NARA; Scobee, *Fort Davis Texas*.
22. General Order No. 13, February 12, 1874; Circular No. 8, July 25, 1874, NMRA 66-783(7675)-3, FODA.
23. Andrews to AAG, January 10, 1873, NMRA 66-783(7576)-1, FODA.
24. Eichner, "Frontier Intermediaries"; "Queering Frontier Identities."
25. Joseph Franklin GCM PP 142, RG 15, NARA.
26. Cooper to Bliss, July 30, 1873, NMRA 66-783(7675)-1, FODA.
27. Minutes of Presidio County Court, Numbers 1 and 2, October 1878, Entry 52, Fort Davis Court House, Jeff Davis County, Texas.
28. Richard Cuff GCM PP-3567 and PP-3773, RG 15, NARA.
29. US Population Census 1870, Maverick County, Texas.
30. Solomon Moore, GCM PP-2875, Henry Jenkins GCM PP-3052, RG 15, NARA.
31. Penningroth, "Freed People's Families in the Age of Emancipation."
32. Solomon Powell GCM PP 3606, RG 15, NARA.
33. Ibid.
34. Collins, *Black Feminist Thought*; Curry, *Man-Not*; hooks, *We Real Cool*; Richardson, *Black Masculinity*.
35. Curry, *Man-Not*, particularly 1–38 and 229–33.
36. Battle-Baptiste, *Black Feminist Archaeology*; Wilkie, *Archaeology of Mothering*.
37. Eichner, "Queering Frontier Identities"; Nelson, "'Right Nice Little House[s].'"
38. Greene, *Historic Resource Study*, 101.
39. See Gero and Conkey, *Engendering Archaeology*; Gilchrist, *Gender and Archaeology;* Joyce, *Gender and Power in Prehispanic Mesoamerica*; Wilkie and Hayes, "Engendered and Feminist Archaeologies.
40. Carlson, *The Buffalo Soldier Tragedy of 1877*; Wilkie, *Creating Freedom*.
41. Billings, *Report on the Hygiene*, xxxvi.
42. Laidlaw, "A Free Gift Makes No Friends"; Mauss, *The Gift*.
43. Wilkie, *Archaeology of Mothering; Creating Freedom*.

44. Eichner, "Queering Frontier Identities."

45. Ibid.; Eichner, "Frontier Intermediaries.

46. Eichner, "Frontier Intermediaries."

47. Wall, "Sacred Dinners and Secular Teas."

48. US Census, 1870 Presidio County.

49. Leiker, *Racial Borders*, 88; Texas State Board of Health Bureau of Vital Statistic Death Certificate George Bentley, February 20, 1923; Us Population Census 1880, Presidio Texas Roll 1323 Page 87A; Warren, "Lines in the Land.

50. Parsons, *Captain John R. Hughes*, 336.

51. Leonard, *Men of Color*, 64.

52. Moore, *Biennial Report of the Secretary of State of the State of Texas*, 146; Marriage Record Robert Fair and Pabla Casey, February 28, 1889, the State of Texas Count of Jeff Davis; US Civil War Pension Index: General Index to Pension Files, 1861–1935, Robert Fayl (alias) Robert Fair, Invalid Pension application no. 752484 certificate 510554, NARA.

53. Anthony Jackson enlistment papers 1870, 1875, US Army Register of Enlistments 1798–1914; 1869-1870, A-O; 1871-1877, H-O.

54. Lucina Jackson Widow Pension, NARA.

55. March 20, 1867, letter, Anthony to Lucinda Jackson, Ibid.

56. Ibid.

57. April 6, letter from Anthony to Lucinda, Ibid.

58. McChristian, *Garrison Tangles*, 46–47.

59. Russell, *Guns on the Early Frontiers*.

60. Herskovits, *Fort Bowie Material Culture*.

61. Martin, Longacre, and Hill, *Chapters in the Prehistory of Eastern Arizona*, 112.

62. Johnson, *Negroes and the Gun*.

63. Rickey, *Forty Miles a Day*, 19.

64. PP-3257 court-martial of James Wilson, NARA.

65. Wilkie, *The Lost Boys of Zeta Psi*.

66. Board of Officers Convened March 17, 1870, transcript, NMRA 66-783(7576)-2, FODA.

67. Dobak and Phillips, *Black Regulars 1866–1898*, 65.

68. D'Emilio and Freeman, *Intimate Matters*.

69. Laqueur, *Solitary Sex*.

70. Miller, *Cameos Old & New*.

71. Haskell and Penny, *Taste and the Antique*.

72. Miller, *Cameos Old & New*.

73. See Wilkie, Hyde, Lowman, and Emerson, "Ode to a Grecian Boy," for a detailed discussion of attribution.

74. Waters, "'The Most Famous Fairy in History.'"
75. Rambach, "The Antinous Braschi on Engraved Gems"; Vout, "Antinous, Archaeology and History."
76. Wilkie et al., Grecian Boy.
77. Dellamora, *Masculine Desire*; Lambert, *Beloved and God*; Waters, "The Most Famous Fairy."
78. Bann, "John Addington Symonds and the Misrecognition of Antinous"; Symonds, *The Memoirs*.
79. Dellamora, *Masculine Desire*; Haskell and Penny, *Taste and the Antique*; Waters, "'The Most Famous Fairy.'"
80. Hubert, "Karl Heinrich Ulrichs"; Kaylor, *Secreted Desires*;
81. Wilkie et al., Grecian Boy.
82. 1870 Population Census, Maverick County, Texas.
83. Martin Pedee GCM PP-2809, RG 153, NARA.
84. Schooley to Andrews, October 20, 1872, NMRA 66-783(7675)-3, FODA.
85. General Order No. 3, January 1, 1874, NMRA 66-783(7675)-3, FODA.
86. Standard Order No. 20, February 20, 1874; General Order No. 19, March 2, 1874, NMRA 66-783 (7675)-3, FODA.

Chapter Seven

1. Southerner was arrested again the following year for shooting at the officer's quarters before being subdued by Sergeant Jonas Cox. Charles Southerner GCM PP-2875, RG 15, NARA.
2. Nankivell, *Buffalo Soldier Regiment*, 193; 1870 US Population Census, Fort Clark, Maverick County, Texas.
3. McChristian, *Regular Army O!*; Wooster, *History of Fort Davis*.
4. McChristian, *Regular Army O!*; Wooster, *History of Fort Davis*.
5. Shafter to Hague, December 17, 1872. NMRA 66-783(7675)-1, FODA.
6. Ibid.
7. Shafter to AAG, April 4, 1872, NMRA 66-783(7675)-1, FODA.
8. General Order No. 58, May 2, 1872, NMRA 66-783(7675)-3, FODA.
9. Endorsement on letter transmitting return of ordinance survey, Company I, Ninth Cavalry. SR-FODA-9, FODA.
10. Endorsement on letter June 3, 1873, Captain of Ordinance to Andrews, SR-FODA-9, FODA.
11. Endorsement, Andrews to Headquarters, June 4, 1872, SR- FODA-9, FODA.
12. Company I, Ninth Cavalry ordnance reports, 1872–75, NMRA-816(8091), FODA.

13. Shafter to AAG, April 1, 1872, post returns June 1872, NMRA 66-783(7675)-1, FODA.

14. Ibid.; Clary, "The Role of the Army Surgeon in the West."

15. Andrews to AAG, July 23, 1872, NMRA 66-783(7675)-1, FODA.

16. Andrews to Patterson, July 5, 1872, NMRA 66-783(7675)-1, FODA.

17. Standard Order No. 105, July 30, 1872, NMRA 66-783(7675)-3, FODA.

18. Andrews to AAG, August 14, 1872, NMRA 66-783(7675)-1, FODA.

19. Post returns, August 1872, NMRA 66-783(7675)-3, FODA.

20. John Sample, H. B. Quimby, NPS-SSS.

21. Hewey GCM, PP-2839, RG 153, NARA.

22. Standard Order No. 158, November 11, 1872, NMRA 66-783(7675)-3, FODA.

23. Standard Order No. 158, November 11, 1872, NMRA 66-783(7675)-3, FODA.

24. Daniel Tallifero first appears in Thompson, "The Negro Soldiers on the Frontier." Thompson situated the case within a discussion of the difficulties of Black soldiers finding sexual partners on the frontier. Thompson cites only Andrews's November 21, 1872, letter to Auger. Dobak and Phillips, in *Black Regulars 1866–1898*, cites the same letter. In *Racial Borders*, James Leiker contextualizes the attempted rape in context of Black sexual needs and stereotypes but never discusses any irregularities in the case (85–86). Wooster, in *Frontier Crossroads*, perhaps the most prolific historian of Fort Davis, cites the letter and makes uncited reference to news of the case "spreading like wildfire" (71). While space prohibits including each description here, each author draws exclusively on Andrews's November 21 letter to Augur as the primary source but freely draws on the mythology of the Black rapist to elaborate and ornament their accounts.

25. Hartman, *Scenes of Subjection*.

26. See Post Mortem of Charles Hill, July 1876; Murder of Abraham Jackson, December 1876; NMRA 63-15(1946), FODA.

27. Andrews to Augur, November 21, 1872, NMRA 66-783(7675)-1, FODA.

28. Edwin J. Stivers, Letter to the Editor, *New York Herald*, December 8, 1872, CA-LOC.

29. Andrews to Augur, July 20, 1872, NMRA 66-783(7675)-1, FODA.

30. Adams, *Class and Race*, 178.

31. Barad, *Meeting the Universe Halfway*; Bennett, *Vibrant Matter*; Chen, *Animacies*; Latour, *Reassembling the Social*; Tsing, *Mushroom*.

32. Entry in surgeon's journal, November 1872, De Graw, NMRA 63-15(1946), FODA.

33. Woodward, February 21, 1874, enclosure in Mary Tallifero mother's pension application number 211669, RG 15, NARA.

34. Physician's report for September 1870, July 1873, NMRA 63-15(1946), FODA; Standard Order No. 24, March 17, 1870, RG 98 66-783(7576)-2, FODA.

35. Katherine Kincopf, personal communication.

36. Skallagrim, "An Antique Percussion Revolver"; Smith, *Warman's Civil War Weapons*; SRPC, "Loading and Firing a Colt 1860 Revolver."

37. See Skallagrim, "An Antique Percussion Revolver"; SRPC, "Loading and Firing a Colt 1860 Revolver."

38. "November 1872 Moon Phases," Moongiant, accessed June 1, 2020, https://www.moongiant.com/moonphases/November/1872.

39. Ibid.; Ordnance and Ordnance Stores in Hands of Troops, May–October 1872, NMRA 816 (8061), FODA.

40. "Visible Proofs: Forensic Views of the Body.

41. Greene, *Historic Resource Study*; Martin Pedee GCM PP-2809, RG 153, NARA.

42. Greene, *Historic Resource Study*,143–47.

43. John Heiner, Site Historian, Fort Davis National Historic Site, personal communication.

44. Goodman, *The Sun and the Moon*.

45. Holt to Andrews, December 18, 1872, NMRA 66-783(7675)-9, FODA.

46. Crane, "Vermilion County Group to Unveil Long-Overdue Tombstone.

Epilogue

1. Limerick, *Something in the Soil*.

2. Barad, *Meeting the Universe Halfway*, 141; Joyce, *The Future of Nuclear Waste*.

3. Binford, *In Pursuit of the Past*; Olsen et al., *Archaeology*.

4. Olsen et al., *Archaeology*.

5. Marshall and Alberti, "A Matter of Difference."

6. Joyce and Gillespie, *Things in Motion*.

7. Bennett, *Vibrant Matter*; DeLanda, *A New Philosophy of Society*; Deleuze and Guattari, *A Thousand Plateaus*.

8. Mbembe, *Necropolitics*; Weheliye, *Habeas Viscus*.

9. Puar, *The Right to Maim*.

10. Dobak and Phillips, *Black Regulars 1866–1898*; Schubert, *Voices of the Buffalo Soldier*.

11. Jasbir, *The Right to Maim*, xiv.

12. Weheliye, *Habeas Viscus*.

BIBLIOGRAPHY

→═◎═←

Manuscripts and Archives

DENVER PUBLIC LIBRARY

Don Rickey Papers, WH986, Western History Collection, Denver Public Library.

LIBRARY OF CONGRESS [LOC]

Douglas, Frederick. "Why a Colored Man Should Enlist." Manuscript/Mixed Material. https://www.loc.gov/item/mfd.22006.

William Branch. Texas United States, ca. 1938. Photograph. https://www.loc.gov /item/99615280/.

NATIONAL ARCHIVES, WASHINGTON, DC [NARA]

US Army Registers of Enlistment, 1798–1914 [database on line at National Archives]. Provo, UT, USA, Ancestry.com Operations, Inc. 2007. [Enlist].

National Archives Microfilm Publication T289. "Organization List to Pension Files of Veterans who served between 1861–1900."

Record Group [RG] 15. Veteran's Administration. Bureau of Pensions. Pension Files.

RG 29 US Bureau of the Census

1860 Eighth Census of the United States, Presidio County, Texas. Ancestry.com <https://ancestry.com>. Accessed 11 June 2016.

1870 Ninth Census of the United States, Kinney, Maverick and Presidio Counties, Texas. Ancestry.com <https://ancestry.com>. Accessed 11 June 2016.

1880 Tenth Census of the United States, Presidio County, Texas. Ancestry.com <https://ancestry.com>. Accessed 11 June 2016

1900 Eleventh Census of the United States, Presidio County, Texas. Ancestry.com <https://ancestry.com>. Accessed 11 June 2016

1910 Twelfth Census of the United States, Presidio County, Texas. Ancestry.com. <https://ancestry.com>. Accessed 11 June 2016

RG 98 US Army Commands 2D Military District 1867–1868. LR 1868 (Book II) s-79-S-301. January–May 1868.

RG 153 Judge Advocate General's Office
General Court-Martial Transcripts.
RG 393 US Army Continental Commands, 1821–1920
Records of the US Regular Army Mobile Units Infantry 26 (1869–), Infantry 1869–1917. Regimental Records. Bimonthly Returns and Inventories of the Effects of Deceased Soldiers, 1869–1881. Box No 1. NM 93 Entry 1804. [RG 393-BRIEDS].

FORT DAVIS READING ROOM [FODA], F
ORT DAVIS NATIONAL HISTORIC SITE, FORT DAVIS, TEXAS

FTD_SoldierDatabase.xlsx. Database of soldiers who served at Fort Davis, Fort Davis National Historic Site Reading Room, Fort Davis, Texas. [FTD Soldier].

Fort Davis Post Trader Ledger 1871.xls Electronic Resource, Reading Room, Fort Davis National Historic Site. [FODA Trader].

NMRA 63–15(1946). RG 94 AGO pdf. Digitized microform of Medical History Posts, RG 94 Records of the Adjutant General's Office. [NMRA 63–15(1946)].

NMRA 65–855 (10427) 2. RG 153 FT DAVIS TX RESERVATION FILE: CHAPLAINS' REPTS (END OF ROLL).pdf, digitized microform of RG 153 Records of the Judge Advocate General's Office, Fort Davis, Texas Reservation File. [NMRA 65–855(10427)-2].

NMRA 66–783(7675) 1. Letters Sent, 1867–1878.pdf Digitized microform of RG 98: Records of the United States Army Commands. Fort Davis, Texas, Selected documents, 1867–1891. Letters Sent, Telegrams Sent, 1867–91. [NMRA 66–783(7675)-1].

NMRA 66–783(7576) 2. Letters Sent, Circulars, Memos, 1867–1890(STARTS DEC 1878).pdf. Digitized file of RG 98 Records of the US Army Commands Fort Davis, Selected Documents, 1867–1891, Letters sent, telegrams sent, microfilm roll 2. National Archives. [NMRA 66–783(7675)-2].

NMRA 66–783(7675) 3. Orders, Circulars, Memo, 1867–1891.pdf. Digitized copy of National Archive microform RG 98: Records of the United States Army Command, Fort Davis, Texas. Selected Documents, Orders, Circulars, Memoranda 1867–1891. Roll 3. [NMRA 66–783(7675)-3].

NMRA 66–783(7675) 4. RG 98 Orders, Circulars, Memoranda, 1875–1884. pdf. Digitized microfilm from National Archives of RG 98 Records of the US Army Commands, Orders, Circulars, Memoranda, 1875–1884. [NMRA 66–783(7675)-4].

NMRA 66–783(7675) 6. Letters Received and Misc., 1868–1891.pdf. Digitized copy of National Archive microform RG 98: Records of the United States Army Command, Fort Davis, Texas. Selected Documents, 1867–1891. Roll 6. [NMRA 66–783(7675)-6].

NMRA 66–783(7675) 7. Letters and Received and Misc., 1870–1891.pdf. Digitized copy of National Archive Microform RG 98: Records of the United States Army Commands. Fort Davis, Texas, Selected Documents, 1867–1891, Letters Received and Miscellaneous Documents, 1870–1891. [NMRA 66–783 (7675)-7].

NMRA 816(8091). Digitized copy of microform of National Archive RG 156, Office of Chief Ordnance, Ordnance and Ordnance stores in hands of troops, various regiments, 1870–1876. [NMRA 816(8091)].

Post Returns 1854–1874 NMRA 172 RG 94, Part 1.pdf Digitized copy of Records of the Adjutant General's Office Record Group No. 94 Fort Davis, Texas Post Returns, 1854–1891. [NMRA-172].

Selected Records-Fort Davis, Texas-RG 92, RG 156, RG 393 1874–1891 Roll 1.pdf, Digitized files of RG 92-Office of the Quartermaster General (1818–1905) Reports of Persons and Articles Hired. [SR-FODA-1].

Selected Records-Fort Davis, Texas-RG 92, RG 156, RG 393, 1868–1891 roll 4.pdf. Digitized file of microfilm reel of National Archive records pertaining to Fort Davis from RG 92, RG 156, RG 393. [SR-FODA-4].

Selected Records-Fort Davis, Texas-RG 92 RG156 RG 393 1869–1883 Roll 5.pdf Digitized copy of RG 393 US Army Continental Commands, 1821–1920 Part 5 Military Installations. Fort Davis. [SR-FODA-5].

Selected Records-Fort Davis, Texas-RG 92, RG 156, RG 393 1881–1883 Roll 6.pdf. Digitized copy of RG 393 US Army Continental Commands, 1821–1920 Part 5 Military Installations. Fort Davis. [SR-FODA-6].

Selected Records-Fort Davis, Texas-RG 92, RG 156, RG 393 1849–1886 Roll 9.pdf. Digitized microform of National Archive selected documents for Fort Davis from RG 92, RG 156, RG 393, selected records (volumes and boxes). [SR-FODA-9].

Selected Records-Fort Davis, Texas-RG 92 1867–1886 Roll 10.pdf. Digitized microfilm RG 92 Records of the Office of the Adjutant General 1870s–1920, selected entries, Roll 10. [SR-FODA-10].

NATIONAL LIBRARY OF MEDICINE.

2008 "Visible Proofs: Forensic Views of the Body: Image 1 of 2 The autopsy of President Abraham Lincoln." Nim.nih.govexhibition/visibleproofs/galleries/cases/Lincoln.html. Exhibition at the National Library of Medicine, closed February 25, 2008.

BEINECKE RARE BOOK AND MANUSCRIPT LIBRARY

Randolph Linsly Simpson African American Collection, Beinecke Rare Book and Manuscript Library, Yale University, New Haven, CT.

Online Database

Ancestry.com

Find A Grave

Sergeant Major John Sample. findagrave.com/memorial/21922912/john-sample.

Library of Congress [LOC]

Chronicling America: Historic American Newspapers. National Endowment for the Humanities and Library of Congress. www.chroniclingamerica.loc.gov. [CA-LOC].

Born in Slavery: Slave Narratives from the Federal Writers' Project, 1936 to 1938. https://www.loc.gov/collections/slave-narratives-from-the-federal-writers -project-1936-to-1938/about-this-collection/.

"William Branch, San Antonio, Texas." In *Federal Writers' Project: Slave Narrative Project, Vol. 16, Texas, Part 1, Adams-Duhon*, 143–146. 1936. Manuscript/Mixed Material. https://www.loc.gov/item/mesn161/.

"William Watkins, Texas." In *Federal Writers' Project: Slave Narrative Project, Vol. 16, Texas, Part 4, Sanco-Young*, 141–143. 1936. Manuscript/Mixed Material. https://www.loc.gov/item/mesn164/.

National Park Service

Soldiers and Sailors Database. Searchable online archive of men who served in the Civil War. https://www.nps.gov/civilwar/soldiers-and-sailors-database.htm. [NPS-SSS].

Newspapers and Periodicals

News-Gazette

Crane, Tracy. "Vermilion County Group to Unveil Long-Overdue Tombstone for Black Civil War Soldier." *News-Gazette*, April 13, 2019. https://www .news-gazette.com/news/vermilion-county-group-to-unveil-long-overdue -tombstone-for-Black-civil-war-soldier/article_f3867587-a28a-5d6b-8337 –0492ca19bde1.html.

Legislation

National Historic Preservation Act of 1966. https://www.achp.gov/sites/default /files/2018–06/nhpa.pdf.

Books and Articles

Adams, Kevin. *Class and Race in the Frontier Army: Military Life in the West, 1870–1890*. Norman: University of Oklahoma Press, 2009.

Alexander, Michelle. *The New Jim Crow: Mass Incarceration in the Age of Colorblindness*. New York: New Press, 2010.

Austermuhle, Martin. "What's the Story behind D.C.'s Old Soldiers' Home, and What's the Future of the Campus?" WAMU 88.5: American University Radio, accessed June 1, 2020. https://wamu.org/story/18/08/02/whats-story-behind -d-c-s-old-soldiers-home-whats-future-campus/.

Bann, Stephen. "John Addington Symonds and the Misrecognition of Antinous." July 12 paper, Henry Moore Institute Online Papers and Proceedings, 2006. www.henry-moore.org/hmi.

Barad, Karen. *Meeting the Universe Halfway: Quantum Physics and the Entanglement of Matter and Meaning*. Durham, NC: Duke University Press, 2007.

Barber, Edwin Atlee. *Marks of American Potters*. Philadelphia: Patterson & White, 1904. http://www.trentonhistory.org/Made/Marks.html.

Barnes, Frank C. *Cartridges of the World: A Complete Illustrated Reference for More Than 1,500 Cartridges*. Edited by Richard A. Mann, n.p.: Gun Digest Books, 2012.

Barr, Samuel D., ed. *Robinson's First Lessons in Mental and Written Arithmetic: On the Objective Method*. Robinson's Mathematical Series. New York: Ivison, Blakeman, & Taylor, 1870.

Battle-Baptiste, Whitney. *Black Feminist Archaeology*. Walnut Creek, CA: Left Coast Press, 2011.

"Battle Unit Details." The Civil War. National Park Service. Accessed June 1, 2020. nps.gov/civilwar/search-battle-units-detail.htm?battleUnitCode=UUS-0064RIOOC.

Bederman, Gail. *Manliness and Civilization: A Cultural History of Gender and Race in the United States, 1880–1917*. Chicago: University of Chicago Press, 1996.

Bell, Andrew McIlwaine. *Mosquito Soldiers: Malaria, Yellow Fever, and the Course of the American Civil War*. Baton Rouge: Louisiana State University Press, 2010.

Bennett, Jane. *Vibrant Matter: A Political Ecology of Things*. Durham, NC: Duke University Press, 2010.

Binford, Lewis R. *In Pursuit of the Past: Decoding the Archaeological Record*. Berkeley: University of California Press, 2002.

Black, Daniel P. *Dismantling Black Manhood: An Historical and Literary Analysis of the Legacy of Slavery*. New York: Routledge, 1997.

Blaszczyk, Regina Lee. "The Aesthetic Moment: China Decorators, Consumer

Demand, and Technological Change in the American Pottery Industry, 1865–1900." *Winterthur Portfolio* 29, no. 2/3 (Summer–Autumn 1994): 121–53.

Billings, John S., ed. *A Report on the Hygiene of the United States Army with Descriptions of Military Posts.* Circular No. 8, War Department, Surgeon General Office, Washington, DC. Washington, DC: Government Printing Office, 1875.

———, ed. *Outline Description of U.S. Military Posts and Stations in the Year 1871.* War Department, Quartermaster General's Office, Washington DC. Washington, DC: Government Printing Office, 1872.

Blight, David W. *Frederick Douglass: Prophet of Freedom.* New York: Simon & Schuster, 2018.

Bowdoin College. "Obituary Record." In *Obituary Record of the Graduates of Bowdoin College and the Medical School of Maine for the Year Ending 1, June 1912,* No. 3 Series 1900–1919, 147. Brunswick, ME: Record Press, 1913.

Bonilla-Silva, Eduardo. *Racism without Racists: Color-Blind Racism and the P ersistence of Racial Inequality in America.* Lanham, MD: Rowman and Littlefield, 2017.

Bradley, Mark L. *Bluecoats and Tar Heels: Soldiers and Civilians in Reconstruction North Carolina.* Lexington: University Press of Kentucky, 2009.

Brock, William H. *Justus von Liebig: The Chemical Gatekeeper.* Cambridge, UK: Cambridge University Press, 1997.

Brooks, James F. *Captives & Cousins: Slavery, Kinship, and Community in the Southwest Borderlands.* Chapel Hill: University of North Carolina Press, 2002.

Brown, Maureen, José E. Zapata, and Bruce K. Moses. *Camp Elizabeth, Sterling County, Texas: An Archaeological and Archival Investigation of a U.S. Army Subpost, and Evidence Supporting Its Use by the Military and "Buffalo Soldiers."* Archaeological Survey Report No. 267. San Antonio: Center for Archaeological Research, University of Texas at San Antonio, 1998.

Browne, Simone. *Dark Matters: On the Surveillance of Blackness.* Durham, NC: Duke University Press, 2015.

Brune. Gunnar M. *Springs of Texas: Volume 1.* Texas A&M University Agriculture Series 5. College Station: Texas A&M University Press, 1981.

Caldwell, Mary Channen. "'Flower of the Lily': Late-Medieval Religious and Heraldic Symbolism in Paris, Bibliothèque national de France, MS Français 146." *Early Music History* 33 (August 2014): 1–60. https://doi.org/10.1017/S0261127913000119.

Carlson, Paul H. *The Buffalo Soldier Tragedy of 1877.* College Station: Texas A&M University Press, 2003.

Carrera, Magali M. *Imagining Identities in New Spain: Race, Lineage, and the Colonial Body in Portraiture and Casta Paintings.* Austin: University of Texas Press, 2003.

Casey, Clifford B. *Alpine, Texas, Then and Now*. Seagraves, NY: Pioneer Book Publishers, 1981.

Cheek, Charles. *The Fort Concho Trash Dump: An Archaeological Analysis*. Archaeological Research Associates Research Report 12. Tulsa: n.p., 1977.

Chen, Mel Y. *Animacies: Biopolitics, Racial Mattering, and Queer Affect*. Durham, NC: Duke University Press, 2012.

Christenson, Andrew L. "A Test of Mean Ceramic Dating Using Well-Dated Kayenta Anasazi Sites." *Kiva* 59, no. 3 (Spring 1994): 297–317.

Cimprich, John. *Fort Pillow: A Civil War Massacre and Public Memory*. Baton Rouge: Louisiana State University Press, 2011.

Clark, Kathleen Ann. *Defining Moments: African American Commemoration and Political Culture in the South, 1863–1913*. Chapel Hill: University of North Carolina Press, 2005.

Clary, David A. "The Role of the Army Surgeon in the West: Daniel Weisel at Fort Davis, Texas, 1868–1872." *Western Historical Quarterly* 3, no. 1 (January 1972): 53–66. https://doi.org/10.2307/967707.

Collins, Patricia Hill. *Black Feminist Thought: Knowledge, Consciousness, and the Politics of Empowerment*. New York: Routledge, 2008.

"County Map of Texas, 1860." Map Collections from the University of Texas at Arlington, University of North Texas Libraries. The Portal to Texas History. Accessed July 5, 2020. https://texashistory.unt.edu/ark:/67531/metapth190739/.

Crenshaw, Kimberle. "Demarginalizing the Intersection of Race and Sex: A Black Feminist Critique of Antidiscrimination Doctrine, Feminist Theory and Antiracist Politics." *University of Chicago Legal Forum* 1989, no. 1 (1989): 139–67.

Cunningham, Jo. *The Collector's Encyclopedia of American Dinnerware*. Paducah, KY: Collector's Books, 1982.

Curry, Tommy J. *The Man-Not: Race, Class, Genre, and the Dilemmas of Black Manhood*. Philadelphia: Temple University Press, 2017.

Custer, Elizabeth B. *Boots and Saddles: Or Life in Dakota with General Custer; With Portrait and Map*. New York: Harper & Brothers, 1899.

D'Arcy, Power. "On Recent Advances in the Surgical Treatment of Syphilis." *British Medical Journal* 1, no. 2473 (April 1908): 1225–30. https://doi.org/10.1136/bmj.1.2473.1225-a.

Deetz, James. *In Small Things Forgotten: An Archaeology of Early Material Life*. New York: Anchor Books, 1996.

DeLanda, Manuel. *A New Philosophy of Society: Assemblage Theory and Social Complexity*. London: Continuum, 2006.

Deleuze, Gilles, and Felix Guattari. *A Thousand Plateaus: Capitalism and Schizophrenia*. London: Continuum, 2008.

Dellamora, Richard. *Masculine Desire: The Sexual Politics of Victorian Aestheticism.* Chapel Hill: University of North Carolina Press, 1990.

Delle, James A. *The Archaeology of Northern Slavery and Freedom.* Gainesville: University Press of Florida, 2019.

D'Emilio, John, and Estelle B. Freeman. *Intimate Matters: A History of Sexuality in America.* 2nd ed. Chicago: University of Chicago Press, 1997.

Dickson, Ephriam D., III. "Museum Spotlight: 'Relics of Barbarism': The Army's Original Enlisted Bunks." *National Museum of the United States Army.* Accessed June 1, 2020. https://armyhistory.org/museum-spotlight-relics-of-barbarism-the-armys-original-enlisted-bunks/.

Dieringer, Ernie, and Bev Dieringer. *White Ironstone China: Plate Identification Guide 1840–1890.* Atglen, PA: Schiffer Books, 2001.

Dobak, William A., and Thomas D. Phillips. *The Black Regulars 1866–1898.* Norman: University of Oklahoma Press, 2001.

Donaldson, Le'Trice D. *Duty beyond the Battlefield: African American Soldiers Fight for Racial Uplift, Citizenship, and Manhood, 1870–1920.* Carbondale: Southern Illinois University Press, 2020.

Douglass, Frederick, and Harriet Jacobs. *Narrative of the Life of Frederick Douglass, an American Slave & Incidents in the Life of a Slave Girl.* New York: Modern Library, 2011.

Du Bois, W. E. B. *Black Reconstruction: An Essay Toward a History of the Part Which Black Folk Played in the Attempt to Reconstruct Democracy in America, 1860–1880.* New York: Harcourt, Brace, 1935.

———. *Black Reconstruction in America 1860–1880.* New York: Atheneum, 1992.

———. *The Souls of Black Folk.* New York: Dover Publications, 1994.

Godden, Geoffrey A. *Encyclopedia of British Pottery and Porcelain Marks.* New York: Bonanza Books, 1964.

Eichner, Katrina Christiana Loening. "Frontier Intermediaries: Army Laundresses at Fort Davis, Texas." *Historical Archaeology* 53 (2019), 138–52. Accessed June 28, 2020. https://doi.org/10.1007/s41636-019-00167-x.

———. "Queering Frontier Identities: Archaeological Investigations at a Nineteenth-Century US Army Laundresses' Quarters in Fort Davis, Texas." PhD diss., Department of Anthropology, University of California, Berkeley, 2017.

Ellis, John H. *Yellow Fever and Public Health in the New South.* Lexington: University Press of Kentucky, 1992.

Ely, Glen Sample. *The Texas Frontier and the Butterfield Overland Mail, 1858–1861.* Norman: University of Oklahoma Press, 2016.

Emberton, Carole. "'Only Murder Makes Men': Reconsidering the Black Military Experience." *Journal of the Civil War Era* 12, no. 3 (September 2012), 369–93.

Emberton, Carole. *Beyond Redemption: Race, Violence, and the American South after the Civil War*. Chicago: University of Chicago Press, 2013.

Eskow, Nicholas. "Sympathy for the Loss of a Comrade: Black Citizenship and the 1873 'Fort Stockton' Mutiny." Honors thesis, Department of Anthropology, University of California, Berkeley, 2018.

Fanon, Frantz. *Black Skin, White Masks*. New York: Grove, 2008.

———. *The Wretched of the Earth*. New York: Grove Weidenfeld, 1963.

Field, Ron. US *Infantry in the Indian Wars 1865–91*. Men at Arms Series 438. Oxford: Osprey Publishing, 2007.

Fike, Richard E. *The Bottle Book: A Comprehensive Guide to Historic, Embossed, Medicine Bottles*. Caldwell, NJ: Blackburn Press, 1987.

Fleck, Ludwik. *Genesis and Development of a Scientific Fact*. Translated by Fred Bradley and Thaddeus J. Trenn. Edited by Thaddeus J. Trenn and Robert K. Merton. Chicago: University of Chicago Press, 1979.

Flewellen, Ayana Omilade. "Locating Marginalized Historical Narratives at Kingsley Plantation." *Historical Archaeology* 51, no. 1 (March 2017): 71–87. https://doi.org/10.1007/s41636-017-0005-7.

Foner, Jack D. *The United States Soldier between Two Wars: Army Life and Reforms, 1865–1898*. New York: Humanities Press, 1970.

Fowler, Arlen L. *The Black Infantry in the West, 1869–1891*. Norman: University of Oklahoma Press, 1971.

Frankenberg, Ruth. *White Women, Race Matters: The Social Construction of Whiteness*. Minneapolis: University of Minnesota Press, 1993.

Fox, Georgia L. *The Archaeology of Smoking and Tobacco*. Gainesville: University Press of Florida, 2015.

Gannon, Megan I. "Unearthing the True Toll of the Tulsa Race Massacre." *Sapiens* 22 (May 2020).

Geier, Clarence R., David G. Orr, and Matthew B. Reeves, eds. *Huts and History: The Historical Archaeology of Military Encampment during the American Civil War*. Gainesville: University Press of Florida, 2006.

Gellar, Pamela L. "Building Nation, Becoming Object: The Bio-politics of the Samuel G. Morton Crania Collection." *Historical Archaeology* 54, no. 1 (January 2020): 52–70. https://doi.org/10.1007/s41636-019-00218-3.

Gero, Joan M., and Margaret W. Conkey, eds. *Engendering Archaeology: Women and Prehistory*. Oxford: Blackwell Press, 1991.

Gilchrist, Roberta. *Gender and Archaeology: Contesting the Past*. London: Routledge, 2012.

Glatthaar, Joseph T. *Forged in Battle: The Civil War Alliance of Black Soldiers and White Officers*. New York: Free Press, 1990.

González-Tennant, Edward. *The Rosewood Massacre: An Archaeology and History of Intersectional Violence*. Gainesville: University Press of Florida.

Goodman, Matthew. *The Sun and the Moon: The Remarkable True Account of Hoaxers, Showmen, Dueling Journalists and Lunar Man-Bats in Nineteenth Century New York*. New York: Basic Books, 2008.

Greene, Jerome A. *Historic Resource Study: Fort Davis National Historic Site*. Denver, CO: United States Department of the Interior, National Park Service, 1986.

Guerin, E. J. *Mountain Charley or the Adventures of Mrs. E. J. Guerin, Who Was Thirteen Years in Male Attire*. Norman: University of Oklahoma Press, 1968.

Gwynne, S. C. *Empire of the Summer Moon: Quanah Parker and the Rise and Fall of the Comanches, the Most Powerful Indian Tribe in American History*. New York: Scribner, 2010.

Hartman, Saidiya V. *Scenes of Subjection: Terror, Slavery, and Self-Making in Nineteenth-Century America*. Oxford: Oxford University Press, 1997.

Harris, Theodore D., ed. *Negro Frontiersman: The Western Memoirs of Henry O. Flipper; First Negro Graduate of West Point*. El Paso: Texas Western College Press, 1963.

Haskell, Francis, and Nicholas Penny. *Taste and the Antique: The Lure of Classical Sculpture, 1500–1900*. New Haven, CT: Yale University Press, 2006.

Hayes, Katherine Howlett. *Slavery Before Race: Europeans, Africans, and Indians at Long Island's Sylvester Manor Plantation, 1651–1884*. New York: New York University Press, 2013.

Herskovits, Robert M. *Fort Bowie Material Culture*. Anthropological Papers of the University of Arizona 31. Tucson: University of Arizona Press, 1978.

Hester, Thomas R. "The Prehistory of South Texas." In *The Prehistory of Texas*, edited by Timothy K. Perttula, 127–51. College Station: Texas A&M University Press, 2004.

Higginson, Thomas Wentworth. *Army Life in a Black Regiment*. Los Angeles: Enhanced Media Publishing, 2017.

hooks, bell. *We Real Cool: Black Men and Masculinity*. New York: Routledge, 2003.

Horne, Gerald. *Black and Brown: African Americans and the Mexican Revolution, 1910–1920*. New York: New York University Press, 2005.

Hubert, Kennedy. "Karl Heinrich Ulrichs: First Theorist of Homosexuality." In *Science and Homosexuality*, edited by Vernon Rosario, 26–45. New York: Routledge, 1997.

Ingold, Tim. "Materials against Materiality." *Archaeological Dialogues* 14, no. 1 (June 2007): 1–16. https://doi.org/10.1017/S1380203807002127.

Israel, Fred L., ed. *1897 Sears, Roebuck & Co. Catalogue*. New York: Chelsea House Publishers, 1993.

Jackson, Shona N. *Creole Indigeneity: Between Myth and Nation in the Caribbean.* Minneapolis: University of Minnesota Press, 2012.

Jenks, Bill, and Jerry Luna. *Early American Pattern Glass 1850–1910: Major Collectible Settings with Prices.* Radnor, PA: Wallace-Homestead Book, 1990.

Johnson, Michael K. *Black Masculinity and the Frontier Myth in American Literature.* Norman: University of Oklahoma Press, 2002.

Johnson, Nicholas. *Negroes and the Gun: The Black Tradition of Arms.* Amherst, MA: Prometheus Books, 2014.

Jones, Jacqueline. *Labor of Love, Labor of Sorrow: Black Women, Work and Family from Slavery to Present.* 2nd ed. New York: Basic Books, 2009.

Jones, Olive, and Catherine Sullivan. *The Parks Canada Glass Glossary: For the Description of Containers, Tableware, Flat Glass, and Closures.* With contributions by George L. Miller, E. Ann Smith, Jane E. Harris, and Kevin Lunn. Ottawa: Parks Canada, 1985.

Joyce, Rosemary A. *Gender and Power in Prehispanic Mesoamerica.* Austin: University of Texas Press, 2000.

———. *The Future of Nuclear Waste: What Art and Archaeology Can Tell Us about Securing the World's Most Hazardous Material.* New York: Oxford University Press, 2020.

Joyce, Rosemary A., and Susan D. Gillespie, eds. *Things in Motion: Object Itineraries in Anthropological Practice.* Sante Fe: School for Advanced Research Press, 2015.

Kaylor, Michael Matthew. *Secreted Desires: The Major Uranians: Hopkins, Pater and Wilde.* Brno: Masaryk University Press, 2006.

Keefer, Justus. *Slavery: Its Sin, Moral Effects, and Certain Death; Also the Language of Nature, Compared with Divine Revelation, in Prose and Verse.* Baltimore: J. Keefer, 1864.

Kenner, Charles L. *Buffalo Soldiers and Officers of the Ninth Cavalry 1867–1898.* Norman: University of Oklahoma Press, 1999.

Kinder, John M. *Paying with Their Bodies: American War and the Problem of the Disabled Veteran.* Chicago: University of Chicago Press, 2015.

Kinevan, Marcos E. *Frontier Cavalryman: Lieutenant John Bigelow with the Buffalo Soldiers in Texas.* El Paso: Texas Western Press, 1998.

King, Eleanor, and Justin Dunnavant. "Buffalo Soldiers and Apaches in the Guadalupe Mountains: A Review of Research at Pine Springs Camp." *Bulletin of the Texas Archaeological Society* 79 (October 2008): 87–94.

Kovel, Ralph, and Terry Kovel. *Kovels' New Dictionary Of Marks: Pottery and Porcelain 1850 to the Present.* New York: Crown Publishers, 1986.

Laidlaw, James. "A Free Gift Makes No Friends." *Journal of the Royal*

Anthropological Institute 6, no. 4 (May 2003): 617–34. https://doi.org/10
.1111/1467–9655.00036.

Lambert, Royston. *Beloved and God: The Story of Hadrian and Antinous*. New York: Viking, 1984.

Lapsansky-Werner, Emma J., and Margaret Hope Bacon, eds. *Back to Africa: Benjamin Coates and the Colonization Movement in America 1848–1880*. University Park: Penn State University Press, 2010.

Laqueur, Thomas W. *Solitary Sex: A Cultural History of Masturbation*. New York: Zone Books, 2003.

Latour, Bruno. *Reassembling the Social: An Introduction to Actor-Network-Theory*. Oxford: Oxford University Press, 2007.

Leach, William. *Land of Desire: Merchants, Power, and the Rise of a New American Culture*. New York: Knopf Doubleday, 2011.

Leckie, William H. *The Buffalo Soldiers: A Narrative of the Negro Cavalry in the West*. Norman: University of Oklahoma Press, 1967.

Leckie, Shirley Anne, ed. *The Colonel's Lady on the Western Frontier: The Correspondence of Alice Kirk Grierson*. Lincoln: University of Nebraska Press, 1989.

Lee, Nedra K., and Jannie Nicole Scott. "Introduction: New Directions in African Diaspora Archaeology." *Transforming Anthropology* 27, no. 2 (September 2019): 85–90. https://doi.org/10.1111/traa.12164.

Lehner, Lois. *Lehner's Encyclopedia of U.S. Marks on Pottery, Porcelain and Clay*. Paducah, KY: Collector Books, 1988.

Leiker, James N. *Racial Borders: Black Soldiers along the Rio Grande*. College Station: Texas A&M University Press, 2002.

Lemelle, Anthony J., Jr. *Black Masculinity and Sexual Politics*. New York: Routledge, 2010.

Leonard, Elizabeth. *Men of Color to Arms!: Black Soldiers, Indian Wars, and the Quest for Equality*. New York: Norton, 2010.

Limerick, Patricia Nelson. *Something in the Soil: Legacies and Reckonings in the New West*. New York: Norton, 2000.

Litwack, Leon F. *Been in the Storm So Long: The Aftermath of Slavery*. New York: Vintage, 1980.

Litwack, Leon F. *How Free Is Free?: The Long Death of Jim Crow*. Cambridge: Harvard University Press, 2009.

Lockhart, Bill. "The Origins and Life of the Export Beer Bottle." *Bottles and Extras* (May/June 2007): 49–58. https://sha.org/bottle/pdffiles/ExportBeerBottles _BLockhart.pdf.

Logan, Thad. *The Victorian Parlour: A Cultural Study*. Cambridge: Cambridge University Press, 2001.

Loren, Diana DiPaolo. "Corporeal Concerns: Eighteenth-Century Casta Paintings and Colonial Bodies in Spanish Texas." *Historical Archaeology* 41, no. 1 (2007): 23–36. https://doi.org/10.1007/BF03376991.

Lyons, Nick. *Montgomery Ward & Co.: Catalogue & Buyers' Guide; 1895.* New York: Skyhorse Publishing, 2008.

Magner, Lois N. *A History of Infectious Disease and the Microbial World.* Westport, CT: Praeger, 2009.

Mahon, John K., and Romana Danysh. "A Diverse Half Century, 1866–1915." In *Infantry, Part I: Regular Army*, 31–41. Army Lineage Series. Office of the Chief of Military History, United States Army, Washington, DC, 1972. https://history.army.mil/html/books/060/60-3-1/cmhPub_60-3-1.pdf.

Marshall, Yvonne, and Benjamin Alberti. "A Matter of Difference: Karen Barad, Ontology and Archaeological Bodies." *Cambridge Archaeological Journal* 24, no. 1 (February 2014): 19–36. https://doi.org/10.1017/S0959774314000067.

Martin, Paul S., William A. Longacre, James N. Hill. *Chapters in the Prehistory of Eastern Arizona, III.* Fieldiana: Anthropology 57. Chicago: Field Museum Press, 1967.

Mauss, Marcel. *The Gift: The Form and Reason for Exchange in Archaic Societies.* Translated by W. D. Halls. London: Routledge, 2000.

Mbembe, Achille. *Necropolitics.* Translated by Steven Corcoran. Durham: Duke University Press, 2019.

McAllister, Lisa S. *Collector's Guide to Yellow Ware Book III: An Identification and Value Guide.* Paducah, KY: Collector Books, 2003.

McChristian, Douglas C., ed. *Garrison Tangles in the Friendless Tenth: The Journal of First Lieutenant John Bigelow, Jr.; Fort Davis, Texas.* Charleston, NC: J. M. Carroll, 1985.

———. *Headgear, Clothing, and Footwear.* Vol. 1 of *Uniforms, Arms, and Equipment: The U.S. Army on the Western Frontier, 1880–1892.* Norman: University of Oklahoma Press, 2007.

———. *Regular Army O!: Soldiering on the Western Frontier 1865–1891.* Norman: University of Oklahoma Press, 2017.

———. *The U.S. Army in the West, 1870–1880: Uniforms, Weapons, and Equipment.* With a foreword by John P. Langellier. Norman: University of Oklahoma Press, 1995.

———. *Weapons and Accoutrements.* Vol. 2 of *Uniforms, Arms, and Equipment: The U.S. Army on the Western Frontier, 1880–1892.* Norman: University of Oklahoma Press, 2007.

McDannell, Colleen. *The Christian Home in Victorian America, 1840–1900.* Bloomington: Indiana University Press, 1986.

McKibben, Carol Lynn. *Racial Beachhead: Diversity and Democracy in a Military Town.* Stanford: Stanford University Press, 2012.

McKittrick, Katherine, ed. *Sylvia Wynter: On Being Human as Praxis*. Durham, NC: Duke University Press, 2015.

McIntrye, C. L., and S. E. Studd. *Terrestrial Vegetation and Soils Monitoring at Fort Davis National Historic Site: Status Report*. Natural Resource Technical Report NPS/CHDN/NRT-2013/753. Fort Collins, CO: US Department of the Interior, National Park Service, 2013.

McPherson, James M. *The Negro's Civil War: How American Negroes Felt and Acted during the War for the Union*. New York: Vintage, 1965.

Miles, Dori, and Robert W. Miller, eds. *Price Guide to Pattern Glass*. 11th ed. Radnor, PA: Wallace-Homestead Book, 1986.

Miller, Anna M. *Cameos Old & New*. 4th ed. Woodstock, NY: Gemstone Press, 2009.

Moongiant. "November 1872 Moon Phases." Accessed June 1, 2020. https://www.moongiant.com/moonphases/November/1872.

Moore, J. M. *Biennial Report of the Secretary of State of the State of Texas*. Austin: State Printing Office, 1890.

Moses, Wilson Jeremiah, ed. *Liberation Dreams: Back-to-Africa Narratives from the 1850s*. University Park: Pennsylvania State University Press, 1998.

Muhammad, Khalil Gibran. *The Condemnation of Blackness: Race, Crime, and the Making of Modern Urban America, with a New Preface*. Cambridge, MA: Harvard University Press, 2019.

Mullins, Paul R. "Racializing the Parlor: Race and Victorian Bric-a-Brac Consumption." In *Race and the Archaeology of Identity*, edited by Charles E. Orser, Jr., 158–76. Salt Lake City: University of Utah Press, 2001.

Nankivell, John H. *Buffalo Soldier Regiment: History of the Twenty-Fifth United States Infantry, 1869–1926*. Lincoln: University of Nebraska, 2001.

Nelson, Dean E. "'Right Nice Little House[s]': Impermanent Camp Architecture of the American Civil War." *Perspectives in Vernacular Architecture* 1 (1982): 79–93.

Newman, T. Stell. "A Dating Key for Post-Eighteenth Century Bottles." *Historical Archaeology* 4 (1970): 70–75. https://doi.org/10.1007/BF03373388.

Noël Hume, Ivor. *Historical Archaeology: A Comprehensive Guide for Both Amateurs and Professionals to the Techniques and Methods of Excavating Historical Sites*. New York: Norton, 1975.

Northup, Solomon. *Twelve Years a Slave: Narrative of Solomon Northup, a Citizen of New-York Kidnapped in Washington City in 1841, and Rescued in 1853, from a Cotton Plantation near the Red River, in Luisiana*. New York: Miller, Orton & Mulligan, 1855.

Novak, Shannon A., and Alanna L. Warner-Smith. "Assembling Heads and Circulating Tales: The Doings and Undoings of Specimen 2032." *Historical*

Archaeology 54, no. 1 (March 2020): 71–91. https://doi.org/10.1007/s41636
-019-00157-z.

Olsen, Bjørnar, Michael Shanks, Timothy Webmoor, and Christopher Witmore. *Archaeology: The Discipline of Things*. Berkeley: University of California Press, 2012.

Omi, Michael, and Howard Winant. *Racial Formation in the United States: From the 1960s to the 1990s*. 2nd ed. New York: Routledge, 1994.

Orth, Samuel Peter. *A History of Cleveland, Ohio: Biographical; Illustrated*. Vol. 2. Chicago-Cleveland: S. J. Clarke Publishing, 1910.

Parker, Richard G., and J. Madison Watson. *The National First Reader; Or Word-Builder*. New York: A. S. Barnes, 1860.

Parsons, Chuck. *Captain John R. Hughes: Lone Star Ranger*. Denton: University of North Texas Press, 2011.

Penningroth, Dylan Craig. "Freedpeople's Families in the Age of Emancipation." Paper presented to Wilson Center, 2011. Accessed June 28, 2020. https://www.wilsoncenter.org/sites/default/files/media/documents/publication/ACF247.pdf.

———. *The Claims of Kinfolk: African American Property and Community in the Nineteenth-Century South*. Chapel Hill: University of North Carolina Press, 2003.

Porter, Kenneth Wiggins. "The Seminole Negro-Indian Scouts 1870–1881." *Southwestern Historical Quarterly* 55, no. 3 (January 1952): 358–77.

Puar, Jasbir K. *The Right to Maim: Debility, Capacity, Disability*. Durham: Duke University Press, 2017.

Quartermaster General of the Army. US *Army Uniforms and Equipment, 1889: Specifications for Clothing, Camp and Garrison Equipage, and Clothing and Equipage Materials*. Lincoln: University of Nebraska Press, 1986.

Raht, Carlysle Graham. *The Romance of the Davis Mountains and Big Bend Country: A History*. El Paso, TX: Rahtbooks, 1919.

Rambach, Hadrien J. "The Antinous Braschi on Engraved Gems: An Intaglio by Giovanni Beltrami." *LANX* 15 (2013): 111–22.

Richardson, Riché. *Black Masculinity and the U.S. South: From Uncle Tom to Gangsta*. Athens: University of Georgia Press, 2007.

Rickey, Don, Jr. *Forty Miles a Day on Beans and Hay*. Norman: University of Oklahoma Press, 1963.

Roberts, Dorothy E. *Killing the Black Body: Race, Reproduction, and the Meaning of Liberty*. New York: Vintage Books, 1997.

Russell, Carl P. *Guns on the Early Frontiers: A History of Firearms from Colonial Times through the Years of the Western Fur Trade*. Lincoln: University of Nebraska Press, 1957.

Schiffer, Michael B. *Formation Processes of the Archaeological Record*. Salt Lake City: University of Utah Press, 2002.

Schlereth, Thomas J. *Victorian America: Transformations in Everyday Life, 1876–1915*. New York: Harper Perennial, 1992.

Schubert, Frank N. *On the Trail of the Buffalo Soldier: Biographies of African Americans in the U.S. Army, 1866–1917*. Lanham, MD: Scarecrow, 1995.

———. *Voices of the Buffalo Soldier: Records, Reports, and Recollections of Military Life and Service in the West*. Albuquerque: University of New Mexico Press, 2003.

Scobee, Barry. *Fort Davis Texas 1583–1960*. Fort Davis, TX: Scobee Barry, 1963.

———. *Old Fort Davis*. Fort Davis, TX: Bartholomew House, 1984.

Sea, W. G. "James G. Birney, A Worker for Freedom." *Negro History Bulletin* 6, 5 (February 1943): 104–19.

Shellum, Brian G. *Black Officer in a Buffalo Soldier Regiment: The Military Career of Charles Young*. Lincoln: University of Nebraska Press, 2010.

Skallagrim. "An Antique Percussion Revolver and How It Works." YouTube video, February 1, 2016. https://www.youtube.com/watch?v=MmLPOBJldyQ.

Smedley, Audrey, and Brian D. Smedley. "Race as Biology Is Fiction, Racism as a Social Problem Is Real: Anthropological and Historical Perspectives on the Social Construction of Race." *American Psychologist* 60, no. 1 (January 2005): 16–26. https://doi.org/10.1037/0003-066X.60.1.16.

Smith, Graham. *Warman's Civil War Weapons*. Iola, WI: Krause, 2005.

Smith, Thomas T., Jerry D. Thompson, Robert Wooster, and Ben E. Pingenot, eds. *The Reminiscences of Major General Zenas R. Bliss 1854–1876*. Austin: Texas State Historical Association, 2007.

Snorton, C. Riley. *Black on Both Sides: A Racial History of Trans Identity*. Minneapolis: University of Minnesota Press, 2017.

Sokolow, Jayme A. *Eros and Modernization: Sylvester Graham, Health Reform, and the Origins of Victorian Sexuality in America*. Rutherford, NJ: Fairleigh Dickinson University Press, 1983.

Somerville, Siobhan B. *Queering the Color Line: Race and the Invention of Homosexuality in American Culture*. Durham: Duke University Press, 2000.

South, Stanley. *Method and Theory in Historical Archaeology*. New York: Academic Press, 1977.

SRPC. "Loading and Firing a Colt 1860 Revolver." YouTube video, January 8, 2015. https://www.youtube.com/watch?v=-llme014E3I.

Stanton, Elizabeth Cady, Susan B. Anthony, and Matilda Joslyn Gage, eds. *History of Woman Suffrage*. 2nd ed. New York: Charles Mann, 1889.

Steward, Theophilus G. *Buffalo Soldiers: The Colored Regulars in the United States Army*. Amherst, MA: Humanity Books, 2003.

Stevenson, Brenda E. *Life in Black and White: Family and Community in the Slave South*. Oxford: Oxford University Press, 1996.

Stocking, George W., Jr. *Victorian Anthropology*. New York: Free Press, 1987.

Stubbs, Mary Lee, and Stanley Russell Connor. "Indian Wars Period." In *Armor-Cavalry: Part 1; Regular Army Research*. U.S. Army Center for Military History Publication. Wikisource. https://en.wikisource.org/wiki/ARMOR-CAVALRY:_Part_1;_Regular_Army_and_Army_Reserve/Indian_Wars_Period.

Symonds, John Addington. *The Memoirs of John Addington Symonds: The Secret Homosexual Life of a Leading Nineteenth-Century Man of Letters*. Edited and introduced by Phyllis Grosskurth. New York: Random House, 1984.

Taylor, Lonn. *Texas, My Texas: Musings of the Rambling Boy*. Fort Worth: Texas Christian University Press, 2012.

Tesh, Sylvia N. "Miasma and 'Social Factors' in Disease Causality: Lessons from the 19th Century." *Journal of Health Politics, Policy and Law* 20, no. 4 (1995): 1001–24. https://doi.org/10.1215/03616878-20-4-1001.

Thompson, Erwin N. "The Negro Soldiers on the Frontier: A Fort Davis Case Study." *Journal of the West* 7 (1968): 217–35.

Tsing, Anna Lowenhaupt. *The Mushroom at the End of the World: On the Possibility of Life in Capitalist Ruins*. Princeton, NJ: Princeton University Press, 2015.

Utley, Robert M. *Fort Davis National Historic Site, Texas*. Historical Handbook 38. Washington, DC: United States Department of the Interior, National Parks Service, 1965.

Veuve Hasslauer Successor of Gambier. Givet: Gambier, 1868. Accessed June 28, 2020. http://tobaccopipeartistory.blogspot.com/2016/03/catalog-vve-hasslauer-succ-gambier-1868.html.

Vout, Caroline. "Antinous, Archaeology and History." *The Journal of Roman Studies* 95 (November 2005): 80–96. https://doi.org/10.3815/000000005784016342.

Wall, Diana diZerega. "Sacred Dinners and Secular Teas: Constructing Domesticity in Mid-19th-Century New York." *Historical Archaeology* 25, no. 4 (December 1991): 69–81. https://doi.org/10.1007/bf03373525.

Warren, Mia. "Lines in the Land: Descendants of the Buffalo Soldiers in Fort Davis." Marfa Public Radio, 2015. https://marfapublicradio.org/blog/lines-in-the-land-descendants-of-the-buffalo-soldiers-in-fort-davis/.

Waters, Sarah. "'The Most Famous Fairy in History': Antinous and Homosexual Fantasy." *Journal of the History of Sexuality* 6, no. 2 (October 1995): 194–230.

Watson, J. Madison. *The Independent Fourth Reader*. New York: A. S. Barnes, 1868.

Webster, Daniel. *The Great Orations and Senatorial Speech of Daniel Webster, Comprising Eulogy on Adams and Jefferson; First Settlement of New England; Bunker Hill Monument; Reply to Hayne*. Rochester, NY: Wilbur M. Hayward, 1853.

Weheliye, Alexander G. *Habeas Viscus: Racializing Assemblages, Biopolitics, and Black Feminist Theories of the Human*. Durham, NC: Duke University Press, 2014.

Weik, Terrance M. *The Archaeology of Antislavery Resistance*. Gainesville: University Press of Florida, 2012.

Weik, Terrance M. "The Role of Ethnogenesis and Organization in the Development of African-Native American Settlements: An African Seminole Model." *International Journal of Historical Archaeology* 13 (2009): 206–38. https://doi .org/10.1007/s10761–009–0079–9.

Wesler, Kit W. "Assessing Precision in Formula Dating." *Historical Archaeology* 48, no. 2 (June 2014): 173–81. https://doi.org/10.1007/BF03376932.

Wetherbee, Jean. *A Second Look at White Ironstone*. Lombard: Wallace Homestead Book, 1985.

White Ironstone Notes 14, no. 4 (Spring 2008): 1–28. http://www.harmonicaguy .com/year14/vol144.pdf.

Wilkie, Laurie A., David G. Hyde, Christopher B. Lowman, and Mark C. Emerson. "Ode to a Grecian Boy: Queering the Fort Davis Antinous." Special Issue, *Historical Archaeology* (forthcoming).

Wilkie, Laurie A. *Creating Freedom: Material Culture and African American Identity at Oakley Plantation, Louisiana, 1840–1950*. Baton Rouge: Louisiana State University Press, 2000.

———. "Glass-Knapping at a Louisiana Plantation: African-American Tools?" *Historical Archaeology* 30, no. 4 (1996): 37–49.

———. *Strung Out on Archaeology: An Introduction to Archaeological Research*. Walnut Creek: Left Coast Press, 2014.

———. *The Archaeology of Mothering: An African-American Midwife's Tale*. New York: Routledge, 2003.

———. *The Lost Boys of Zeta Psi: A Historical Archaeology of Masculinity at a University Fraternity*. Berkeley: University of California Press, 2010.

Wilkie, Laurie A., Katrina Eichner, and Erin C. Rodriquez. *Report of the University of California Berkeley 2015 Archaeological Research at Fort Davis National Historic Site*. Unpublished report, 2016.

Wilkie, Laurie A., Katrina Eichner, Erin C. Rodriquez, and Leah Grant. *Report of the University of California Berkeley's 2013 Archaeological Research at Fort Davis National Historic Site; Report Prepared for Fort Davis National Historic Site, National Parks Service, Under Federal Archaeological Permit 13-FODA-1*. Unpublished report, 2015.

Wilkie, Laurie A., and Katherine Howlett Hayes. "Engendered and Feminist Archaeologies of the Recent and Documented Pasts." *Journal of Archaeological*

Research 14, no. 3 (September 2006): 243–64. https://doi.org/10.1007/s10814 –006–9005–4.

Williams, Heather Andrea. *Self-Taught: African American Education in Slavery and Freedom*. The John Hope Franklin Series in African American History and Culture. Chapel Hill: University of North Carolina Press, 2005.

Willis, Deborah, and Barbara Krauthamer. *Envisioning Emancipation: Black Americans and the End of Slavery*. Philadelphia: Temple University Press, 2012.

Wilson, Rex L. *Bottles on the Western Frontier*. Tucson: University of Arizona Press, 1981.

Wooster, Robert. *Frontier Crossroads: Fort Davis and the West*. College Station: Texas A&M University Press, 2006.

Wooster, Robert. *History of Fort Davis, Texas*. Southwest Cultural Resources Center Professional Papers 34. Santa Fe: Division of History, Southwest Cultural Resources Center, Southwest Region, National Park Service, Department of the Interior, 1990.

Wynter, Sylvia. "Unsettling the Coloniality of Being/Power/Truth/Freedom: Towards the Human, after Man, Its Overrepresentation–An Argument." *CR: The New Centennial Review* 3, no. 3 (Fall 2003): 257–337. doi:10.1353/ncr.2004.0015.

INDEX

~⇒○⇐~

Page numbers in *italic* text indicate illustrations.

Printed in the USA
CPSIA information can be obtained
at www.ICGtesting.com
LVHW041307291123
765187LV00005B/57